Master or Servant is an extraordi... ...by Joe Frazzette that is inspiring and uplifting.
A story for the ages; it will help to change your life.
Rena C. Winters, Author
"In Lieu of Therapy:"

With Master or Servant Joe Frazzette proves that his first outstanding novel was not a fluke. He delivers top quality writing from start to finish, and a story you won't soon forget.
Robert M. Cawley, Author
"Treasure of La Dura"

MASTER or SERVANT

Lessons Learned at the Wisdom Café

JOE FRAZZETTE

Master or Servant, Lessons Learned at the Wisdom Café - copyright © 2015 by Joe Frazzette.

ISBN: 1942688180
ISBN 13: 978-1-942688-18-1

Perfect Publishing

Cover design by A.D. Cook
www.adcookdesign.com

All rights reserved. No part of this book may be reproduced in any form or by any means without written consent of Joe Frazzette, except as provided by the United States copyright law or in the case of brief quotes used in articles and reviews.

The scanning, uploading and distribution of this book via the internet or via any other means without the permission of Joe Frazzette, the publisher, is illegal and punishable by law.

Printed and bound in the United States of America.

DEDICATION

This story is dedicated to my good friend
Doctor Dave Hill, DCH.
You are truly a master.

ACKNOWLEDGMENTS

Thank you to Yukari Howard for believing in me and my life's passion. My heart belongs to you. I love you.

Thank you to the man I would acknowledge as my mentor, Robert Cawley, for your expert guidance and encouragement to continue with my passion to write, write, and continue to write some more.

To Rena Winters for your editing skills and creativity, I greatly appreciate all your input and assistance. Thank you so much for your time and experience.

Thank you to my friend Dr. Dave Hill. Your wisdom, experience, and guidance are always greatly appreciated. You have helped me in so many ways that cannot be listed here, but especially in my search to pave my own special path in this life.

To all of my family, friends, classmates, and fellow writers who participated in the process and generally supported my vision. The experience and input from all of you was instrumental. I thank each one of you.

A special thanks to my good friend, Josie Settimo, for your time, collaboration, and sharp insight. I value your contributions.

Thank you and cheers to my designer and good friend A.D. Cook. Your talent, creativity, and imagination are unsurpassed. You are the best at what you do and I look forward to further projects with you working at my side.

For as a man thinketh in his heart, so is he.

Proverbs 23:7

MASTER or SERVANT - BOOK 1 **JOE FRAZZETTE**

PREFACE

Certain people would have you believe every life has a specific destiny. However, the likelihood each individual will execute their pre-determined plan is improbable. Unless of course we tap into that most powerful aspect of our being, the subconscious mind. Yes, it is in the subconscious mind where all behaviors and habits are formed and imprinted on our being to then be manifested into the physical realm of our conscious existence. Therefore, one can conclude the subconscious mind is the center in which human beings imagine, develop, and create the lives we choose to live. Our path in life can be tenuous and difficult to realize, and if we can't get there solely on our own effort, we can certainly turn to outside sources and experiences learned from others to assist us along the way. While uncertain, these variables may help lay the breadcrumbs that form a path to the ultimate prize; a life fulfilled; full of surprise, intrigue, and splendor.

Mind control is an interesting concept men have been curious about for centuries. What is it that enables one person to achieve great success, and for some at incredibly enormous odds, while others wallow in the mire of their retched lives and get a daily kick in the ass from a life so uncertain, they can't possibly know what to expect from their efforts? Does each one of us actually possess the power to change our life's course or is there a predetermined plan in which we have no control? Is life all packaged up with a "free will" and no handbook on how to use the machinery we come equipped with? These are just a few of the questions posed by seekers throughout the centuries. One thing we are certain of is the cumulative experiences life has to offer are things we all can learn from. While some do, many more let life and all those experiences within it go by the wayside without a second thought and learn nothing at all from them. That would include their own personal incidents, as well as occurrences observed or learned from others.

This story is about one man's life changing experience at the hands of one of the most powerful mind control techniques known to man, hypnosis. Doctor Jefferson Paul is the world's greatest hypnotist and when he meets a total stranger after one of his premiere Las Vegas shows, the ensuing friendship they develop will have a life-long effect on one of them for sure, and quite possibly on both. David Christian is an average guy who developed a drug habit at a time in his life when he should have developed a plan for his future. The effects his drug use has had on him are clearly evident in that it lessened his ability to realize his dreams and live a life of his own choosing. He is unlike any other person with a habitual drug habit, with one exception, in that David seemed to always detect an internal voice which attempted to guide him out of his troubled existence.

All the while, he struggled with his addiction as it seemed to take hold in a manner that allowed life to kick him down the road with no direction at all. That is until he meets Jefferson Paul. It is from that point in his life, David began to learn the secrets to creating significant change in his direction and he began to realize his dreams rather than just live, or better yet survive through the daily challenges life brought him. His newfound friendship has a powerful impact that will inspire him to change his life forever. He sets out to embark on a mission in an attempt to bring a new consciousness to the world.

It is not often that people have the opportunity to experience, or better yet create an extraordinary life change like the one David Christian is about to go through. At the start, he is naïve and ignorant of the great potential he has within but there is one man that will bring it forth in a manner he could never have anticipated. That man is Doctor Jefferson Paul, a master of mind control. Under his guidance David Christian's life will take such a dramatic turn and be so mind-blowing it will even amaze him to see the type of person he will become.

MASTER or SERVANT - BOOK 1　　　　　　　　JOE FRAZZETTE

CHAPTER ONE
LAS VEGAS, NEVADA

The lights in the theater were dim, with only a spotlight shining on the master hypnotist at center stage. His tall, statuesque frame and command of presence created an eerie feel of intrigue which engulfed the entire audience. To each it felt as if they were being controlled by someone or something mysterious and outside of themselves. In a line behind the master sat the usual suspects in anticipation of what lie ahead for them. Each one willing to be a prop for the duration of the show, and not at all concerned with the outcome. They would each have their fifteen minutes of fame and that's all that mattered to them at the moment.

"Sit back, close your eyes, relax your mind, your body and be comfortable."

The calm, calculated, and rhythmic patter came from out of the darkness, as the selection of participants hung onto every word flowing over them like a soft, warm, summer shower.

"In a moment you will begin to feel more relaxed than you have felt in a long, long time."

With those words, the World's Greatest Hypnotist began to take control of his newest subjects in a manner he had grown to love. He was truly the best in the world at his craft. Thousands, if not millions who came to witness and let this man perform his magic on them were a testament of this very proof every time he appeared. The show, Mind Bending Illusions, continued along in the usual fashion with one man being induced to strut across the stage and cluck like a chicken, a young sexy lady made passionate love to a chair, and another young woman got to meet "Denzel" for the first time, only in this show, Denzel Washington was a stuffed teddy bear.

"Sheila, give me that teddy bear."

The master hypnotist commanded his young female subject.

"No, no, this is Denzel and he's all mine."

Sheila turns her body from Jefferson Paul; hugs and hides the teddy bear in her grasp as she maneuvers away. The crowd roars with laughter and approves with screams of delight. As each comedic and illusory sketch plays out, the audience breaks out into more laughter, cheers their approval and encourages the master hypnotist to give them more. They love the entertaining way he controls his subjects and cringe at the thought of being in the situation of embarrassment the people on stage had put themselves in. For each of the participants on stage, the short lived fame was all that mattered. They were at the center of the biggest show on the Las Vegas Strip. The opportunity for them to be "on stage" and garner the attention of everyone present was their only objective. For the next hour all that mattered was they would be at the center of the most entertaining hypnotic extravaganza in Las Vegas, the city known for entertainment.

Each and every night, the World's Greatest Hypnotist would take a group of participants in his show, Mind Bending Illusions, and turn them into virtual puppets with a craft that he had mastered twenty-five years before under the tutelage of the best known hypnotist on the planet at the time, Gil Boyne. Now, the master hypnotist had taken that position as the World's Greatest Hypnotist and millions flocked to the showroom at the Stardust to see him perform his magic and execute with the skill only the master hypnotist possessed. On this particular night, David Christian sat in the audience in amazement at the precision and timing of each spectacle he observed. He wondered just how was it possible, a man who appeared to be normal in every way could lose complete control at the hands of the master hypnotist. Even to the extent of not resisting when asked to perform the most embarrassing and hilarious comedic acts for an audience full of strangers. It seemed as if their behavior had become automatic and someone else was at the controls. They were on autopilot, or were they? The power of suggestion had been extended to the master hypnotist, and without resistance, each of the participants performed whatever acts he asked of them. With their eyes wide open, one would swear they were either sleepwalking or they must be shills for the show.

For David, there was more to it than just being entertained and the questions sped through his mind. He wanted to know how the craft of hypnosis was executed to achieve the desired results. Exactly how was this master of mind control able to take over another person's will? More importantly, can anyone do this or is it only an exclusive club of especially talented individuals that have the ability? Can the power of suggestion be applied to one's own mind? If it could, David wanted to find out how. By the end of the show he was determined to get answers to his questions, to his persistent curiosities.

David had decided he would stop at nothing to get those answers. It was in that absolute moment David Christian made a conscious choice that would have a long term effect on his life. He unknowingly began his own life change with the simple act of making a choice. It would vault him in a direction that would change his life forever and it would take him beyond anything he had dreamed could ever happen to him.

MASTER or SERVANT - BOOK 1 　　　　　　　　JOE FRAZZETTE

CHAPTER TWO

"In a moment I am going to wake you. I'll count to three and tap you on the shoulder. You will awaken feeling refreshed as if you had just had a deep, sound, long night of restful sleep. You will feel as you did when you walked into the auditorium tonight, only very rested. Finally, you will not recall a thing from your experience on stage tonight."

With those words, the master hypnotist began to awaken the participants in the Mind Bending Illusions show. The crowd buzzed, giggled, and cheered each one of the participants for their contribution to the night's entertainment. They stood and roared with approval at the master hypnotist's ability to perform at such a high level as he mixed visual intrigue with hilarious comedy. The effective combination resulted in the best show currently playing on the world-famous Las Vegas Strip. David stood up tall and applauded along with the mass of fans tucked into the showroom at the Stardust. Jefferson Paul took his bows and walked off the stage to the right of the audience, his left. A brief moment later he re-enters from the opposite side of the stage and the audience, still cheering and in complete wonder of how he maneuvered so quickly, let out a big roar of laughter and applause.

"Thank you; thank you ladies and gentlemen."

The applause continues and Doctor Paul raises his arms to quiet the crowd. Moving his arms in an up and down motion to bring the crowd noise down, he waves downward a couple times before the crowd silences to a low whisper.

"Thank you all very much for that generous

applause. You have been a wonderful audience tonight. Please give another hand for the volunteers in tonight's show. They were wonderful."

As the loud applause rose to engulf the room, The World's Greatest Hypnotist moved forward to the center and front of the stage to address the audience. The crowd begins to go silent and Jefferson Paul starts.

"Now, at the conclusion of each show I give the audience an opportunity to purchase CD's, DVD's or any of my published works that may be of interest to you. If you have a desire to purchase any of these items, please proceed to the back of the theater and I'll meet you there in a few minutes to sign them for you. Thank you again for a wonderful evening."

As the crowd roared with applause one more time he gives them a big wave of his hand, he mouths another thank you for their participation and generous applause and then turns and walks off stage. David slips through the crowd and heads for the tables loaded with the wares to be sold in the rear of the theater. This was the opportunity he had come for and he didn't want to jeopardize his potential for meeting with Doctor Paul. This was a man he believed possessed a power that not only intrigued him, but had such an effect on him in a short period time that he had become extremely focused for the first time in his life. The change happened so quickly and was so evident that if he had been on the outside looking in, he would hardly recognize himself.

The crowd gathered around and formed lines in front of the table where the master hypnotist would soon appear to sell his materials. David decided to hang back a bit and attempt to be one of the last to purchase in hopes he would get some time to converse with Doctor Paul about the skill he had mastered. A few minutes went by before Jefferson Paul arrived and greeted the crowd with a warm hello and a loud clap of his hands. Some in the crowd wondered if he had attempted to 'put the spell on them' with the loud clap, but it quickly became evident nobody was being hypnotized. He was only expressing gratitude for the folks who came back to meet with him to purchase his wares. Several minutes went by as he greeted members of the audience and sold CD's, DVD's, and books to all the interested and curious people. Finally, after about fifteen minutes had passed, most of the crowd had dissipated and David stepped up to the table to meet Doctor Paul. He put out his hand and introduced himself, all the while keeping his eyes locked on the master.

"How do you do, I'm David Christian."

With a smile and a piercing look into David's eyes Doctor Paul responded.

"How do I do what David?"

The two men chuckled and their instant rapport was evident. Being the perceptive man he was, Doctor Paul sensed David may have some questions on his mind, so he nodded in the opposite direction and pointed toward the two young women who stood to the left of him waiting to make a purchase of the products on the table.

"Do you have a minute David, let me take care of these young ladies and I'll be right with you."

"Oh yeah, sure, I can wait."

David was anxious to speak with the doctor and actually happy to wait. He stepped away as Doctor Paul turned to greet the last two audience members that stopped to meet him and purchase CD's for friends they felt had smoking problems. When they mentioned that to Jefferson, he responded with soft laughter and some friendly advice.

"You know, this will only work for them if they

want to quit, if they are not committed to make that change, it will not happen."

Both young women looked at him with puzzled stares on their faces and giggled as he continued to give them his verbal guarantee.

"I'm just telling you this so you don't waste your money on something your friends may have no conviction to change."

The two made the purchase anyway, walked away from the table and giggled some more as if they were going to play tricks with their friends and get them hypnotized with the newly purchased CD's. Jefferson shook his head and laughed as they wandered into the casino and away from earshot. Turning toward David, he stated frankly.

"Oh well, I gave them fair warning."

David was slightly dumbfounded by the statement and asked Jefferson Paul the first of what would be many questions from him over the next several hours, weeks, months… even years.

"So when the person listens to the CD they may not be hypnotized or changed by what they listen to?"

Jefferson broke out in a broad smile and explained the process to David in a brief answer.

"Absolutely not David; you see the subject has to want to be hypnotized for one, and secondly, they must have a conviction to make the change they say they want to make."

With that, the two men started a conversation that would ultimately lead to, and even accelerate a dramatic change in David Christian's life. A change that would head to his dreams being realized, as well as the development of his company; a company that would ultimately be responsible for changing the lives of many others he would come into contact with over the course of the next several years. David looked at Jefferson with a puzzled look. The questions came flooding into his mind and he began to blurt them out one at time.

"So how does it work Doctor Paul?"

"David, please call me Jefferson."

He paused for a brief moment and smiled with a curiosity of his own before he asked David.

"How does what work?"

David pursed his lips in a sign of impatience as if Jefferson had begun to play a mind game with him. He took a step back, shuffled his shoulders a bit and started over again.

"Hypnosis, how does it work?"

Jefferson is amused at David's curiosity of his mastery and decided to invite him for a drink at one of the casinos nearby watering holes. To avoid interruption they took a table tucked away in the back of the cafe to evade the gawking patrons that would assuredly recognize Doctor Paul and interrupt their conversation. A waitress quickly scurried over and took their drink order, a couple ice teas with lemon wedges. As she turned away, Jefferson directed his attention back to David and began to explain the facts of hypnosis.

"Well David, I guess the best way for me to answer that question is to first explain to you all hypnosis is self-hypnosis."

David eyed Jefferson with raised eyebrows and heightened curiosity. The questions began to roll into his mind, but rather than ask, he gestured for Jefferson to explain further so the doctor took his cue and continued.

"You see David, each individual is entirely in control of his or her own mind and all I am is the facilitator for their movement into what I will call the state of trance."

"So are you telling me you don't actually hypnotize people?"

"Well yes and no. What I do as the hypnotist is facilitate the process. I lead them into the state of hyper suggestibility, or hypnosis. It's a state of pure relaxation, and in that state the subject's subconscious mind is then accessible to suggestion."

David stares at Jefferson with a confused look on his face, but he isn't sure what his next question will be, or should be, so he just sits quietly and allows Jefferson to continue with his detailed explanation.

"You may not believe this and most likely are not even aware of it, but the fact of the matter is you are hypnotized every day of your life."

"Come on Jefferson, how can that be?"

Doctor Paul leans in and begins to explain this concept as clearly as he could without creating more confusion for his newly found pupil.

"You see David, over the course of our lifetime we develop habits that get seeded in our subconscious minds. It is the action created by the thoughts buried deep inside your subconscious mind that bring you into the state of hypnosis on a daily basis. You do things each day of your life without ever giving them a second thought. You're actually in the state of hypnosis as that occurs."

"But I am wide awake, how can I possibly be hypnotized if I'm awake?"

"Well then let me ask you; were those people you witnessed on the stage tonight not wide awake?"

David paused to consider what he witnessed on stage earlier that evening.

"I'm not sure Doctor Paul, they appeared to be awake, but they also acted like they were out of their minds or had no control over their actions."

"Please David, call me Jefferson."

Doctor Paul peered into David's eyes as he made that request a second time and then continued to explain.

"I can assure you David they were all very much awake, wide awake. Being hypnotized is not like going to sleep; as a matter of fact it's a relaxed state in which your focus becomes even more acute."

Jefferson watched David's reaction as he spoke and sensed he was still not sure what to think of as he listened to the explanation from this master of one of the world's oldest and most intriguing crafts, hypnosis. David had a curious and somewhat confused look on his face. He wasn't sure if the master was playing mind games with him or if he was being straight and truthful about the craft he had mastered over the last two and a half decades. Jefferson decided to change the subject for the moment and asked David if he wouldn't mind telling him about himself. David nodded in agreement and the Doctor began to ask him questions about his personal life, marriage, children, and other personal tidbits, which left David feeling unguarded and somewhat apprehensive, but he wanted this meeting so he went along with the doctor's request and answered each question.

"So David, what kind of work do you do?"

"I'm a regional sales manager for an industrial gas company."

"That sounds interesting, what types of gases do you sell?"

David was unsure of where Jefferson was going with the conversation, but he patiently complied and continued to answer his inquiries.

"We have a couple divisions in the company, one handles medical and industrial customers; the other which

I am part of, is focused primarily on CO2 for food service and beverage applications."

"How long have you been in that business?"

Why does he want to know this? David thought to himself before he answered.

"I've worked in this industry for twelve years, all with the same company. I've been their west region sales manager for five."

Just then the waitress arrived at their table with two tall ice teas and a small basket of trail mix for the men to snack on. As she sets their drinks down she turns to Jefferson,

"Will you be ordering food off the menu tonight?"

Jefferson raised his open hand, much like he did at the conclusion of his show, and gestured across the table toward David.

"David, please go ahead and order if you're hungry for anything on the menu."

"No thank you. I'll just snack on the trail mix. It'll be fine."

Jefferson turned back to the attractive, young female and gave her a broad smile.

"I guess were fine Sheri, thank you."

"OK, I'll be around if you need anything, just flag me down."

Jefferson nodded and turned back to David with a keen interest in learning more about this man who seemed to approach him with a personal mission in mind earlier in the evening.

"So David, are you from Las Vegas?"

"No, but I do come here often on business. I travel the southwestern states, managing current accounts, and prospecting for new opportunities."

Jefferson nods and then continues with another of

his probing questions.

"I see... is business good?"

"It's not bad, but to listen to our Vice President of Sales you would think business was absolutely awful. He's never satisfied with our results, just a real prick to work for."

"So why do you put up with it?"

David responds somewhat sarcastically.

"The paycheck Jefferson, I'm certainly not independently wealthy yet."

David's attempt at a sarcastic response, one that would indicate he never expected to be independently wealthy, prompted Jefferson to use the opportunity to begin with his first lesson as he continued to inquire.

"Do you want to be?"

David, being unsure of the line of questioning, reacted somewhat impatiently.

"Want to be what?"

Jefferson looked him directly in the eye and asked candidly without pause.

"Do you want to be independently wealthy... or rich David?"

David had picked some of the finer morsels in the trail mix bowl, but the question gave way to his immediate halt and he looked up as if the good doctor had made him an offer.

"Why, do you have something in mind?"

Jefferson laughed out loud and threw his arms up as he leaned back into his chair.

"I'm just asking David, that's all, just asking."

Jefferson's broad smile displayed those pearly whites that shone brightly when the spotlight beamed bright his image earlier on stage. In the blink of an eye Jefferson got serious and looked straight into the eyes of

David Christian.

"Okay David, what's the deal? Why did you come to the show tonight and why did you want to meet me? What are you so curious about, hypnosis? Is there something you haven't told me?"

David hedged uncomfortably in his seat and repositioned himself. He suddenly felt as if he was a criminal experiencing an interrogation with the barrage of intrusive questions. Suddenly the doctor's manner seemed to shift to a more serious disposition as he asked some pointed questions that pushed David to come clean with regard to his true intentions. David sat back, took a deep breath, and after a brief pause, he started to explain his motivation for seeking out his encounter with Doctor Jefferson Paul.

"I want a change in my life. I saw a commercial one night that pitched stop smoking in thirty days. I want to know if that is something that can truly happen or is it just a scam?"

Jefferson took a moment to size up the man seated across the table from him before he responded in straightforward fashion, which was the typical style for the master.

"David I can't tell you the answer to that but I will tell you this, if you seek a change in your life it won't just happen. If on the other hand you want to create a change in your life, I can help you with that."

David was actually more desperate than he had led on during the conversation and without hesitation he blurted out.

"OK, so how does it work? What do I have to do create a change?"

Jefferson smiled broadly at his apparent, eager new student and gestured with his hand held up in a stop signal position all the while shaking his head.

"Whoa, whoa, not so fast grasshopper."

He gently laughed at David's excitement as to not insult him, paused and then continued.

"Why don't we start at the beginning David, tell me what it is you have in mind that you want to change."

David was unsure if he should open up and be truthful with Jefferson about everything, including his issue with substance abuse, so he started with a vague answer to the question and hoped it might bring an answer with some wisdom from the master that would aid him in his current state of confusion.

"I just feel as if I am going nowhere with my life. I need to find something that I am passionate about. My job pays okay, but the work bores me to death and my personal life is a train wreck."

Jefferson sensed David had some serious issues he wanted to deal with but he was hesitant to bring them up. He wanted to pry some more in an attempt to genuinely help, but he didn't want to intimidate David so he kept the conversation light and a bit more general.

"Well David, it sounds to me like you want to create a major overhaul."

"Yeah, I guess I do but I don't know how to do it or even where to start."

"Let me tell you something I learned from a wise man many years ago, it goes something like this.... "You don't follow your passion, you bring it with you."

Now, even more confused than when they had started the conversation, David asked.

"I don't get it Jefferson, isn't that the goal in everyone's life, to follow their passion?"

Jefferson proceeded to explain.

"Most people don't have any idea what their

passion is, so what do they do? Let me ask you David, do you know what your passion is?"

"I guess not, that's what I had hoped to find out with your help."

Jefferson laughed again in a loud boisterous way and some of the patrons in the café and bar looked over to their table as if they had missed out on a very good joke.

"That is precisely why I stated, you don't follow your passion; you bring it with you. You see David, if you don't know what your passion is, then exactly what are you going to follow?"

David looked at him with a blank stare as if he was not sure if Jefferson had solicited an answer from him or just threw out a rhetorical question. The Doctor doesn't wait for him to respond to the question and promptly continued with his tutorial.

"On the other hand, if you bring your passion with you and be the best you can be at whatever it is you're doing in the moment... can you begin to see how that may open the possibilities for better opportunities and a better life?"

The good doctor paused a moment to allow David to reflect on the question and then quickly proceeded.

"You see David, if we incorporate passion in every facet of our life and we bring that passion to whatever it is we are doing, whether its work or play, life starts to take on an entirely different meaning. Our perspective changes things dramatically. I am sure you've heard the old saying 'change the way you look at your life and your life begins to change.' Well my friend, it all begins with you. Commit yourself to begin now and bring the passion you hold inside into every day and apply it to whatever it is you do."

"But what if I don't like what I do?"

"What did I just say? If you change the way you view your life, I assure you, your life begins to change."

David, still unconvinced, did not totally buy it but he stayed engaged for the moment.

"How do you get passionate about a job you don't want to do anymore, or otherwise hate?"

"The only way to answer that is you find the passion deep within you, not in the work you do, and just focus on the single purpose in the moment. If you allow yourself to be miserable I assure you David, you will be."

"What's that supposed to mean?"

Jefferson, exhausted from the performance of two shows a night for five straight nights, was not in the mood to be challenged and so he brought the conversation to a conclusion for the evening.

"David I have a book I want to give you, but you have to promise me you will read it before we speak again, or at least get started on it."

David was pleasantly surprised to hear Jefferson allude to the possibility they would meet again and he made a move to confirm.

"So are we going to meet again?"

"Well that's entirely up to you David, but yes, I am willing to meet if you are."

David perked up and was excited at Jefferson's confirmation they would meet again.

"That sounds fair enough; what's the title of the book Jefferson?"

"It's one of my own books which I sold tonight after the show, 'Lessons of the Mind.' Let's take a walk back to the theater and I'll give you a signed copy."

"OK, thank you. I appreciate it"

The two men slide free from their chairs, exit the café and head toward the theater in which Jefferson performed nightly. As they walked through the casino, some of the patrons recognize Jefferson and point, wave, and ask for autographs. He stopped a couple times for brief introductions and signed autographs for his most loyal fans. When the two men arrive in the backroom of the theater, Jefferson walked up to a large cabinet opened the doors and pulled out a soft cover book. He signed it on the inside cover page and handed it over. David looked down at the book titled 'Lessons of the Mind' and opened the cover page to read the inscription.

It read...

Move in the direction of your thoughts. Keep your thoughts on your objective in life.
Your Friend,
Jefferson Paul.

Doctor Paul also handed David a card with his contact information on it.

"I'll tell you what David. I don't do clinical work anymore, but I still sell some of this stuff at my shows. I believe you're a good guy, so I will make this one exception. If you're interested I'll help you in any way I can within reason, but if you accept, I'll ask you to do one thing for me."

David looked at him curiously and asked.

"What can I possibly do for you?"

"Pay it forward. You've heard that before, right? Just pay it forward."

David pondered Jefferson's request as he reached into his pocket for his own business card. He always carried a few with him wherever he went because one never knows where or when a good opportunity might arise. He handed it to Jefferson.

"Thank you Jefferson. Thank you very much for taking your time to meet with me."

Jefferson nodded his head and acknowledged David's gratitude with a warm smile. The two men shook hands and David quickly turned to head out the door of the backstage area. He was anxious to get back to his room and see just what it was this book had inside that would be helpful to him in his quest for a life change.

Back in his hotel room David wasted no time as he sat comfortably in the lounge chair and cracked the book open. 'Lessons of the Mind' is Doctor Paul's brief synopsis of the intricate workings of the human mind and how human beings can manipulate their reality through the control of thought. Throughout his career and study of hypnosis, Jefferson compiled what he knew to be the rules that governed human behavior. The book was a thorough study of the twelve rules that, if understood completely, could be used to significantly enhance or otherwise dramatically change one's course in life.

As David read through the first half of the book, his eyes got heavy and he began to dose off until he finally fell into a deep sleep in the lounge chair seated in the corner of his room. David drifted deep into a dream and saw himself on a stage while he spoke to a small crowd of onlookers about the rules that he was now reading about and would soon learn to utilize. He shares with the crowd his own life experience and how these lessons impacted him, gave him the foundation for a life change that ultimately vaulted him in a completely different direction and started him on a path completely changed from the one he was on. The faces in the crowd are fixed on his every move, his every word. He seems to guide them with the same relative ease the master hypnotist displayed the night David was in attendance at his Mind Bending Illusions hypnosis show. David falls deeper and deeper into a restful sleep and doesn't wake until the next morning.

CHAPTER THREE
FIVE WEEKS PRIOR (NEW YEARS EVE)
JANUARY

The clock on the wall read a quarter to one in the morning. David sat on the recliner in the den of his townhome watching the television screen with a blank, hypnotic stare on his face. The mirror on the end table had a small mound of white crystalline powder on it and two lines approximately three inches in length were drawn at an angle from the middle of the glass to the top left corner. There was a small drop of blood on the bottom edge of the mirror and smears from his fingerprints left evidence from when he dabbed at the cocaine residue drawn from previous lines to rub onto his gums for a quick numbing effect.

David's head was tucked back into the padding of the recliner. His nose was outlined with dried dark red blood and the top of his lip was lined with the same. The New Year's gala celebration was the fourth in a row he had watched alone, in the seclusion of his townhome. The scene was just as pitiful as the previous three years in which he lingered in a drunken, coked-out haze. It had been exactly three years and five months since the break-up with his ex-girlfriend Laura Mangiani. Since then he hadn't made any attempts to change the course of his life or stop using drugs. In fact he ended up getting busted for a first offense charge, possession of a small quantity of cocaine, in that time. He was lucky to get a lenient judge who would only have him pay a large fine and do community service while on his two years of probation. He was fortunate not to have to serve any time behind bars. The episode was past him now but the nightmare continued. Since the end of his probation he was back into the constant drug use that led him to his troubles, and the uncontrolled lifestyle that drove a wedge between him and Laura.

She loved him very much, but her experience living with a drug addict led her to know their relationship could not continue in that condition and last long term. She pled with him to get help and warned him she would leave, but he was a functional drug addict and didn't believe the problem he had would cause a significant breach in their relationship. That was until the day she delivered the news that she couldn't take his lifestyle anymore and would abscond without him. It was at that moment David realized the path he was on would come to a difficult end if he didn't change. Regardless of the news she brought, he still did not or possibly could not change and she left him as she warned she would do.

Deep down in his soul, David knew he had to either make significant changes in his life or it would continue to spiral out of control into a grave, dark abyss and potentially end prematurely. As he sat and lingered in a dazed state brought on by the coke and alcohol he had consumed, David rifled through the television channels until he came to an infomercial that seemed to have seized his focus. It was a featured pitch for smokers to stop their habit in thirty days. For some strange reason it caught his attention. After all it was New Year's and all those ads which pitched New Year's resolutions would flood the airwaves in the next couple of weeks. Weight loss, start a new career, stop smoking, and so many more; he had seen them all and questioned if any of them could really work. Even though he struggled with his demons, David gave time to thinking about what he believed were life's truths.

He often pondered the purpose of life and whether each individual was just on autopilot or if they truly had the capacity to control what happened to them in the course of their lifetime. Between his cocaine and alcohol binges, David would find time to read material on the subject and search for answers to these profound questions few people even gave thought to. It would be in the process of contemplating and asking his self these types of questions that he would find his way back to a meaningful life. One which would be filled with all the trappings he had dreamed of many times in his current, lonely, torn world.

Awkwardly slumped in the recliner, he faded in and out of his drunken induced sleep. Finally, David slipped off and quickly delved into a dream of days gone by with Laura, his one true love. In years past, they were good together but his escalating cocaine and alcohol use was at the center of their break up. It left both of them devastated and each wondered what had happened. His failure to address his insidious addiction left her with no other option but to leave him. It pained her to abandon David, but she had to move on with her life and put distance between them or she would continue to enable him to live in the manner she detested and it would ultimately cause her to resent him even more and hate herself as well.

As he slipped further into his dream, he held her beautiful face in his hands. Suddenly, a cold shiver coursed through his body and he awoke only to find himself alone, slumped in the recliner. Drool dripped from the corner of his mouth as the stop smoking infomercial still played on the television. David felt another chill pass throughout his entire body as he attempted to stand up. The alcohol obviously affected his equilibrium and he lost his balance as he rose and fell forward out of the recliner and onto the floor. As he lunged forward his face hit the floor with a thud and caused his nose to bleed profusely. He ended up on his knees with his head bent over in a position accustomed to Muslims attending temple prayer service. He began to weep like a child and then spoke in a low, but firm measured voice.

"God if you are real... and out there listening, please help me. I need you to help me now."

David wept like he had never done before. He realized his life was out of control and at the point in which he would either make a significant change in direction or it would continue to unravel, likely to end up in a devastating crash. He remained on his knees, his body hunched over and he cried while he spoke with whatever or whoever was out there to listen to his pleas.

"My life is wrecked. I can't continue to live like this anymore, I need a sign... I need your help..."

As he continued to plead for help from some omniscient force, the stop smoking infomercial ended. An instant later an ad for a Las Vegas hypnosis show, which featured 'The World's Greatest Hypnotist', appeared on the screen. David heard the advertisement for the show, 'Mind Bending Illusions' and stopped to look up at the television with his water filled eyes. He wiped away the moisture with the back of his hand to get a better look at the ad. Something unexplained had happened in that single moment of time which diverted his attention over the next few minutes and would most assuredly change the course of David's life. He was suddenly drawn to the content of the ad and wrote down the information to purchase tickets to the show. He immediately reached for the phone and made a call to the Stardust Hotel and Casino in Las Vegas. On the other end the operator politely answered his call.

"Thank you for calling Stardust Hotel and Casino, how may I direct your call?"

David was anxious to order a ticket to see the World's Greatest Hypnotist featured in Mind Bending Illusions, but he was still lingering in a drunken haze from his drug and alcohol consumption which made him slur. His voice was barely audible and difficult to understand as he attempted to purchase a ticket for one of Las Vegas' most popular shows.

"Uhh, yeah, one show ticket for the Greatest."

"Is that Mind Bending Illusions with the World's Greatest Hypnotist sir?"

"Yeah, yeah that's the one."

Somehow the operator deciphered his request and forwarded the call to the theater ticketing office. A soft voice can be heard on the other end and the conversation with David continues.

"Main event tickets, how may I help you?"

In a slurred voice, and somewhat impatient, David stammers out his request again.

"Juzz one pleeze for Worlz Greatest Hypno…"

His voice faded off, but surprisingly the young female agent also understood exactly what David had asked for and she responded.

"One ticket for the Mind Bending Illusions featuring The World's Greatest Hypnotist; did you have a date in mind sir or do you want our first available?"

"Firz available pleez."

She proceeds to advise David.

"This is a very popular show sir; it's sold out for the next five weeks; the earliest I can get a ticket for you is Friday, February ninth; will that work?"

"Yeah, yeah tha'll be good; one ticket pleez."

The operator proceeds to complete the ticket purchase and provides David with all the details before she closed the sale. He began to fade back into a sleep as she completes the call, advised him his ticket would be sent regular mail and should arrive within five business days, well before the show date. David hung up before he passed out, but didn't realize he had made a purchase to see Mind Bending Illusions featuring the World's Greatest Hypnotist.

The next morning David awakened on the couch with an expected, severe headache and cotton mouth that felt like a dry desert wind had blown through his respiratory system. He rolled over and noticed scribbled notes on a yellow pad of paper by the phone which sat on his coffee table. There was a barely legible phone number and the word "hypnotist" written on the pad. He wasn't sure what the note alluded to or if he had made the ticket purchase for Mind Bending Illusions featuring the World's Greatest Hypnotist the previous night, but less than one week later it was confirmed when his ticket arrived in the mail. His date with destiny was set. He was now going to see for himself how this so-called master of the mind took control of others through the use of hypnosis. He didn't realize it in the moment, but David would soon be on a personal mission that would take him in a direction even he would have a hard time imagining. With no thought given to what had taken place the previous night, his quest for the significant change in his life that he had prayed to God for had begun.

CHAPTER FOUR
FEBRUARY
LAS VEGAS, NEVADA

David awoke early the next morning and reflected on the sequence of events that led him to meet with Jefferson Paul the previous night. He made several attempts in the past couple years to change the direction of his life and shed his habitual drug use, but to no avail. David now felt the breakup of his relationship with Laura could well have been the impetus he needed to finally seek the type of help he would need to make a permanent shift in his life's path. He was uncertain of the impact Jefferson's book 'Lessons of the Mind' may have, but he decided he would dedicate himself and focus his efforts to realize the change he so desperately sought.

For some unexplained reason, David sensed he had a special destiny which awaited him. Since his breakdown on New Year's Eve he seemed to be in search of how he would find it and develop the path to fulfilling what he felt lie ahead for him. That's where Jefferson would enter into his life and provide the help he would need. David realized just how fortunate he had been to have had enough awareness on that fateful New Year's Eve to buy a ticket to Jefferson Paul's show. He also had the courage and took the opportunity to meet with him, which could possibly lead to getting Jefferson's help in what would eventually turn out to be his mission in life. As he thought of the sequence of events that had played out over the course of the last few weeks, it seemed as if there may be something greater than his self at work in the background. It appeared to be a mysterious force beyond his control that led him to this point.

The long nights rest did him a world of good, but he woke with a slight kink in his neck from the awkward position he had been in while he slept on the lounge chair. He called down to the spa to schedule a late morning massage to work out the stiffness in his neck and the tension in his shoulders.

"Good morning, how may I direct your call?"

The hotel operator eagerly asks with a sweet southern draw to her voice. As she spoke, David thought to himself, there were so many transient or relocated people in Las Vegas she must be a southern belle from Louisiana or maybe Alabama.

"Hi, this is David Christian in room #1226. I would like to schedule a massage for later this morning."

"Absolutely Mister Christian, let me forward you to the spa for scheduling."

The phone rang into the spa and a women's voice answered softly.

"Good morning, it's a wonderfully relaxed day at the Stardust Spa. How may I help you?"

David leafed through the pages of the book in his hands as he stated his request to the spa receptionist.

"Yeah, I'd like to schedule a massage for later this morning, say around eleven or eleven-thirty, if you have an opening."

"Yes sir, let me check that time. We do have a couple of openings at eleven, can I get your name and room number?"

"David Christian, room 1226."

"Mister Christian, do you have a preference for male or female therapist?"

"Female preferred, but it's not necessary."

"Yes sir. Will you be billing direct to your room?"

"Yeah, that'll be fine."

"OK sir, we have you down for eleven with Susan Hunter. See you then."

"Thank you."

David starts for the bathroom and runs the shower to warm the water before he steps in. He lets the soothing, warm, rain wash over his head and shoulders as he begins to wash the sleep from his eyes. After a thorough cleanse, David dresses and heads down to the lobby of the hotel. He looks around and spots the familiar café off in the distance. It's a perfect spot to get a bite and relax awhile before he heads to the spa for his massage. David strolls across the casino floor and walks up to the counter. The young female hostess reaches for menus.

"Will anyone be joining you sir?"

"No just myself."

"Right this way please."

The pretty young woman leads David to the rear of the café and seats him at the same table he shared with Jefferson the previous night. She sets his menu down on the right side of the table and smiles at him with a bright sparkle in her eye.

"Your server will be right with you. Can I start you with a coffee?"

"That sounds terrific, thanks."

David grabs the menu and spots the daily special, two eggs, bacon, sausage, or ham, hash browns and a muffin for less than three bucks. That'll be it. He brought Doctor Jefferson's book with him to the café and opened to where he left off the night before. Just as he starts to read his mind flashes back to the dream he had as he slipped into a deep sleep the night before. It all seemed so real now, the faces of the crowd, his presentation, and they hung onto his every word. David remembered the last words Doctor Paul asked of him when he offered his help. Jefferson had asked him to 'pay it forward.'

He paused for a moment to contemplate the request. Just what did the Doctor mean by that? Did he really expect David to go on and help others in the same manner the master was capable of? Hell, David didn't even know if he would be able to turn his own life around with this new information he was being exposed to, let alone help anyone else. How could he possibly pay it forward? In that moment, David was oblivious to the realization of the previous night, but he would soon find the answer was revealed in his dream.

"Good morning sir, my name is Rhonda and I'll be your server. Are you ready to order?"

David's concentration is broken and he looks up to see a middle aged woman with a bright smile and sparkling blue eyes. She notices the cover of his book as he closes it and begins to place his order with her.

"Yes Rhonda, I'll have the special with ham and eggs over medium."

"Very good, I'll get you a coffee refill too."

David had gulped down the first cup while he daydreamed and didn't realize it was empty until Rhonda mentioned a refill.

"Oh yeah, that would be great, thank you."

Before she leaves Rhonda made a gesture toward the book in his hands.

"How is Doctor Paul's book?"

David, a bit surprised, smiled at her reference to the master and responded.

"I just started to read it last night and I'm almost halfway through. It's interesting, but I am sure I'll give it at least a second look to thoroughly understand the subject he discusses."

Rhonda nods and continues.

"He comes in occasionally for coffee or a meal. He's an interesting man. Is he a good friend of yours?"

The question caught David by surprise. He wasn't sure how to answer. After all, Doctor Paul did offer to help him in any way he could and even signed 'your friend' in the book. Did that really qualify him as a friend? After a slight pause to contemplate he replied.

"I actually just met Jefferson last night after the late show. We spent some time together here in the café and discussed hypnosis. He shared the book with me and gave me his card so I guess you can say it was the start of a friendship. At least I hope it is."

She smiled, turned and walked off to place his order. David opened the book again and started to read where he had left off. The subject was one that certainly intrigued him and he had read several books from various authors on topics related to self-realization. The problem with most of the material available in that subject matter was that it was typically based in theory and never gave practical steps to take or applications to execute in an effort to make a significant change. David grasped the concepts, but never applied practical methods to make the changes he sought. The other issue was he would not, or could not make the effort to stop his drug use. In the years since college, David had become a functional drug addict and if he was going to experience the significant transformation in his life that he sought, he would have to make a commitment to go about it with a clear mind. He was an intelligent man and performed well enough at his occupation to make a decent living, but there was always the subject of drug use that kept him from really excelling and creating a life based on his choices rather than just make a living. David bore that crutch and he knew it was an obstacle he would have to overcome. He had begun the process and quit using after his New Year's crash, but weeks later he struggled to stay off the substances. He knew the road to recovery would be long and arduous and he would have to find an effective method that would last long term. He wondered if hypnosis could aid him as it did for those who used it to stop smoking.

As he read the pages, his focus continued to move back to the thought of obtaining the assistance of Doctor Paul in hypnotic therapy as a means to overcome his issue with drugs. Even though Jefferson had advised him he no longer did clinical work, he decided to address the topic and would discuss it with him the next time they spoke. David stopped and turned back to the previous page, knowing full well his mind was not on the words he had just read. As he started over once again to read the words he hypnotically breezed over, Rhonda approached with his breakfast and a fresh thermos of hot coffee. She set the warm plate down in front of him and filled his cup with the hot brew.

"Here you go honey, one special breakfast with ham and eggs over medium. Will there be anything else?"

David closed the book and looked down at the plate full of steaming hot breakfast food.

"Mmm, it looks good. That'll be fine for now. Thank you."

"Sure thing sweetie, you enjoy."

Rhonda turned and walked away as David devoured his breakfast with the vigor of a hungry cheetah ripping into the hide of a freshly caught cottontail. He consumed the meal in minutes and turned back to his reading until his bill was delivered. David signed it off to his room and headed out of the café onto the casino floor. It was ten minutes after ten in the morning and he had less than an hour to kill before his massage, so David decided to play a few hands of blackjack to pass the time.

He pulls up to a table with a five dollar limit and places forty dollars on the table. The stone faced dealer counts out an equivalent amount of chips and slides them in front of David. As he plays out his first couple hands, his mind inadvertently goes back to the book he has been reading. Lesson five, what you expect tends to be realized. You become what you think about. He starts to think about being dealt winning hands and as luck would have it, he hits a blackjack on the third deal. He thinks to himself, maybe there is something to these lessons after all. A smile comes across his face as he focuses on hitting another winning hand. After several hands have been dealt and he wins an additional forty dollars, he notices the time and has to get to the spa before his massage appointment. David cashes out his chips and collects his winnings at the cashier's cage. He doesn't give much more thought to the pattern he developed at the table, but he feels good about winning and now looks forward to a thoroughly relaxing session with the massage therapist.

David arrives at the spa five minutes before his scheduled massage and checks in with the female clerk at the front desk.

"Hi, David Christian, I have an eleven o'clock."

"Yes sir, I see we have you with Susan. I'll let her know you're here. Please have a seat; would you like a bottle of water?"

David nods as he turns toward the padded couch in the lobby area.

"No thanks, I'll get a bottle on my out though."

"Sure thing, just stop by and we'll have it waiting for you."

David sits down in the soft cushioned couch and

no more than a minute passes, when in walks Jefferson Paul. He immediately spots David on the couch and with a broad smile across his face he greets his new friend.

"Well, well David. Are you getting a massage?"

"Yeah, I called down this morning after waking up with a couple kinks and some tension in the neck and shoulders. And you?"

"Certainly, I try to make it in at least once a week. They have a great team of massage therapists here. Any one of them will do a tremendous job."

He pauses a brief moment before asking.

"So did you start reading the book?"

Jefferson questions to see if David is serious about changing or if it was all talk. He isn't interested in offering his help to someone who isn't going to take a primary roll and act on their stated desire. After all, it's going to be up to David to do the work if he wants to experience any real transformation.

"Yes, as a matter of fact I did."

Jefferson was very pleased to hear that answer and he nodded his approval with a pat on David's shoulder and offered encouragement to continue with his quest.

"That's good David. You took the first step toward the transformation you stated and did so without hesitation. I'm very glad for you. Now just keep it up and let me know if you have any questions as you go through the lessons."

David hadn't planned to return home until Sunday and would be in Las Vegas for another day, so he considered asking Doctor Paul to meet again. He didn't want to be intrusive in asking, but he figured what the hell, after all he did offer his help.

"I'll be in town until early Sunday afternoon; would you have time to meet again tonight or maybe

Sunday morning for breakfast? I'll buy."

Jefferson smiles and gives him the answer he was hoping to get.

"Absolutely David, what works best for you? I will be free tonight after my nine o'clock show or we can meet in the morning for breakfast at the café."

"Let's plan breakfast. I don't want to impose after you perform again tonight."

"That'll be fine David. Let's meet at the café Sunday morning at nine. Enjoy your massage."

David extends his hand and grips Doctor Paul's in a firm handshake.

"Thank you Jefferson."

Doctor Paul nods, turns away from David and walks into the back room and disappears into the bowels of the spa. Just then, Susan Hunter comes out of the back area and eyes David sitting on the couch as he leafs through a local 'Las Vegas' magazine.

"David Christian?"

He looks up from the pages and is surprised, actually delighted at the young beauty standing in front of him. A quick thought runs through his mind as he stands. He quietly wonders if she provides customers with the oft talked about Las Vegas 'happy ending.'

"Yes I'm David."

Susan extends her hand and they politely shake. She is medium height with a slender build, but has a firm grip when they shake. Her long blonde hair is pulled back in a ponytail and clipped into a ball onto the back of her head. She has piercing blue eyes and full mouth with pursed lips, a real natural beauty. David is a bit mesmerized at first and then snaps out of it. He smiles and thinks he could not have selected a better therapist if he had the opportunity to do so.

"Nice to meet you David, I'm Susan. I'll be your therapist today."

David smiles and nods his approval. His mind now cleared; his thought immediately changes… this will certainly be an enjoyable massage.

CHAPTER FIVE

The next morning David arrives at the café ten minutes early and sits on the bench in front so as to not miss Jefferson when he arrived. So many beautiful women in this town he thought as he watched couples and single ladies stroll around in the casino area. Jefferson glides up from behind him and startles David.

"Good morning David. How was your massage with the incomparable Miss Hunter?"

With a broad smile David gestures to Jefferson to lead the way into the restaurant. David wondered how Jefferson already knew who he was paired with in the spa. Jefferson grinned and fished to get some feedback on the details. The smile never left David's face as he started to describe the efficacy of what turned out to be one of the best massages he had experienced.

"Well as you know, I had Susan Hunter; you've had her before?"

"Ahh yes, absolutely; she's the beautiful young blonde with strong hands."

Jefferson laughs out loud, then sits back to take in the rest of David's description of the session he enjoyed with the lovely Miss Hunter.

"Strong hands indeed; she is a very good therapist as you already know, and quite the looker too. When she had me flip over onto my back I was worried I was going to pitch a tent with my hard dick poking upward in that sheet they cover you with."

Jefferson let out another boisterous laugh and shook his head in approval. He had experienced the beautiful Susan Hunter's massage a number of times previously and envied the fact David got her before he could select his masseur.

"Ahh yes indeed, she has that way with men, at least the straight men she rubs down."

Just then Rhonda walked up to their table and noticed David.

"Hey there, so good you couldn't stay away huh? And I see you brought the master with you this morning."

The two men exchange pleasantries with Rhonda as she takes their drink order, Cranberry juice and coffee for both. She walks away briskly and they quickly continue their conversation about the massages.

"So you have had Susan Hunter before?"

David asks.

"Oh yes, I have had a massage from every one of those woman in that spa and Susan really is the best therapist. She's a lovely young lady, not to mention she's easy on the eyes too, as you indicated."

"Boy you can say that again."

Jefferson laughs and repeats it again as if they are high school adolescents in discussion about the hot girls in the class.

"She's easy on the eyes."

Rhonda arrives back at the table with a hot pot of coffee and two tall glasses of cranberry juice. She sets the juices down in front of each man and picks up Jefferson's cup to fill it with the hot steaming brew. She places the cup down and grabs David's while she refers to the comment he made the previous morning.

"So David, I guess you were right."

At first David isn't sure what Rhonda had referred to but then he remembers the comment he made with regard to the start of a friendship with Jefferson. He smiles and nods his head up and down to acknowledge the fact she remembered. Rhonda gives him a wink and turns away to deliver the coffee pot back to its position on the hot plate. She returns a moment later to take their order.

"Have you decided what's for breakfast?"

Jefferson gestures to David.

"Go ahead David, please."

David looks up from the menu and wonders if she would remember.

"I'll have my usual."

Rhonda giggles and recites the special.

"You got it, eggs over medium with a slab of ham and an English muffin."

Jefferson looks at David with surprise as David smiles at Rhonda for remembering.

"So you've been here before?"

He then turns his attention to Rhonda and places his order.

"I'll have the special as well, only scramble my eggs. I'll have the slab of ham too, and wheat toast."

"Okay, I'll get this order in; how is everything else, alright?"

She checks out their coffee cups. Both men nod affirmative and she leaves them to continue with their conversation. David starts by telling Jefferson he has completed the book and asks if they can go over the lessons briefly. Jefferson nods his agreement.

"Of course David, we can discuss whatever you would like to talk about."

David conveniently pulls the paperback from the back of his pants and lays it on the table. Opening to the first chapter he looks up and says.

"Let's start at the beginning."

Jefferson gestures and waits for David to ask his question. Struggling for the right question, David looks at

Jefferson and blurts out.

"Everything begins in thought? What exactly does that mean?"

"Well David, we know that everything in the material world must first begin with a thought and thoughts are things. There is actually scientific evidence that points to this fact. Thoughts have a physiological, as well as psychological impact on our actions."

David listens intently and nods as if he is in agreement with Jefferson.

"You have heard the old saying keep positive thoughts and good things will happen. Well that is true to a degree. It is true that positive thoughts induce action, progress, and productivity while negative thoughts create passivity and procrastination."

Inquisitively, David interrupts and asks.

"So just by thinking positive thoughts, we will create change?"

"No, not entirely; you see David, that is just the start. To create real change takes much more than just positive thinking. You need a plan and included in that plan, you need action steps to bring you to a level of change that you desire. Just thinking positive thoughts, while it is a good start, is not enough."

David has a puzzled look on his face as Doctor Paul continued to explain the first lesson, so the good doctor stopped to clear any questions David might have lingering in his head.

"Do you have a question David? You look like you may need something clarified."

David hesitates briefly and then asks.

"You just stated that positive thoughts induce action, correct?"

"Yes, that is correct. However, if you have no plan

to follow then what action will you take? You need to view the cumulative effect of the lessons and not just one lesson at a time."

David smiles and nods as if a light bulb went off in his head. Jefferson continued.

"If you maintain a positive frame of mind you are much more inclined to execute the plans you create to make a change or to move your life in a certain direction. But it is critical to know that a plan of action is as important to the process as is the first lesson, which is everything begins in thought. Think about it."

Jefferson smiles at David as he struggles to fully grasp the concept. Rhonda arrives at the table with a tray of food. She pulls two large plates of eggs, ham and hash brown potatoes from the tray and sets them in front of each patron.

"There you go gents, can I get you anything else for now?"

David slides his coffee cup out to the edge of the laminated table.

"I can use another shot of caffeine. I'll be driving home later and I definitely don't want to nod off while I'm on the highway."

"No you don't. I'll be right back with that refill right away."

Jefferson all the while is looking at David with a grin on his face and when he has his full attention he continues with his teaching.

"Do you get what I have stated here in lesson one? The thought is only a piece of the puzzle. You have to have thoughts to get things started and the best way to proceed in a productive way is to have positive thoughts. It's really just that simple."

David pauses from shoveling eggs and ham in his

mouth and looks up to ask Jefferson another question.

"How do you control whether the thoughts you have are positive or not? I mean, you know how we have a continual conversation going on inside our heads? Sometimes I have a negative thought that just pops in my head without my knowing its coming."

"You must learn to let it go and replace it with a positive thought."

David sets down his fork and grabs his coffee cup, not realizing it hasn't been refilled yet.

"You make that sound like it's no big deal."

Rhonda arrives with the pot and pours a hot cup for each of them and turns away as Jefferson continues the conversation.

"It really is simple David. Have a standard positive thought ready at all times, what I like to call my 'go to thoughts.' When something negative pops into your head, let it go and turn your attention immediately to one of those 'go to thoughts.' You will find over time you'll become better at controlling your thoughts and very efficient at replacing a negative thoughts. This process will keep you at a higher frequency; remember, think positive thoughts and execute your creative plan."

Jefferson pauses to take a few bites of his breakfast and lets that last statement settle with David before he continues. David looks across the table with a scrunched brow as if he is thinking real hard about what Jefferson has just explained to him when the doctor proceeds to explain lesson two and how it all ties into the first lesson.

"I mentioned to you that thoughts are things. Do you understand this or is it something that just goes by you without your giving it serious consideration?"

"Wow, you don't have to be mean about it and

insult my intelligence."

Jefferson gives him a slight chuckle and proceeds.

"I am not being mean or attempting to insult you; I just want you to get this David. It is very important to the process to know that thoughts are things and they produce emotions in us that affect the way we go about our daily lives. Do you ever wonder how two people can view the exact same event and have two entirely different reactions to it?"

"What do you mean?"

"Well let's just take an automobile accident as an example. One person may see it happen and through her continued thoughts of the event, will go on to have a miserable day. She just repeatedly thinks of those poor people in the wreck and relives the situation over and over. Those negative thoughts she continues to dwell on create a negative feeling or emotion in her being and her day spirals downward as a result. Whereas another woman may experience the same event and not give it a second thought. She says a quick prayer for the individuals involved, lets it go and replaces the memory of the accident with a positive 'go to thought' and thus continues to have a pleasant day and executes on the plans she had for the afternoon. It comes down to knowing how to filter your thoughts and having the ability to dispatch those that take you off course."

David slowly chews on a piece of ham as he listens intently to Jefferson's explanation. He stays focused on the doctor through the discussion and keeps eye contact without allowing the environment that surrounds them to distract him from the topic he is so interested in. Jefferson pauses and keeps the eye contact as well. He gives David a look as if to ask, 'do you get it?' and places both of his hands with palms faced upward, shrugs his shoulders as if he is the Robert Dinero character in the cast of the 'Goodfellas.'

"Capice?"

David breaks out in laughter and confirms he does understand these first two lessons.

"Yes, I understand. Though I can see this process will take some time and practice to develop the habit of replacing bad thoughts with good ones."

"Of course it will take time David, but not as much as you may think. Stick to what I have told you. In thirty days you will find you have developed a new positive habit that will impact you in a way that will start the change you've said you seek in your life."

The two men sat in silence for several minutes while they finished their meals. Once done, Rhonda dutifully comes by their table to gather their plates and refill coffee cups. The mood has turned somewhat uncomfortable and David wants to breech the topic of drug abuse to inquire if Jefferson has had any clinical experience with clients who faced addictions. A smile crosses Jefferson's face and he senses David is searching for the words by the way he shifts.

"David, go ahead and ask."

"Ask?"

"Well you're shifting in your seat and I can see from the look on your face you have something on your mind, what is it?"

That was David's cue to ask what he had waited to get an answer to since the moment he met Jefferson. He had a problem with drug and alcohol abuse and needed help to eliminate the habit. David paused and wondered if this would change the budding friendship the men had begun to establish. The last thing he wanted was to burden Jefferson with his personal problems, but he decides to continue anyway since he wouldn't know if he didn't ask.

"I actually need your advice on how to break a habit... a bad habit."

"Is that what has bothered you for the last several minutes? I see it in your expression."

"Well, yes. I haven't been totally forthcoming with my story."

Jefferson, having done prior work in clinical hypnosis has dealt with this situation many times over. He isn't overly concerned yet, but probes to get the information he needs to make a judgment on whether he can help David or not.

"So let's hear it David, what have you held back? Are you gay?"

Jefferson realized he may have just insulted his new friend and immediately raised his hand to stop any response from David.

"I'm sorry for that remark; it was an insensitive comment to make. Please, go ahead and tell me what is weighing heavy on your mind."

"I have dealt with a drug and alcohol problem for several years. It has undoubtedly held me back in my career and has also created issues in my personal relationships for most of my adult life."

David felt the weight come off his shoulders as he spoke the truth. He even felt a sense of strength that he could overcome the issue by virtue of his admittance to the problem. More than he knew, he was correct. Admit you have the problem and you have taken the first step in the process of recovery; Jefferson reinforced that fact.

"Well that's not as bad as murder, now is it?"

They both laughed at Jefferson's sarcasm and the tension was put to ease.

"David, you have just taken the first step to recovery. Kick the habit by first admitting you have a problem. Now I don't know how bad your drug use is but I can say this, it usually depends on the drug you use as to whether it can be either easy or more difficult to quit. You see some drugs create physical withdraw that complicates the situation, but we can work through it and see how committed you are to changing the circumstances in your life. I also want to make this perfectly clear; you are the one that will do the work and you can kick a habit with self-hypnosis, even a drug habit."

David sat slumped and looked at Jefferson with a puppy dog look on his face and continued to explain his personal drug habit.

"I have smoked weed and snorted coke for several years. Not every single day, but I use one drug or the other at least three or four days a week, sometimes more. It may seem like a lot to some and not much to others, but if I am going to make a change in my life, it has to stop."

"I agree David, and if you have a conviction to end it, you will stop."

Jefferson was firm in his comment and displayed his concern with a stern look as the two men sat across from one another. He decided to move the conversation from David's drug use.

"Have you made any decision as to what it is you want to do with your life?"

David had a vague idea and attempted to explain it, but he wasn't crystal clear or focused in his explanation and that left Jefferson with only one thing to do.

"Let's do this David, take some time over the next couple weeks and really give this question a lot of thought because it is critical that you have a single minded purpose and are willing to work toward achievement of your objective without distraction. If you can't do that, it will be virtually impossible to make a significant change; without clear focus it just won't happen for you."

For some unknown reason, David felt disappointment when he heard that statement and knew their meeting would come to an end soon. Upon deep reflection into his soul he knew Jefferson was correct to point this out to him. He shook his head in agreement and before they would part ways he asked one more question.

"Jefferson, can I call you before I return to town next month?"

"Of course you can David, you can call me anytime you like."

CHAPTER SIX

On his return drive home from Las Vegas David stopped in Baker for a gas refill and a bite to eat at the local Denny's. Baker is a small desert town that most refer to as the gateway to Death Valley located in the Mojave Desert. Typically, this would be a nice stop for David to venture off the beaten path and attempt to find the perfect spot to get high, but after his discussion with Jefferson he decided to give it his most concerted effort and change his ways. Before he left town, he flushed what weed he had down the toilet in the hotel room. If he was going to experience the life transformation he wanted, it had to start immediately as Jefferson indicated, and without reservations about giving up old habits. David knew Jefferson would not hang around and waste his time if he continued to abuse drugs and ignore the advice he had received from the master of hypnosis.

As he wandered into the diner he noticed the room was practically full and he wondered if there was some special reason for the abnormal numbers at this small desert stop. Then it hit him, Valentine's Day was around the corner and couples were traveling to Las Vegas to spend the romantic date together. The thought of Valentine's Day with Laura brought memories to the forefront of his mind. He reminisced of days gone by and the great times they had spent together. It was only distant memories now and David knew he would have to focus on himself before he could ever get back into a loving relationship with any type potential for commitment. His only commitment now was going to be to himself. David needed to be the best he could be if he was going to make the life change he so desired, and for that matter be a help to anyone else.

The hostess spotted him and came up from the counter to offer him a seat.

"Hi, will it just be you today?"

David smiled and replied.

"Yep, I'm flying solo today. Actually, I can just sit at the counter and you can save the table or booth for a larger party."

"OK, that's great. Go ahead and seat yourself then. Here's a menu for you and a server will be right with you."

Taking the menu from her hand, David looks into her eyes and smiles before he turns and heads for a seat at the counter. There are many open stools and he takes one close to the end of the bar, next to the hallway that led to the restrooms. Just as he sat down a young, dark haired female walks up from the other side of the counter. She is an attractive woman with fiery green eyes to go with her medium length dark brown hair. It's pulled back in a small bun and clipped to the back of her head. Setting a glass of ice water in front of him, she asks.

"Hello, would you like anything else to drink besides water?"

David settles into the barstool with a low back and takes a deep breath before he answers.

"I'll have a Diet Coke, and I'm also ready to place my order if you're ready to take it."

"Sure, go right ahead."

She responds as she pulls the pad from her apron.

"I'll have the double cheeseburger with fried onion rings."

"How would you like that prepared?"

He places the menu down on the counter, looks up

and replies.

"Medium, please and thank you."

She grabs the menu and before she turns to place his order with the head cook, she introduces herself.

"By the way, I'm Tina and I'll be your server."

Smiling at her impromptu intro David replies.

"I'm David, and nice to meet you Tina.

She giggles slightly as she makes the turn toward the kitchen and calls out his order to the cook who is diligently at work in front of the grill.

Feeling fatigued from his previous late nights as well as the drive, David stands up, maneuvers around the stool and heads down the hallway to the restroom. He walks in and steps up to the sink, turns the water on and cups his hands together to splash his face with the cold liquid. He then washes his hands and rinses them off before he throws one last splash of cold water across his face to awaken himself. Several minutes after he returns to his spot at the counter his meal is prepped and set under the heat lamp. Tina moves quickly from the opposite end of the counter, grabs his plate and sets it in front of him.

"Can I get you anything else David?"

"Oh no, this looks good. Thank you."

David is surprisingly hungry after the large breakfast he had earlier and begins to devour the juicy burger and crispy fried onion rings. Just as he stuffs the burger into his mouth for another bite Tina walks up to make sure all is well.

"How is everything?"

Immediately realizing his hands are full with the juicy, dripping, burger and his mouth is stuffed, she giggles and apologizes for her bad timing.

"Oops, sorry about that; it looks like you're enjoying it though."

He sets the big burger down on the plate, finishes chewing the mouthful and swallows as he waves his approval to her.

"Great, it's great. Thank you."

Tina is intrigued with David and wonders why he is on the road alone. She is hesitant to get too personal, but asks anyway.

"So where are you headed David?"

"Back home to Oceanside."

"You were in Las Vegas I take it?"

"Yes, I went to see Mind Bending Illusions featuring the World's Greatest Hypnotist on Friday night. It was quite an amazing show to see."

Tina nods with peeked interest, and continues with her inquisitive questions.

"You went alone?"

With a smile on his face, and a sudden realization that this young woman is interested in him, David responds in a manner which let her know the timing was just not right.

"Yeah, I recently came out of a relationship and need some time to myself."

His message was loud and clear even though he didn't state it verbally. He was not interested in any type of committed relationship at this time, but she was nice to speak with. Tina, ever the intuitive server got the message and with a slight smile on her face, she turned and left him to enjoy the rest of his meal.

"Well… enjoy; if you need anything else just flag me down."

"Thanks Tina, I appreciate it."

He was appreciative of the solitude she gave him. He wasn't the same guy that left his home in Oceanside for a weekend in Las Vegas three days ago. David was somehow different and he had begun to feel it. Could one meeting with the master, Jefferson Paul, have had such a dramatic impact on him that he was already a new man? It was too soon to make that observation, but he definitely felt a slight transformation from the man that bought a ticket to the Mind Bending Illusions show on that miserable and dreary New Year's Eve. While David finished his meal, Tina stopped by to leave his bill.

"It's no rush David, but anytime you're ready, I'll take care of this for you."

David looked into her eyes, smiled, and thanked her at a barely audible level. He finished up within a couple minutes and gulped down one last swig of his diet Coke. The check total was eleven dollars and thirty-one cents. He grabbed the pen sitting on the plate the check was on, scribbled a short note on one of his business cards, and left it there with a twenty dollar bill he pulled from his pocket. David looked around and didn't see Tina, so he turned and headed for the exit. Just as he opened the front door to exit Tina spotted him walking out and he looked back and waved to her. She gave him a quick wave and slightly turned up smile. Tina was disappointed he hadn't stopped to say goodbye, but she realized they just met and her feelings weren't first on his mind. When she looked down at the plate were he left the check and money, she noticed he also left his business card. She picked it up, flipped it over and noticed there was a short note written on the back of it.

It read…

Thank you Tina, I'll see you again soon. Call me if I can help you with anything.

That was odd, she thought. He wasn't much in the

mood to get to know her but he offered her help. For what, she thought. Oh well, it was nice of him to leave a note and hopefully she would see him again. She noticed he left a twenty. Her tip was significantly higher than what is commonly expected and she smiled at the thought of his generosity. Just then one of the cooks yells out "pick up" for one of her orders and she snaps back into action and leaves the thought of David in the back of her mind for the time being.

The Highway #15 was crowded with travelers headed to and from Las Vegas, but the pace was quick and not the usual stop and go David was accustomed to in the Southern California traffic he dealt with regularly. As he drove through the dusty, windswept desert, he couldn't keep his mind from drifting back to the diner and his interaction with Tina. Maybe he should have taken some time to converse more and get to know her, he thought. Then again, he knew the challenge of his current mission and it was going to take all his focus and attention to make significant steps toward a change of the path he was on. The last thing he needed right now was a relationship that might divert his attention from what he intended to accomplish with his life and career change.

Back at the diner in Baker, a couple hours had passed and Tina Crevino had ended her shift. She shared a common bond with the small group of people she worked with. They all had their own story of escaping from a small hometown somewhere in the vast United States in an effort to come west and live the 'California Dream.' Only this wasn't the California they all dreamed of. Baker was a small, dusty, out of the way town that had a population of less than one thousand residents. It wasn't quite the coastal resort city of Newport Beach or even the big city metropolis of Los Angles that some in this group had dreamed of. No, Baker was a pit stop; or even better described as an arm pit of Southern California. But why or how did Tina end up in this town of travelers and transients? She seemed to be a bright young woman, well-grounded with a friendly personality. This couldn't be her final destination and lord knows she hadn't aspired to be a server at Denny's in Baker, California for the rest of her life. Could her chance meeting with David Christian be her possible ticket out?

Her real story went something like this. A young girl with dreams of going to Hollywood to become a successful actress on the big screen; it took a wrong turn and stalled in Baker. She now looked for her next move to get out of town and in to the city where she could resume her quest for the dream she had temporarily let go of. Tina was from a family of seven children in a small town outside of San Antonio, Texas. She was the middle child and reared with four brothers, three that were older and two younger sisters. Her childhood was tough at times and she dreamt of the day she would be far away from that hell-hole. With a large family to support, her father jumped from job to job as he struggled to provide for his family. He was frustrated and drank to deal with his failures, which led to his abuse of his children. As each child grew older, they all searched for a way out of their miserable situation and all seemed interested to leave the small town for bigger cities and higher aspirations. Tina was no different. She had dreamed of a career in theater. Drama was something she took up in high school and continued to participate in while attending community college. It was her escape and she actually had raw talent for the craft. It was there at Brown Mackie College in San Antonio where she had met her boyfriend and planned an escape with him to the bright lights and big opportunities in the City of Angels, Los Angeles, California. They both wanted the same thing, or so it seemed, but as they traveled away from the small town outside San Antonio and pressures mounted, he became abusive just as her father had been. When they arrived in Baker, he realized he no longer had an interest in their individual pursuits and decided to take another direction without Tina.

One morning at dawn, before she rose, he left a note for her. He was headed back to Texas and California was no longer in his plans. He left her with no money and no transportation to get out of Baker. Tina was stuck and she needed a plan to survive until she could get back on her feet and resume her dream of becoming a notable actress. The immediate plan was to get a job that would support her for the time being while she worked out the details to get her potential acting career back on the forefront of her life's objectives. Denny's needed a server and that's where Tina could be found for the last two and half years. The job provided her with enough income to survive in the small town, but not nearly enough to save and make the move she so desperately wanted to make. Every day that went by was one more day she would slip further behind on her dream. She had to find a way to make a change, but was too proud to call on her family for their help. Anyway, she knew they wouldn't have the resources to assist her if she made that call. It was going to be up to her to work this matter out for herself.

As she walked from the diner to her apartment a couple blocks from the restaurant, Tina stopped at the local grocery store to pick up some items for dinner. She enjoyed cooking her own meals and it gave her a respite from the miserable life she lived at the time. Gourmet chef she wasn't, but she could whip up some tasty dishes on her tight budget and often had her best girlfriend from the diner over to enjoy the meals together. Tonight was different though she would eat alone and enjoy an evening of quiet solitude. It would give her an opportunity to think about her situation and ponder her earlier meeting with David. He was friendly and seemed to be a good guy, but she too, did not want to jump into a relationship that would just take her further from her life's dream. She pulled the card he left her from her clutch and flipped it over to read the message one more time...

Thank you Tina, I'll see you again soon. Call me if I can help you with anything.

Tina's eyes welled up with tears as she read his message. For a brief moment, she hoped he would be her knight in shining armor and come back soon to save her from her broken life. Quickly, she halted her thoughts and regained her composure before she let herself break down in tears. She realized nobody was going to save her but herself and she would have to rely on her own strength and determination. Tina was a strong, determined young lady and would persevere as she had for the last two and half years. She was going to find a way out of her current situation and it would come soon. She placed the card on her small dining table and went about preparing her dinner for the night. Maybe I'll give him a call in a few days, she thought.

CHAPTER SEVEN

It had been a week since David met Jefferson for breakfast and discussed the first couple of chapters from his book, "Lessons of the Mind." Since that morning in which they shared a couple hours over breakfast, David had given much thought to what Doctor Paul had instructed him to do. He had developed a special interest in the subject of self-realization from all the material he had read over the past few years. What really caught his attention the most was how so many people, he included, didn't seem to grasp the reality that they were ultimately in control of their life's destination. It was a simple concept to understand, but one that became more complex to execute because the mind and the use of one's thoughts were not an easy thing to control. What Jefferson had provided him, through a quick education in the use of self-hypnosis, was a very real method in which he could control his thoughts and thus create a path to what ultimately would be his real dream or the destination he desired most in life.

David walked into the den and picked up his copy of "Lessons of the Mind" which sat on the coffee table. Just as he opened the book to review, the phone rang. He set the book down, turned and walked into the kitchen where he had a phone on the wall by the cupboards.

"Hello"

"Hello David, its Jefferson."

"Doctor Paul, how are you?"

"David, stop with the formalities and please call me Jefferson."

That was the third time he made the same request.

Jefferson hoped it would be the last.

"Okay, so Jefferson how are you doing?"

"Doing well, but more importantly how are you doing? Have you been giving much thought to what we spoke about?"

David, somewhat intimidated by the Doctor, slightly paused, took a deep breath and spoke.

"Yes I have been and I think I have an idea I would like to consider for development."

"That's pretty weak David."

"You haven't even heard my idea yet."

"No I haven't, but that statement you just made is pretty weak. Remember David, you have to have a strong conviction to even begin to make a change. Consider the words you used in the statement you just made."

Jefferson paused to allow David a moment to digest what he said. David, on the end of the phone, sank to the floor and sat with his back to the wall. He suddenly felt frustrated or better yet, felt defeated before he even started the game would be a more accurate description. What did he not get that the "Lessons of the Mind" should have taught him?

Before he could respond, Jefferson continued.

"You see David, when you use words and phrases like 'I think I have an idea' or 'I would like to consider developing,' those are weak statements that have no conviction behind them. I realize you are at the start of this process, but you must understand the words you use when you speak or think have a significant impact on your ability to achieve what it is you decide to pursue. Take the statement you made for example, how would you turn that into a strong statement that you could develop a plan around and then act on it?"

David, now even more confused, thought hard and

as he started to speak he was cut off by his mentor.

"I'm not..."

"David, consider this statement; I have an idea I have begun to develop."

He paused to let it sink in for a moment.

"Do you see how that statement is one of conviction versus the statement you made earlier? There is actually commitment in the second statement, nothing is left to question."

As if a light just went on, David smiled and suddenly understood the lesson Doctor Paul was personally providing him.

"I get it. I see what you mean by that."

"Good, I am glad. Just keep in mind, there are certain words and phrases that are passive or weak and they tend to make your entire statement weak; phrases like 'I'll try,' or 'I think' which you just used. They are passive and show no conviction. Once you decide the object of your pursuit, make sure you leave those weak, passive statements out of your thoughts or spoken words. It becomes very important when planting the right emotional content in your subconscious mind."

David walked over to the coffee table as Jefferson spoke and picked up the book, opened it to chapter three and commented.

"Chapter three, correct?"

Jefferson chuckled on the other end of the line and continued with the lesson.

"Yes, lesson three. Your thoughts impact all the functions of your body and because the subconscious mind is a feeling mind, thoughts with strong emotional content always reach that part of you. Once accepted by your subconscious mind, these thoughts or ideas will produce the same reaction over and over. Knowing that, it's imperative that you keep a close watch on your thinking and speaking. Use positive, active, phrases and words, and you will find over a surprisingly short period of time this practice will begin to produce positive physical reactions automatically."

Jefferson paused a moment and then asked.

"Does this make sense to you David?"

David was lost in his own thought on the other end of the phone and the question caught him off guard.

"Uh, yeah I guess so."

"You guess so? Have you been listening?"

"Yeah, but it's a lot to absorb in a short call."

Not one to waste his time and a bit frustrated with David's response, Jefferson changed the topic.

"David, how's business going?"

A little surprised by the sudden shift in conversation, David pulls the phone from his ear and looks at the receiver quizzically, then places it back to his ear and responds.

"Geez Jefferson, that was a sudden change in the topic of conversation."

"Continue your study grasshopper."

Jefferson stated jokingly and then continued.

"A little at a time and you'll soon be a master of your own mind."

David shrugged his shoulders and slid back down on the floor with his back to the wall.

"Yeah, right; I'll be the master."

"David, do you see what you just did to yourself. This is why I told you to pay attention to your thoughts and words."

"What, what did I do?"

"You used words in a negative manner against yourself. What kind of reaction do you suppose that will create? Better yet, how do you feel about the statement you just made about yourself? It can't be good."

"Holy cow, I was just kidding," David stated to avoid the wrath of his mentor.

Jefferson decided to let him off the hook for the time being and went back to his initial question.

"OK, so how's work going? When will you be back in town?"

For a moment David flashed back to his meeting with Tina at the Denny's in Baker. He didn't want too much time to pass before he stopped in to see her again, so he planned to make a business trip to Las Vegas real soon. Even though a relationship wasn't in his immediate future, he was determined to start and maintain a friendship with her if possible. His mind quickly shifted back to the question.

"Not long Jefferson. I expect to make a trip to Las Vegas in another week or two at the most. When I do you can be sure I will call you beforehand."

"That sounds good David. Let's plan to speak before then. Call me if you get stuck on anything pertaining to the lessons."

"Oh I will, you can count on it."

On the other end of the call, Jefferson just smiled and shook his head at his new student.

"I occasionally do classroom trainings for those interested in hypnosis and self-hypnosis. I happen to have one scheduled in five weeks and you may want to consider going through the course. It will be very beneficial if you do complete it. Information we cover in the three day curriculum will bring everything together in a way that will help you in your quest to create change in your life."

"That sounds interesting. Is it a large class? What

do you charge?"

"No, I limit the class size to a half dozen so that everyone gets a fair amount of attention. I'll give you a special 'friend rate,' so it won't kill your pocketbook."

David was sure he would benefit from the special course and if it could help him with his desire to create a new path in his life, he was committed to attending.

"Count me in."

"Great David, we'll speak about it when I see you in Vegas. Stay the course and I'll speak with you soon."

"Thanks Jefferson. Thank you for calling."

They both hung up and it dawned on David that Jefferson never asked him about his drug use. That was a hurdle he would have to rise above and it presented Jefferson with some concern when they first met, but the doctor left the subject for another day. He was more concerned with the way David approached the lessons and even more important, with the change in his thinking. He knew David had the capacity to change anything he wanted as long as he understood the process of shifting his thoughts in the right direction. The phone call from Jefferson to David came at a critical stage. He wanted to follow up with his friend within a short period of time before David lost his passion to succeed in his effort to make the changes he sought. Jefferson knew he had to make it very clear for David; this wasn't theory all over again, what he presented was a practical method for David to implement, as well as a strategy to utilize in his quest for creating real changes for his future. Jefferson knew as he hung up from the call, he had made an impact and now it was up to David to do his part.

As he placed the phone on the receiver David reflected on the conversation he just had. Jefferson had actually taken a genuine interest in his new friend and wanted to see him achieve the objectives he would eventually set for himself. That thought made David even more committed to his new venture to create a life change that would ultimately have a significant impact on both friends. Just then a knock at the door broke his concentration and took him away from the daydream in which he reflected on his conversation with Jefferson.

Still somewhat distracted from his daydream and his earlier discussion with Jefferson, David approached the front door of his condo. He opened the door to find his old drug supplier standing there with a clear baggie of shinning white rocks and powder. Penny, a street wise hustler, holds up the bag and with a broad smile on his face blurts out.

"Are you ready to party brotha?"

David's mind immediately snapped from his preoccupation and he felt a shiver run up his spine as he stepped back from the entry to allow Penny to step into the condo.

"Penny, what are you doing here?"

"Haven't heard from you in a while bro, so I just thought I would come around and check you out. Whassup man, you in or out?"

"Penny, you can't do this. I can't have you show up at my front door waving a bag of cocaine for all of my neighbors to see."

"Chill out man, nobody saw anything."

Penny saunters into the kitchen and places the bag of coke on the counter. He turns to see David not far behind him with a look of concern on his face.

"What's buggin' you brotha? You look like you seen a ghost."

Penny chuckles as he slips open the zip lock on the freezer bag filled with high quality cocaine. He helps himself to the kitchen utensils and pulls a small spoon from the cabinet drawer that holds the silverware.

"Get your mirror bro, let's try some of this shit."

David steps forward and takes the spoon from Penny's hand. He looks him in the eye and with a serious tone begins to inform Penny of his commitment to quit drugs. The coke in the bag looks like it is definitely high quality and David wondered just how pure it was. Penny had been known to get some of the best coke on the streets, the best David had ever used, and this batch was going to be a test for his will being that it was right there in front of him for the two of them to indulge in. Penny looked at him cross and wondered what the hell happened to David since he last sold him a score of this white crystalline powder.

"Penny, I can't do this anymore. I've made a commitment to quit drugs and change the direction of my life. This is a dead end for me."

Penny had a look of disbelief on his face.

"What the hell are you talking bout man? This is some of the best shit I've scored in quite a while. You sure you don't want to have a taste?"

David hesitates as Penny grabs for the spoon again, but he recoiled and pulled his hand away which left Penny grabbing for air. David felt the turmoil inside of him and it took all his strength to stay on course and not succumb to the urge he was experiencing in his gut. He wanted nothing more than to take a mound of that pearl white powder and snort it up his beckoning nostrils, but in a moment's notice he shifts his thoughts to the conversation he just had with Jefferson. There is no way he is going to spoil the friendship he has initiated with him and disappoint the man who took a risk to help him find the tools to turn his life around.

"I can't Penny. I won't. You have to go."

Penny looks surprised that David has declined his offer to party on his finest score in some time, but he nonetheless turns toward the counter to pack up his drugs and heads for the door.

"You sure man? This is some fine shit."

Penny waves the freezer bag full of cocaine in front of David's face. David turns away and asks him to leave once more.

"Penny, it's nothing personal, but you really have to go now."

Penny shakes his head and laughs softly as he walks slowly toward the front door. He opens the door and before he steps out turns to David.

"You be cool bro. Call me if you decide to come back to the wild side."

He chuckles, turns away from David and steps out the door without looking back. David is close behind and closes the front door as Penny saunters off and walks along the pathway to the visitor's parking area. Back inside, David turned to face the entry into his condo and fell back against the door. He takes a long drawn breath and leans back as he slides down the door onto the cool tiled floor. He sits with knees bent and his head in his hands as he softly sheds a few tears. David now realized the war for his soul would not be easy, but he just won a critical battle when the drugs were in his presence and he could have easily succumbed to the temptation. The feeling that coursed through his body was one of mixed emotion. David shook uncontrolled, but felt an inner strength at the same time. He knew it would be tough to stay the course on his quest to end his drug abuse, but each day gone by would bring him more and more comfort as he would come to know he had the will to proceed in the direction he intended to head. He sat a few minutes and then picked himself up, headed to the kitchen and took a quick observation of the space. There was some coke residue left on the counter and he quickly sapped it up with a moist towel and continued on to his business for the remainder of the day.

CHAPTER EIGHT

Another week passed and David actually began to develop a plan for his future business. His interest in self-realization and personal development had led him to focus on what he ultimately would create; a business centered on self-help through hypnosis. His intention was to create and sell affirmation CD's as well as published works on the benefits self-hypnosis with practical methods included for use in one's daily life. This was clearly a way he could pay it forward as Jefferson asked him to do. All the while he gave thought to his plan, he never forgot the one request Jefferson had made of him and he certainly didn't want to let him down. If this method of self-hypnosis he had begun to learn could help him, he wanted to share it with others. Creating products that could be useful to others who faced the same issues David had dealt with was the best way he knew he could pay it forward. He was excited about his new venture and couldn't wait to share the news with Jefferson.

David was in the middle of making his plans and scheduling business appointments for his upcoming trip to Las Vegas when the phone rang. He was completely focused on his work as he sat at the desk in his home office and became startled at the loud ring. After a brief pause and recollection of his attention, he reached for the phone, grabbed the receiver and placed it gently to his ear.

"Hello, this is David."

A female voice on the other end responded.

"Well hello there David, it's been a while."

At first David doesn't recognize the voice, but then he suddenly remembers he had left Tina a card with a short note on the counter at the diner. David is hesitant as he asks.

"Is that you Tina?"

"Yes David, how are you?"

"Good, good, I'm glad you called. Your timing is perfect. I'll be heading to Las Vegas next week and had planned to stop in at the diner to see you."

Tina brimmed with joy at the sound of those words and beamed a big, bright, white smile as she responded to the good news she had just heard.

"That's great, when will you pass through?"

She kept her emotion in check when she asked. She didn't want give away the fact she was delighted that he reacted in the manner he did to her call. Even better she thought, he had been thinking of her and planned to stop and see her. Her joy was about to burst and she did all she could to contain herself and act cool and calm as he responded.

"I'll leave Oceanside early Tuesday morning and will probably be passing through Baker around eight in the morning. Perfect time for breakfast, don't ya think?"

Tina smiled on the other end of the phone. She was elated at the news of his visit and the joyful emotion coursed through her body much like Jefferson had explained to David with regard to lesson three.

"I don't work the breakfast shift Tuesday morning, but I could meet you there."

"That sounds like a plan. Let's have breakfast together at eight."

David's confirmation made her dance inside. Tina wanted nothing more than to get to know David and this would be a good chance for them to spend a little time together without her having to wait on other customers. It was perfect.

"I look forward to seeing you David."

Somewhat curious as to the primary reason for the call, David probes a little before he lets her go.

"So what have you been up to Tina? I wasn't sure you would call."

"Well you did leave a note on the card you left, so I figured I would check the number."

He laughed, but still curious and suspect since his note stated "call me if I can help," David digs a little bit deeper to see if there is a specific reason for the call.

"Tina, was there something in particular you called for or wanted to talk about?"

Tina didn't have the nerve to tell him she needed help to get out of that desolate town of Baker, so she left it alone for the time being.

"I just wanted to say hi and see when you might be headed our way again, that's all."

David knew there must be a reason for her call, but he didn't pry anymore and would wait to see her.

"OK, well I'll be there next Tuesday morning at eight. Look forward to seeing you then."

"See you then David, bye."

"Bye Tina."

After she hung up Tina jumped to her feet and started to pump her legs in a running motion like the dancer from the old film "Flash Dance." She was elated and couldn't contain it. She danced around her apartment like a child who just received her favorite toy for Christmas. Tina danced into the walk-in closet which held all the clothes she owned. They were either hanging on the rods or folded and placed on the shelves built into the sidewalls. She started to comb through each piece, already thinking about what she would wear. Nothing to flashy, she wanted to keep it casual and tasteful. She pulled out her best pair of Calvin Klein jeans, form fitting with a rustic look to them, and a silky emerald green button down top. That's it she thought. That's my outfit for the Tuesday morning breakfast with David. She giggled knowing full well she would change her mind several times before Tuesday would come around. With the joy still coursing through her body, Tina ran her fingers like a comb through her hair. She waved them through the thick, dark mane while she shook her head back and forth to fluff it out in the manner Marlo Thomas used to do at the start of her hit show "That Girl." At the very moment, Tina was "That Girl."

The day had quietly slipped by and by early afternoon David decided to turn his attention to the business at hand, specifically the affirmation recordings he planned to create. Searching for leads on studios or companies that specialized in that type of recording, he came across a firm in Los Angeles that advertised various specialties for self-publishers. That seemed like the type of company he wanted to connect with, so he placed a call to inquire about their specializations and rates for the different services they provided. David was interested in printing his own books if he wasn't able to get published in the traditional manner. He also would need to know what the cost of studio time would be for the recordings he planned to do. The entire venture was going to take some investment, but he wasn't sure how much so he started to do the leg work needed to get started, all the while he never gave a second thought to doing any drugs. It hadn't been that long, but in the week since he had the unexpected visit from Penny, he hadn't had any desire to indulge. He picked up the phone and started to dial.

CHAPTER NINE

    Monday mornings always seemed tougher to get started than any other day in the week, but this Monday was different than most. Later in the day, David would pack and gather his business materials as he readied himself for another business trip to Las Vegas. He planned to leave Tuesday morning around five and he would stop off in Baker to have breakfast and visit with Tina before he would continue on to Las Vegas. The thought of his visit with Tina made this Monday morning much easier to deal with. Actually, he really wanted to see her and test his desire to either stay single and on course with his new business idea or succumb to the pull of a possible relationship with her. He knew she was interested in him, but he wanted to take things as slow as possible being that he had changes taking place in his life that required him to keep focused and on track. Those changes included a business plan and he was excited to share his idea with Jefferson and looked to get some feedback from his newly found mentor.

    The clock on the wall in David's office struck ten in the morning and he remembered he had to call Jefferson to advise him of his planned trip into town. Just as he reached for the phone to make the call, it rang. David picked up with his usual greeting.

    "Hello, this is David."

    "Is this David Christian, soon to be master of his own destiny?"

    David broke a smile and laughed at the remark that came from the other end of the line.

    "Yes it is Jefferson. It's good to hear your voice."

He paused and then continued.

"It's strange but I had just reached for the phone to call you."

Jefferson, always looking for an angle to give him an edge commented.

"I know you were. We share the same thoughts and I decided to jump on that call first."

"I believe it. You scare me sometimes."

David quipped and the two men laugh and then continue with their conversation. David was happy to advise Jefferson he would be on his way to Las Vegas the next morning.

"I was going to call to let you know I'll be in town tomorrow and staying through Friday. I hope you have time to get together while I'm there."

"Of course David, we'll make time to meet. How are things going?"

David sensed Jefferson had asked just to see if he had made any progress on his plans to make changes in his life. More specifically, he wanted to know if David's awareness of his thoughts and spoken words had been raised since their last conversation. Jefferson was interested in the level of progress David made since they last spoke. Without asking directly, he sought that information with his open ended question.

"Well Jefferson, I have made decisions with regard my career, or more specifically a plan to start my own business. I won't share it with you now if that's okay, but we will have plenty of time to discuss it when we meet."

"That's fine David. I'll look forward to hearing all the details."

Before they hung up Jefferson wanted to get feedback on one more detail.

"David, regarding your other issue, you know I am concerned and I have to ask..."

David cut him off before he could even finish the question. He knew what Jefferson wanted to know.

"I have been clean and sober since the night we met Jefferson. I have no intention of going back now, there's just too much for me to accomplish and drugs will only inhibit my progress."

David sounded sure of himself, but Jefferson knew it was only three weeks since they met and the true test would come over time and especially when David was faced with adversity. For now, he was happy to see his friend make a commitment and stay with it. He intended to encourage David and help in any way he could, to keep him on course.

"That's great to hear David. Stay the course and we'll see you in town tomorrow."

"Thanks Jefferson, see you then."

The two men hung up and David went back to his list of business "to do's" for the day. He wanted to wrap up early, get his bags packed and take the rest of the evening to work on his business plan. Being prepared when he met with Jefferson was important to him. He knew he was receiving the benefit of a friendship with someone who could truly help him and he didn't want to spoil it by not following through on his stated plans. The cat was out of the bag now and Jefferson would want to hear all about the plans David had for a start-up business. David worked into the night and wrapped up around ten o'clock before he took a warm shower to relax and spent thirty minutes to watch the late news. He was fast asleep by eleven and would be up early the next morning to head for Las Vegas. But first there was the stop he would make in the small town of Baker. It was a stop he anxiously looked forward to making and included a certain young lady in town that he looked forward to seeing.

CHAPTER TEN

The moonlight shined through his bedroom window just as David's eyes popped open around four-thirty in the morning. He woke with his usual morning erection and wished he had Tina lying next to him now. That wasn't the case so the solution would be a quick cold shower. David shivered as he stepped out of the shower and grabbed for the soft fluffy towel hung over the towel rack. He dried off quickly, shaved and brushed his teeth at the bathroom sink before he dressed in his normal "business casual" attire, dark suit with a button down shirt and no tie. He hated to put that tie on; it felt like a noose around his neck and every time he was pressured to sell more he felt the noose tightened.

David went to the kitchen and made himself a tall cup of instant coffee and popped an English muffin into the toaster to hold him over until he would meet Tina for breakfast. He drank most of the coffee and took three bites from the muffin before discarding the rest in the trash bin as he headed out the door. The morning cloud cover was thicker than usual and it was brisk. If he hadn't woken by now, the cool air which hit him in the face as he strolled to his auto would certainly do the trick.

David liked his life on the coast, but the morning cloud cover was something he never could get used to. He really enjoyed the clear afternoon skies once the cover receded back into the marine layer and out to sea. It was still dusk when he hit the road and the bright sun flickered over the peaks in the direction of Pala as he took Mission Road to Highway #15. The bright flicker of light streamed into his face caused a glare and his tired eyes needed the protection of his handy Ray Bans. As he slid them on, his memory served him at that very moment and reminded him it was Laura who gave him those sunglasses one Christmas a few years ago. It all seemed so long ago now. He reminisced for a few minutes and quickly let the thoughts go. Laura was a distant past memory and he had more important things to focus his attention on now, primarily a safe drive to his first destination, Baker.

The early morning traffic was light and moved along at a speedy pace up Highway #15. Climbing through the Cajon Pass was always an adventure as he weaved around the large rigs that pulled their heavy loads. David would cruise through the traffic and reached the top of the mountain pass in less than two hours from the time he left his home in Oceanside. The desert air was clear, cold, and crisp as the spring season approached. Strong winds blew against the automobiles as they raced up and down the highway and David could feel the gusts move his vehicle as he gripped the wheel tighter to maintain his direction. It would take less than two hours for him to arrive to the Denny's in Baker.

Tina was already inside and waited in the lobby for David to arrive. She had decided on the Calvin Klein jeans and green silk top after all. It was a simple outfit and the top was a stunning compliment to her beautiful green eyes. She looked good and felt confident, which was rarely the case in the past two years of her struggle. The wind still blew hard as David pulled in and when he opened the door to step into the diner, a strong gust pulled the door from his hand and swung it open further. He lunged forward, reached for the handle, grabbed it and pulled the door shut while turning to see Tina as she stepped forward to greet him.

"Hi David, how was the drive?"

David gave her a short hug which actually surprised Tina, but at the same time it was absolutely welcomed. It felt very good to be hugged, even if it was for only a brief moment.

"The first leg of the drive was not bad, but when I hit the top of the Cajon Pass the wind started to blow harder. I could feel the car being pushed by the strong gusts. Hopefully, it dies down soon."

Tina felt a real connection with David and the hug he gave her reinforced what she had sensed. She knew from their previous conversation David wasn't looking for a relationship, at least that's what he told her, but she wondered if he may have changed his mind over the weeks from the time they met. He looked for the hostess and gestured for Tina to lead the way when the young female turned to show them to their table. The booth they took was close to the window and the strong winds blew dust and debris against it. Tumble weeds were thrashed across the parking lot and paper trash was strewn all over. David searched for something to start the conversation.

"This wind sure makes a mess of things, huh?"

Tina smiled and nodded in agreement, then quickly changed the direction of the conversation. She wanted to bypass all the small talk and figure out what David's intention was with regard to her.

"So David, you really surprised me when you gave me that hug?"

The comment caught him off guard and he slightly paused before he answered.

"Uh... well I... uhh I like to give friends a hug when I greet them. Why, you no like?"

He stated jokingly with a foreign accent.

She giggled at his comedic line and peered at him with a twinkle in her eyes. Tina felt comfortable around

David and though they only met a couple weeks ago she has a sense that she has known him for a long time. He makes her feel relaxed and at ease. It's a feeling that she had once before with her ex-boyfriend, so she is cautious and doesn't want to be fooled again. She hopes her sense of David is accurate. He certainly doesn't seem to be the type that would want to play games. He was open and honest when they initially met and she is willing to believe his story unless she learns otherwise. Tina continues the conversation.

"I liked it David, it's nice to be hugged. I don't get that too often living out here on my own."

"Well I'll have to come out and give you a hug more often."

David did not want to get too sappy so he grabbed the menu in front of him and buried his head in it to view the breakfast choices before she could respond to his comment. He quickly decides to take the special 'grand slam' breakfast with bacon. When the waitress approaches the table she immediately notices Tina opposite David.

"Hey girl, you can't stay away huh?"

Christie is one of Tina's close friends from the diner and a frequent dinner guest at Tina's house when she cooks up her home made specialties. She knows Tina's story and suspects she may be working a plan to get out of Baker. What she doesn't know is Tina isn't working a plan. She actually has a genuine interest in David, either as friend or boyfriend if something more serious develops. Christie asks for drink orders to get them started. They each order the same, coffee and cranberry juice then smile and laugh at one another before she leaves.

"I'll get those drinks out for you laughing birds."

Tina turns her attention to Christie.

"Thank you Christie."

David's curiosity is now peaked and he wants to know more about this young lady he met a couple weeks ago. She certainly seems out of place in this small dustbowl of a town between Los Angeles and Las Vegas. He wonders what brought her here or is she just a native of the town that won't venture away for a better life in a bigger city.

"So Tina, you know a little about me from my last visit, why don't you tell me your story, I mean why Baker, you couldn't have been raised here correct?"

Tina laughs at the question and begins to tell him how she came to California from a town outside of San Antonio, Texas.

"No I wasn't raised here. My boyfriend and I had big plans for our life together until we hit the town of Baker. He decided California wasn't what he wanted after all so turned around and headed for home. He left me in the middle of the night. When I woke the following morning there was a note and twenty bucks on the dresser in our hotel room."

Surprised that someone would do that to this lovely young lady, David pried further.

"So what did your plan hold for you? Why were you headed for California?"

"Well I always had an interest in drama, both in high school and college. I set my sights on an acting career and Hollywood seemed to be the best place to make that happen, unless my only ambition was to act in Community Theater productions, which it is not."

David nods as she continues with her story.

"I still want to act, but with my circumstances, I had to put that dream on hold."

Christie arrived as Tina finished her last comment and set the drinks down. As she turns to look at Tina, she pulls out her small pad and pen.

"What will you have for breakfast Tina?"

"I'll have the Denver omelet."

She turns to David.

"What can I get you sir?"

David chuckles at being called sir.

"Please, that makes me feel old."

They all laugh and David continues.

"I'll have the grand slam with bacon and an English muffin."

"Ok, I'll get your order in."

As soon as Christie left, David immediately turned his attention back to Tina.

"So, you were telling me you still have plans to act. Why not get out of here and make your way for Hollywood if that's what you want?"

As the question rolled off his tongue, David realized he had just stepped into the role of mentor and Tina was his first student, much in the same way as Jefferson was his mentor. The obvious difference with him and Tina is a possible romance may loom, but David doesn't want to lead her or him in the wrong direction if there is that possibility. He wondered if she called him for help since he did leave the note on his card the last time he passed through town so he decided to address the elephant in the room directly.

"Tina is there anything I can do to help you?"

She sits back in the booth and takes a breath before she answered his direct question. The last thing Tina wanted to convey was that she couldn't handle the situation herself or she was unable to make her dream come true. She is strong and has the will to persevere as she had for the last two years since being left in this out of the way desert town.

"It has been tough for me to get my feet under me. Working a job to survive isn't my idea of a good life. It's been a struggle to put together the resources I would need to move and be able to take time to find work in a new city. But no David, just be my friend. That's all I want from you. I don't want handouts or sympathy. I'll be fine; I just need to keep working hard and save where I can."

This was not a good situation for Tina and David realized that immediately. He wanted to tell her to pack her bags and he would pick her up on his way back from Las Vegas and take her to live with him. He actually considered it for a moment but then let the subject go for the time being.

"I can help if you want, but I won't interfere in your life if you don't want me to. If you ever need anything though, just ask."

Tina's eyes welled with tears as he spoke those words. Her awful experience at home with her father, as well as her boyfriend. They never treated her with the same compassion as this man she recently met and it had overwhelmed her.

"Thank you so much David."

She smiled at him with tears streaming down her cheeks. As she fought back sobs, she continued with a heavy breath and wiped at her eyes.

"You're very kind to make that offer. I mean, you hardly know me and here you are with an offer to help me when the guy I came here with two years ago abused me and snuck out in the middle of the night. He left me stranded with nothing."

David felt a surge of compassion and would have hugged her again if not for the table between them. He reached across the table and took her hands into his to soothe her as he peered into her emerald green eyes and gently stated.

"Tina, you can do anything you want in this life. Just take the reins and go for it. When I wrote that note to you last time I was in, I really meant it. If you need anything to help you in your quest to realize your dreams I am here. Don't ever hesitate to ask."

"But why, Why me David? I'm just a waitress you met three weeks ago. You don't even know me very well or owe me anything, why do you want to help me?"

"Let's just say I'm paying it forward."

He smiled at her and sat back to take in the moment. David realized he was doing exactly what Jefferson had asked him to do and it elicits a genuine feeling of satisfaction mixed with a compassionate yearning to do more. What he feels in that moment is something he wants to capture in a bottle and recreate over and over again. He suddenly becomes very clear on his mission and the business he envisioned just one day earlier. He intends to help people for the rest of his life and nothing will stand in the way of his desire to execute his plan to do just that.

Tina and David finish their breakfast over lighter conversation and when it's time to go they both feel a bit saddened that their time together had to end. Each is now experiencing a real chemistry and the connection they have is unmistakable. It isn't sexual tension, even though they are attracted to one another, it's more like old friends that have been in each other's life for the longest time. So long in fact, you know the other persons next move or phrase. They were interesting to watch as they walked out of the diner together. The early maneuvering to avoid too much physical contact became obvious. Although David was physically attracted and even desired Tina, he kept a distance that was almost strange to her. Any normal female would have probably thought something must be wrong with them, but David didn't want to show his full hand just yet. Tina walked with David to his car and it was then he realized she did not have an automobile and typically walked to get around the small town.

"Can I give you a ride anywhere?"

"Home James."

Tina replied with her sharp wit and a smile on her face. David laughed and they both climbed into his company vehicle. Tina lived in the apartment house around the corner from the diner and could have just as easily walked home, but she wanted to get as much time as she could with her new friend. She wished she could leave with David and go to Las Vegas with him for the week, but she had a work schedule for the week and desperately needed the pay, not to mention the tips she earned with her pretty smile, friendly demeanor and uniquely attractive looks.

"Thank you for putting up with me over breakfast David. I really didn't mean to break down like that while airing my sad story."

David caught her by surprise again with another physical gesture. He gently patted her on the lower thigh as he spoke words of encouragement.

"Don't be silly Tina. I know it hasn't been easy for you, but you'll turn things around. I can sense that in you and know you will."

David sounded so sure of himself and yet just weeks earlier he struggled with his own life issues and wasn't sure what his next move would be. The time he spent with Jefferson proved to be most valuable and it definitely got him on track to create the changes he was intent on creating. Even though he was at the early stages, he had a new confidence that would continue to carry him forward in his newfound mission. The drive took only minutes and when they arrived at Tina's apartment David pulled into a parking stall and turned the car off. He stepped out and walked around to give Tina another hug and say his goodbye. Tina felt good that he took the time and got out to give her another hug. She really hadn't expected it, but it was pleasant and gave her a feeling of comfort to know he genuinely cared for her.

"Tina I'll be in Las Vegas until Friday. I would like to stop by to see you on my way home if that's alright with you."

Tina was happy to hear that he wanted to see her again on his return trip and hoped he would be passing through after she ended her shift. The opportunity to spend time with David was a premium and she didn't want to have to share his time with customers.

"What time do you expect to be in town?"

David had the same objective on his mind and suggested he plan to be in town after she got off work so they could spend their time together outside of her work.

"When will you be off? I can plan to come to town after you get off work."

"That would be great David. As a matter of fact, why don't you plan to arrive around seven in the evening; I could have dinner ready for you."

David didn't plan to stay that late in Las Vegas, but the additional time with Jefferson would be to his benefit. To be able to have dinner with Tina made it even more appealing.

"Dinner at seven it is. I'll look forward to it."

"Be safe David, I'll see you Friday evening."

Tina turned and walked down the pathway toward

her apartment just about twenty yards away. She was already figuring what special dish she could make to impress David. It would be tough on her small budget, but she had a short list of economical dishes her mother use to make for their family when she was just a little girl. Tina's family struggles in her early life taught her to be thrifty and how to cook tasty dishes on a small budget. She would have a special meal, one of her best, selected before Friday.

CHAPTER ELEVEN

David jumped back into the car, started the engine, and placed the car in gear. Tina looks back and waves as he backs out of the parking space and heads out the lot onto the side street that leads to the main road in town. The wind had eased somewhat and the traffic is light as David merged back onto Highway #15 and accelerates to a comfortable speed before he places the car into cruise control. He would arrive in Las Vegas in less than two hours so he decided to call Jefferson to see if he had lunch plans. He caught him at home as Jefferson worked to schedule students and participants for his upcoming "Lessons of the Mind" hypnosis training seminar. Jefferson held two or three of these courses per year and only took a handful of people at a time. The average attendance was only five or six and that gave him the ability to spend time with each student and teach the technical details in a manner they would not get in a larger seminar filled with crowded classrooms of inquisitive, yet uncommitted people. Most students that took Jefferson's course were serious about using hypnosis either on stage or in a clinical setting. He had a very lucrative career with the show and income was not his motivator so he was very selective with the students he would mentor. David's objective would be slightly different than most that took his course, and he looked forward to sharing his ideas with Jefferson when they met. The call went through and Jefferson recognized the number on his phone.

"Hello David, are you in town yet?"

"I'm an hour and half away Jefferson. Do you

have plans for lunch?"

Lunch sounded good and Jefferson quickly responded to the implied offer.

"Meet me at Nora's Restaurant on Flamingo and Jones. They have great Italian food, probably the best in town off the strip."

"Sounds good Jefferson, I'll see you there."

David hung up and turned his undivided attention back to his drive. He was anxious to get to town and share his news with Jefferson. The idea for the business venture was going to be a new experience for David, but his expectations were solid for the mere fact he had Jefferson to consult with as he would work his plan. David's confidence had grown quite a bit since he met Jefferson and he continued to believe in his own ability much more as each day passed. Also, to have a friend and consultant who had mastered life through the knowledge of how the mind worked felt like he held an ace in the hole at a high stakes card game. The one thing he didn't anticipate he would hear from Jefferson was ultimately any success David would experience was going to be solely up to David, and not come from anything Jefferson taught him or indirectly did for him. Success would come with hard work and execution of his plan, not just knowledge.

The time passed quickly on the final leg of the drive and David pulled into the strip mall parking lot near the corner of Flamingo and Jones. Nora's was a small quaint place, with authentic Italian dishes cooked in old southern Italian and Sicilian style. The aromas in the air rushed to fill his senses as soon as David entered the restaurant. Jefferson had arrived a few minutes earlier and was already seated at a table not far from the entrance when David walked in. Jefferson spotted his friend as he stepped through the doorway and waved him over.

"David, how was the drive?"

Somewhat exhausted from the early morning start, but filled with purpose, David sits down and takes a long, deep breath.

"Not bad Jefferson, traffic was light and no accidents to slow me down. I left early this morning and stopped off in Baker to have breakfast with a new friend."

Jefferson stared into David's eyes with an inquisitive look on his face. He's familiar with the town of Baker and wondered who he could have befriended in that desolate part of the desert.

"A new friend huh; so who is she David?"

They both laugh as David squirmed in his seat. He knew he couldn't hide much from the man who set across the table from him. Jefferson was the most astute person he had ever met and he possessed a very good read of people, especially when they attempted to hide something from him.

"I stopped in at Denny's on my last trip back from Las Vegas. She was my waitress. I left her a card on the counter with my payment and included a note to call me anytime. Surprisingly she did."

Jefferson smiled and displayed a curious look on his face as he continued to pry for more details. His concern was for David's welfare and more importantly, that he continued with a focus on what he is in the process of doing. A new friend is fine as long as she is supportive and doesn't become a distraction to the changes David is intent on creating.

"So is this your new love interest or just a road stop quickie for the back and forth travel from Oceanside to Las Vegas?"

"No, no, it's nothing like that Jefferson. She's just a nice young lady that had a situation go bad with her ex-boyfriend and she found herself stranded in Baker. She took the waitress job to raise funds and ultimately wants to head west to Hollywood."

Shaking his head in disbelief, Jefferson breaks out in a boisterous laugh.

"Oh David, how many times have I heard that one? Small town girl wants to hit it big in the movies and ends up prostituting herself on Sunset Boulevard to make ends meet."

David was slightly irritated and taken aback by Jefferson's comment, but he remained composed and quickly advised Jefferson that Tina was not the type to end up on the boulevard selling blow jobs to old perverts to support herself.

"Jefferson, you have it all wrong with this girl. Tina is a good person who just got a raw deal when her boyfriend ran out on her and the dreams they made together. Anyway, you told me to pay it forward and that's what I plan to do. Pay it forward to Tina, and get her restarted in the direction of her own dreams."

"Okay David, I'll stop and give you a pass on this one. I did ask you to pay it forward and it sounds like your head, and heart, may be in the right place."

Just then their waitress steps up to the table.

"Hi guys, I'm Lily and I'll be your waitress today. Can I start you with drinks?"

Both order an ice tea with lemon wedge and Lily scurries away to get the drinks as Jefferson turns his attention back on David.

"Forget Tina for the moment and talk about what you have been up to. How are things going for you?"

"It's going well. I have decided to participate in your hypnosis training course. I know it will be beneficial in what I plan to do."

"That's wonderful David, and I noticed the declaration you made was a firm statement. So tell me what your plans include."

David was anxious to share his plan with Jefferson, but he hesitated slightly for fear of being shot down. Self-confidence and assurance were two things he would have to master, but for now he continued slowly with a brief description of his business plan.

"I have an idea for a business that I intend to create. I would like to get your input and direction for the start-up. Then if you would, we can discuss some ideas on how to elevate it to reach a large audience."

"Sounds like you have a big idea David, let's hear some details."

David takes a breath but before he can get started Lily arrived at the table with their iced teas. She set the drinks down and pulls her pad from the front pocket on her apron.

"Have you decided on lunch?"

Jefferson extends his arm outward.

"David, please go ahead if you're ready."

David grabbed the menu, opened it up, and picked out the first thing he recognized.

"I'll have the sausage and peppers."

She turns to Jefferson and he orders an antipasto salad. Lily turns away and heads for the kitchen to place their order. Jefferson nods to David.

"So David, continue please and tell me about this big idea of yours."

Now David is even more hesitant than ever, but he takes another deep breath and let's out the knot in his chest, leans back in his chair in search of comfort and begins to speak.

"I'm interested in doing what you do Jefferson,

but not from an entertainment perspective. I want to use hypnosis in a way that allows me to help others realize their dreams."

Jefferson stares intently as David continues to speak about his plan.

"Initially, I plan to produce and sell three recorded affirmation discs and a book on the subject of self-hypnosis. To get started, I will write a book on the subject and record the affirmation tapes, which will be the first of a series of products that I will produce for the business. The subjects for the three affirmations will be 'how to improve concentration', 'how to build self-confidence', and 'how to grow your creativity'. I plan to build a website to market the products, but I'll also advertise in various trade magazines, and sell the book as an e-book or a print on demand through Amazon. I'll also make myself available for speaking engagements and even schedule seminars on the subject as well."

Jefferson nods his approval and leans forward before he speaks.

"David, this all sounds exciting but let me warn you, internet businesses come and go by the thousands each day. The big trick there is how do you drive an audience to your website, and then capture their attention to buy your products. If you're going to rely on the website as your primary revenue driver, the business stands a good chance of failure. I don't want to discourage you from taking this leap forward, but I want to see you succeed. If you want my advice I would suggest you direct your energy at creating a business centered on self-help seminars and then sell the ancillary products as a bonus."

David felt slightly frustrated at what Jefferson had just stated, but he knows Jefferson would only give him sound advice. It certainly wasn't the feedback he had hoped to get, but he is adamant about his business idea and still plans to continue. Although he may have to adjust his initial idea, he senses it is still the direction he wants to take. He then realized Jefferson may have planted the seed for an even larger venture than he initially envisioned.

Lunch arrived just as Jefferson finished his explanation of the difficulties David would face and so the two men ate their lunch over some small talk. David had actually made a couple of appointments with customers for that afternoon and he would need to leave Jefferson soon after lunch to handle his business with them. During the meal, he shrugged off the initial dose of reality that Jefferson hit him with and regrouped for a meeting with Jefferson later that night.

"Jefferson, we're not done yet. I would like to meet later tonight if you have the time."

Jefferson was pleased to see David's resilience and decided he would meet David after his late performance. It was going to be around eleven, but David was on a mission and time was not going to keep him from learning everything he could from the master of hypnosis.

"David, if eleven o'clock tonight is fine with you let's meet at that café we went to the first night we met."

"That would be great Jefferson. I'll be there. I would like to stay longer, but I have appointments to see a couple customers this afternoon."

He glanced down at his wristwatch.

"The first one is probably waiting on me now. I'll see you tonight."

David paid the lunch bill and excused himself. Jefferson just nodded and stayed behind to enjoy the double cup of espresso he ordered to finish off his lunch.

CHAPTER TWELVE

David was exhausted when he arrived at the hotel that afternoon. He decided to stay at the Stardust to make it easier for him to meet with Jefferson before and after his nightly shows. After he checked in and made it to his room, David laid down on the bed before unpacking his bag and fell fast to sleep. The early morning start on the road had finally caught up to him and he needed to get some much needed rest before his meeting with Jefferson later that night.

While he slept, David drifted into the same dream he had previously in which he stood in front of an audience and spoke about the benefits of self-hypnosis. The crowd is keenly set on his every move as he paces the stage like a caged cheetah while placing emphasis on his words in a way that will inspire them to make a decision to create a life of their own and stop being a slave to their uncontrolled thoughts. Just as he comes to the end of his presentation David awakens and realizes he has had the same dream once again. He suddenly realizes the dream is a validation for what Jefferson had advised him with regard to his business. He is even more steadfast now than he had been earlier at lunch. His conviction now clear, he decides to pursue a business in the field of self-hypnosis, but it will be similar to what Jefferson had described. He wasn't looking to be a stage hypnotist or even a clinical hypnotherapist. David's vision was different and he had a dream that took him in a direction which held much bigger plans and could potentially impact larger numbers of people. He wanted to educate, inspire and bring people out of the doldrums of their miserable lives. His would be a quest to show them a new direction is easily attainable if you have the necessary information and utilize the tools each and every one of us come equipped with. David's vision was actually a dream for the realization of others to experience and not necessarily for himself alone. Acting as his mentor and consultant, Jefferson would be a considerable benefit to his efforts as David would seek to develop products that could be mass marketed to a large audience. He was now even more anxious to begin Jefferson's hypnosis training seminar, because he knew the information he would receive in the course would be exactly what he needed to get his business launched in the right direction.

 The clock read seven-thirty and David decided to take a quick, cool shower to clear out the cobwebs in his mind from the two hour nap. After a refreshing cleanse and change of clothes, he decided to grab a quick bite to eat in the food court and kill some time playing blackjack before he headed to the café for his scheduled meeting with Jefferson. The crowd on the casino floor grew and became dense as the night moved into the later hours. David had some success at the table and when it was time to leave for his meeting he was up over one hundred dollars. Not bad, he thought, and then wondered if he could apply the same techniques Jefferson had taught him to the card game. He chuckled as he walked away from the table. Silly for him to think he could actually influence the deal by just thinking of the cards he needed to win a hand.

 It was ten forty-five when David arrived and the crowd in the café was sparse. He took a seat on the bench just outside the café entrance and waited there for his friend to arrive. Las Vegas is a wonderful town to people watch and David took in the sites as if he was a foreigner from another part of the world, even though this was a regular work stop for him. He was intrigued with the way the passers-by interacted with their partners or in the groups they traveled with. David wondered, as he watched these people, if any of them might be in pursuit of a similar quest as the one he was on. He was struck by the casual, careless manner in which many of them went on about their business, or in this case their pleasure. His life was skirting along in the very same way at one time, and then he had the fortunate opportunity to meet Jefferson Paul. That meeting and the ensuing friendship seemed to lead him into a different dimension. It was as if his life had suddenly gained purpose. Actually, he knew for quite some time that he had something on fire inside of him. With Jefferson's help he would now develop the tools he needed to help him spark that fire and turn his dream into a reality.

Time passed along as he watched the passers-by and before long Jefferson walked up from an angle that left him in David's blind spot. As he approached David, Jefferson noticed his friend was taking in all the interesting sights and especially the amusing people who walked by.

"Interesting, aren't they?"

David, his concentration broke, looked up a bit startled and laughed softly.

"Yes, this is certainly an interesting place to people watch; you're bound to see all types."

David reached out and took Jefferson's hand in a firm handshake as they both chuckled.

"So how was the show tonight?"

Jefferson was delighted to be the star of the biggest show on the Las Vegas strip and he knew he had the good fortune of a long run in the most competitive entertainment market on the planet. His life was exactly where he would have it had he planned it, and truth be told, that's exactly what he did. He shook David's hand and peered into his eyes he replied.

"David the show was splendid. I am thrilled every night to get the opportunity to do what I truly love to do; to entertain crowds of people with the craft of hypnosis."

David smiled and quickly retorted.

"It sure must be nice to be able to do what you love to do."

"Well my friend, isn't that what we are all here to do after all? Do what we love to do."

"I guess so, but for most us, getting there is quite the challenge."

"Nobody said it would be easy David. Come on, let's grab a table and relax a bit."

Jefferson took David's shoulder and spun him in the direction of the hostess who was waiting to greet them. The pretty young female walked them to a table in the rear of the café so they wouldn't be disturbed and could enjoy their privacy for as long as they desired. The table in the rear of the cafe had become their spot for collaboration. They took their seats across from one another and got comfortable just as the waitress approached. It was Sheri, working the late shift as usual.

"Well good evening gentlemen, couldn't stay away huh?"

It seemed like all the waitresses had that line ready for repeat customers.

"Good evening Sheri, yes your bright smile and wonderful service has us coming back for more."

Jefferson smiled as he leveled the compliment.

"So what can I get you two tonight?"

Jefferson looks over to David with a nod of his

head and pointed finger.

"I'll have an iced tea with lemon wedge."

Jefferson orders the same and she quickly rushes off to fetch the teas for the two men. As she turns away from the table, Jefferson brings his attention back to David and the last statement he made prior to them entering the café and sitting down.

"So David, let me address the statement you made before we walked in, you remember the one, about doing what you love as being a challenge."

David has his eyes locked on Doctor Paul and he was all ears. If the coming advice can eliminate or even ease the challenge he perceives everyone to have, it will be all the advice he would need for the night. He leaned into the edge of the table and placed his elbows down as Jefferson continued.

"Do you recall the information from the next two lessons, six and seven?"

"If you remind me it will be helpful. I don't have them all memorized."

Jefferson smiles and passionately reminds David the information is only good if you truly know it and put it into action.

"It would benefit you enormously to know these rules David. I realize it's all new information for you, but if you know this stuff it makes execution in the moment automatic. No thinking, just being."

David shrugs his shoulders and nods while he shakes off the direction he is being given.

"Okay, I know, I know."

"I won't harp on it anymore. It's up to you to learn these key techniques. You have to do the work or change doesn't occur."

Jefferson states firmly.

"Now, let's get back to the lessons and identify the impact they will have as you attempt to make a significant change or improvement in your life. Why don't we start with lesson six David, words and thoughts have no power over you, the only power they have is the power that you give them."

David, listening intently, breaks his silence and interjects before Jefferson can continue with his detailed explanation of the lesson.

"So how does this lesson ease the challenge of doing what one loves to do?"

Jefferson pauses and takes a breath before continuing to explain.

"Have you ever heard the famous Henry Ford quote 'whether you believe you can or you can't you're correct.' In other words, your thoughts lead to the actions you take which end up delivering the results you create."

Jefferson paused again to let his last statement resonate with David, who looks across the table with a strained expression on his face but it softens as that statement comes clear.

"This lesson can also be taken in another way. Have you have ever had someone say something to you that might otherwise be offensive?"

David nods.

"Yeah, sure I have."

Jefferson continued.

"Well those words only have power over you if you give them power. You see David, it is you alone that is in complete control of your emotions and if you relinquish that power to someone else or to your own negative thoughts, that becomes your reality."

David's face lit up at that moment as if a light went on in his head. He sat up tall and then leaned back into his chair. Rubbing his chin with his left hand, he states out loud.

"Ahhh, I get it Jefferson. This is a great segway into the method you taught me about letting negative thoughts pass through my mind and replacing them with positive thoughts."

Jefferson smiles proudly at his new developing student and hopeful prodigy.

"Exactly David, it's the thoughts you harbor and give power to, those are the ones that create your reality. Whether they come from you or as a form of words from someone else, those are the thoughts and words that will form the way you begin to think about yourself, which is very important in anything we set out to do in life. As Ford stated, whether you believe you can or you can't, you're right."

They both smiled and shook their heads in agreement. David was at the start of his quest and this newfound information would be critical to build his confidence and know that he could indeed do whatever it was he set out to accomplish. The important first stage is to believe you can and then begin to develop and execute the plan. Jefferson sipped from his tall sweating ice tea and sat back to continue the discussion.

"Should we continue?"

Excited to gain even more knowledge David states without hesitation.

"Yes, if you're fine with it Jefferson I can stay as long as you have."

"OK then, let's move to the next lesson and dive into the way we overcome obstacles and naysayers as we move to create our own reality. How does that sound?"

Jefferson doesn't wait for a response and continues. He knows David has read the book, but could not repeat the lessons in order or at all if he was asked to at that moment.

"So David, let's take a look at lesson seven; imagination is more powerful than knowledge when dealing with the mind. Reason is easily overruled by imagination. Whenever imagination and logic are in conflict, imagination usually wins."

Jefferson stares at David's blank expression and smiles as his pupil struggles to follow what he has just been told. David sits quietly and shakes his head as if to say 'I need more information, please continue.' So Jefferson promptly takes his friends cue and continues to explain in a more thorough manner.

"This is a very important rule when using self-hypnosis David. Reason is easily overruled by imagination and especially if it is accompanied with strong emotional content."

He paused again to let those words resonate with David before continuing to explain further with more supporting examples.

"David, it is important to learn this because it's this lesson that drives people to blindly rush into unreasonable acts or situations, such as crimes of passion due to their overactive imagination. Can you see that when we tie a strong emotion to the imagination, human beings can be driven to do things that go beyond our use of reason?"

Without stopping, and in an effort to make this lesson as clear as he possible can, Jefferson continues his explanation further.

"Knowledge is the means of the conscious mind to communicate with the subconscious mind through use of reason. The subconscious mind is the realm of emotions, dreams, and aspirations. Together with knowledge they form imagination. The two forces together are more powerful than either force alone and therefore, imagination easily overrules reason. You can use the example I gave you regarding a crime of passion and flip it over to a positive action. Rather than a crime of passion, human beings can perform acts of passion that end in positive results."

Jefferson takes a brief pause to inhale softly and then continues.

"The point I am making is this; if you attach strong emotion to your imagination the world is virtually at your beck and call. Do you understand the power in that David?"

Jefferson sat back and just took in the moment. He wanted to allow David the time to fully grasp this concept and know that it was really as simple as using the tools within ourselves that allow us to formulate a life we want. And it all begins with an idea or thought accompanied by a strong emotion. Virtually any thought in the conscious mind may be manifest in the physical world if you continually feed your subconscious mind that imagination and attach the strong emotion to it.

It is in the subconscious mind, or the feeling mind that we form images that can remove, amend, or otherwise alter old ideas. This is the foundation for making changes to behavior patterns or beliefs about one's personal self.

"I do understand what you're saying Jefferson. For me, the challenge is going to be execution. It seems so simple, yet why is it most people do not follow this simple method to create positive change in their life?"

"Let's focus on you for now and when the time is right, we'll turn your attention to helping others understand these lessons."

The two men sat back and laughed softly and looked each other in the eye. David knew he had made a breakthrough with Jefferson at this meeting and the knowledge he gained would be instrumental in the weeks to follow as he continued to develop his business and implement lifestyle habits that would impact him in ways he could not conceive of at the moment. As much as he wanted to continue with the discussion, he knew he had some work to do in the morning and Jefferson had a long day as well. He didn't want to impose on Jefferson being it was now close to one in the morning, so David suggested they meet again the next day.

"It's getting late Jefferson and I do have some business to tend to in the morning, so what do you say we wrap and meet again tomorrow. We can pick up where we left off?"

"David that would be fine with me; how about a late lunch right here at the café. I can go prep for my early show afterward and if we want to meet again, we can convene after the late show, at around eleven again."

David was pleased that Jefferson was so willing to give him this much of his time and he was exuberant in his response.

"Great, what time should I be here tomorrow?"

"Let's plan for three o'clock; I think that will give us enough time to cover another couple lessons before I have to leave for show prep."

David picked up the check Sheri left earlier and signed it off to his room. The men slid out of their chairs and shook hands before they parted ways.

"Thanks again for everything Jefferson."

Jefferson just smiled, turned and walked toward the tunnel the show personnel would use to enter the stage area. Moments later he was gone and David was on his way up to the twelfth floor and a good night's rest. But not before he opened the book and reviewed the two lessons they had discussed earlier that night. He also made a mental note to be sure to review the upcoming lessons before their meeting the next day.

CHAPTER THIRTEEN

The next morning David woke early and made coffee with the portable room percolator. It wasn't the best brew, but it did the trick and he got a quick jolt from the caffeine infusion. After a long cool shower, review of his daily appointments, to do list, and quick review of his e-mails, David headed into the Las Vegas market and on to his customer visits. He had scheduled calls with a few small franchise operators that used the bulk CO_2 service his company offered, as well as a local industrial gas company that he worked with on a regular basis to steadily grow the markets business. After making his morning calls, David checked in with Jefferson to confirm their three o'clock lunch at the café was still on. The phone rang and Jefferson picked up after the second ring. He always let the phone ring twice, just a strange habit he developed years ago.

"Hello David, how's your day going?"

David was bored with his work, but he remembered the discussion in which Jefferson advised him to bring his passion with him and so he turned up his enthusiasm a notch.

"Doing great Jefferson, just wanted to touch base and confirm we're still on for three."

"Of course we're still on. That is unless you have other more important things to attend to this afternoon."

Jefferson smiled as he made the statement. David was not going to let anything get in the way of his meetings with Jefferson. He knew how fortunate he was to have a mentor the likes of Doctor Paul and he quickly responded without hesitation.

"No way, our meetings are my primary focus these days and nothing is more important."

"Well then I'll see you at three o'clock."

"I'm looking forward to it Jefferson."

The two hung up and David continued to make his early afternoon calls, but before he got started he stopped at the corner convenience store to pick up snacks. A small bag of almonds, pack of beef jerky and a bottle of water should be enough to hold him over until he had lunch with Jefferson. David planned to arrive early and take some time to review the next couple lessons he anticipated they would discuss over lunch. The early afternoon breezed by and before he realized it was close to two o'clock. David made his way to the Stardust where he would meet Jefferson at the cafe. When he arrived the lunch crowd had been thinned out already and David requested their usual table in the rear of the dining area. He took his same seat and pulled the book from his duffle bag and began to thumb through the pages to the chapter that would be topic for their discussion during lunch. Just as he starts to read a waitress arrives at his table to take his drink order.

"Hello, I'm Alba and I will be your server today. Can I get you a drink to start?"

Alba Reyes was a youthful looking woman in her late thirties with a slight accent, possibly from south of the border but David couldn't pin it to any specific country. She was an attractive lady with a thick, wavy mane of medium brown hair and voluptuous build. Her dark brown eyes sparkled and when she smiled the contrast of her pearl white teeth against her dark tanned skin enhanced her natural splendor even more. David, a bit mesmerized by the woman's beauty, took a long pause while staring at her and then snapped out of his temporary trance and ordered an ice tea with lemon wedge.

"I'm meeting someone else but I'll have an ice tea for now. We'll order lunch when he gets here."

"Of course sir, that will be fine."

Alba skirts away and David takes one more look at her from behind before he dives back into the "Lessons of the Mind." A couple minutes pass and Alba returns with David's ice tea, sets it down to the right of him and asks if he would like anything else while he waits.

"No, this is fine for now. Thank you Alba."

The two exchange smiles and David turns his head back into the pages of the book as she walks in the direction of a young couple seated at a table close by. The time passes quickly and Jefferson arrives at the café just before three. The hostess walks him back to the table where David is reading and waiting for his friend and mentor to arrive.

"Good afternoon David. I see you're reviewing the next couple of chapters for our discussion today. Before we start into those next chapters, tell me, how was the carbonation business today?"

"Not bad at all Jefferson. It's sure good to see you again though."

Alba was not far away and spotted Doctor Paul as he strode up to the table and she was right behind.

"Hello Doctor Paul, how are you today?"

"Hello Alba, I am doing splendid dear and thank you for asking."

Alba smiles and captures David's attention again with those beautiful pearl white teeth against her tanned brown skin. Her natural beauty was captivating and had David in a spell. She looked at Jefferson and then turned back to David with a surprised look pasted on her face.

"You didn't tell me you were meeting the great

Doctor Jefferson Paul."

Jefferson quickly chimes in.

"Oh Alba, please."

He gives her a hug, pauses and then gestures toward David to take attention off him.

"So you have met my friend David."

"Not formally, no."

She turns to face David and extends her hand as she speaks.

"It's nice to meet you David."

David smiles at Alba while he gently shakes her hand and is now even more intrigued than he was previously. This beautiful woman knows Doctor Paul and the two seem smitten with each other. She takes Jefferson's drink order and heads to the fountain for his usual, an ice tea with lemon wedge.

"So Jefferson, do I detect a little something between you two?"

Jefferson laughs and sits down across from his pupil. He leans in before he starts to explain his relationship with Alba.

"Let's just say I helped her kick a smoking habit and she has been very thankful."

David chuckles, shakes his head and leaves it there without prying further.

"So David, tell me what have you been reading and learning about?"

Jefferson asks to see if he has retained any of the information contained in the next two chapters they had planned to discuss over lunch. He stares into David's eyes with a serious look on his face and waits for an answer to his inquiry. David glances into the book and then looks up at Jefferson, who still intimidates him. He begins to explain his perception of the tenth lesson as Jefferson settles into his chair without changing his expression.

"Well, I guess the best place to start is to say that emotions have a powerful effect on our physical being and that's the foundation for implementing change. In other words, if we do not attach emotion to our thoughts, creating change in our behavior will be much more difficult, or virtually impossible."

Jefferson displays a proud look on his face and reinforces David's statement with supporting evidence from the lesson they are referring to.

"Yes indeed David, emotions are key to everything we experience in the physical realm. This lesson is actually a supplement, or an add-on to lesson's one and two. You see, our body, mind, and spirit are inseparable and we have built in protections, but if we attach negative emotion to negative thoughts, these protections can be over-ridden. It is because of this, many physicians will admit that seventy percent of human ailments are emotionally based rather than organic. The same can be true for the opposite. If we attach positive emotions to our positive thoughts, we will most assuredly have a positive experience."

Jefferson pauses for a brief moment as Alba approached with his ice tea.

"Will you be ordering lunch?"

Jefferson gestures to David.

"Please David go ahead if you're ready."

"I'll have the chopped salad with the dressing on the side please."

Alba turns to Jefferson.

"That sounds good. I will do the same Alba."

"Well that was easy. I'll be back to refill your tea as well."

Alba turns and walks away and Jefferson places

his attention back on the subject at hand as he re-establishes eye contact with David.

"So David, a most important key in this whole series of lessons can be summed up in this lesson. An emotionally induced symptom tends to cause organic change if persisted long enough. Keep in mind, the change can be positive as well as negative and this is what is at the center of the cause for many who develop disease or psychosomatic illness."

David, curious that an individual can actually bring upon their own illness, cuts in to ask.

"So are you're saying here that people can actually make themselves ill or can even potentially heal themselves as well?"

"Certainly; it's all in the way we attach emotion and repetition to those thoughts we feed to our subconscious mind. You see David, your subconscious mind functions in somewhat the same way a computer works. Repetition, and because we are human, emotion are the keys to programing the subconscious mind. The emotion that gets attached to our repetitive thoughts directly impacts the behavior or result we experience in the physical world."

David nods his head in acceptance and seems to grasp the concepts within the lessons with much more understanding as Jefferson thoroughly explains them. Jefferson smiles at David's acknowledgment and continues on with the tutorial.

"That brings us to lesson eleven which states each suggestion acted upon creates less opposition to additional or successive suggestions."

Jefferson pauses briefly and let's that statement sit with David for a moment before he continues to explain in more detail what this actually means.

"Essentially, once you experience acceptance of a mental habit, each successive attempt to establish mental habits is met with success. It goes something like this David, when you begin to use self-hypnosis to create mental habits and you stick to a systematic method with an established repetition you will experience over time, the longer a habit remains unbroken the easier it becomes to establish more mental habits and to maintain them without breaking the habit. In other words, once you are successful with your subconscious mind accepting self-suggestion, it becomes easier with every additional self-suggestion. A good process to follow is to take simple suggestions at first and as you experience success move on to more complicated or challenging suggestions. Each success will lead to more success and over time it becomes easier to change a behavior or implement a behavior that you desire. Does that make sense?"

David, clearly focused and listening intently, begins to nod.

"Yes, it does. One question though. How long does it normally take to establish a behavioral change using this method of self-suggestion?"

"Well that all depends on the individual and the manner in which you execute the process. For some it takes longer than others, but the average time it takes to experience a change in habit is twenty-one to thirty days. If the change sought is more complex, it may take a little longer than that."

Just then a thought popped into Jefferson's mind and he paused to ask.

"By the way David, how have things been going for you with regard to your drug use?"

David puffed his chest out a bit and was proud to announce he had been clean for the duration of time since he and Jefferson first met. It wasn't without its challenge though as he had experienced some of the normal withdrawal from the chemicals, as well as the subtle craving he experienced in his impromptu meeting with Penny. He dealt with the withdrawal by diverting his attention to his work or doing more research into the subject of self-hypnosis and the development of products he had in mind for his business plan. As for the craving he had in his meeting with Penny, he ended it as quick as he could by kicking him out before he broke down and succumbed to what could have been a bad decision.

"I won't say it's been easy, but I have stayed clean since we met over three weeks ago."

Jefferson was glad to hear David had made a genuine effort to stop and he had no reason to doubt David wasn't being honest with him. It would be critical to his advancement.

"It won't be easy at the start, but stay the course David and these things will get easier as you go. If you ever feel tempted and need to talk, don't hesitate to call me. Other than if I am doing a show, I will always take your call and do what needs to be done to change your course of action if you even consider using drugs again."

"Thank you for your support Jefferson. It helps to know I have someone like you to lean on if the temptation ever gets that tough."

Jefferson gives him a nod of the head and points his finger across the table at David.

"Don't ever question it David, I am in your corner. You have displayed a commitment to change your life and it's the least I can do as your friend."

Just then Alba shows up with their salads and a pitcher of tea for refills.

"Are you boys ready to have some lunch?"

She sits the salads down on the table in front of each of them and grabs their glasses to refill with tea.

Jefferson sits back and takes in the beautiful presentation of food before them.

"Ahh, the salads look wonderful Alba."

"I slave over them Jefferson; only for you."

She jokingly states in her Latin accent.

They all enjoy a good laugh at her joke. Alba refills their tea and leaves the men to continue their conversation and enjoy their lunch. Jefferson raises his glass of iced tea and proposes a toast to his new friend and pupil.

"Here's to your success David. You have the power within to make any change you desire; stay the course and you will master the life you seek to create for yourself rather than be servant to one dropped on you by your uncontrolled thoughts."

David smiles and raises his glass and the two click their ice teas and drink to the toast.

"Thank you. You know it wouldn't be possible without your help. I really can't thank you enough for everything you have done and especially for all the time you have taken to mentor me in this process. It has been more than I could have ever hoped for when I set out to see your show over a month ago."

Jefferson smiles and the two dig into their salads without another word for the next several minutes. Jefferson checks his watch and the time reads five thirty-seven. The two men finish their salads and it's now time for Jefferson to head for the backstage dressing room and prep for the evenings shows. Alba comes to the table with their bill and David immediately reaches for her to hand it to him.

"I'll get that Alba."

She hands it to him with friendly gesture and another beautiful smile.

"Certainly, here you go. You can bill to your room if you would like."

David was familiar with the process and fills the ticket out before he and Jefferson excuse themselves and head in opposite directions. Before leaving Jefferson asks.

"Do you want to meet again tonight or should we plan for lunch tomorrow?"

David is anxious to get as much time with Jefferson as possible during his trip, but he realizes the late nights can be grueling on both their schedules and concedes to meet for lunch.

"Let's meet again for a late lunch tomorrow. Will three o'clock work?"

Jefferson nods and reaches for David's hand and a firm handshake before they part ways.

"See you at tomorrow at three David. Have a wonderful night."

"Thanks again for everything Jefferson. Enjoy your show tonight."

"I always do my friend, I always do."

With that Jefferson heads for the theater and David points himself to the elevators and on to his hotel room where he will finish up his daily reports and address his unopened e-mails.

CHAPTER FOURTEEN

Back in his room for the evening David settles into the lounge chair and turns on the television set to catch the evening news. He has a bit of work to complete, but the day has drained him mentally and the brief rest is much needed before he gets on with finishing his daily reports and e-mails. As he cozies back into the soft pillowed lounge chair, his eyelids become heavy and David spills off into a deep slumber. He again slips into a dream and the scenario is the same, in which he is on stage and speaking to an interested group of onlookers about his life story and how his use of self-hypnosis helped him overcome his demons and gave him the tools to focus his life in the specific direction he chose, planned, and executed. Only this time as he is speaking to the crowd his old drug supplier Penny steps up and shouts in an angry manner.

"You're a fraud you drug addict!"

Immediately David's eyes pop open and he sits up with a startled look on his face and breathes a heavy sigh. Sweat is beaded up on his forehead as his imagination takes hold. David struggles with the mental image of the drug hustler calling him out in front of an audience of admiring fans and potential students of his teaching. He pauses briefly, then settles back into the chair, closes his eyes and drifts again. Within minutes he is back to sleep and entering into a dream that takes him to a place he feels warmth and comfort. He is under a large Oak tree on the shady shore of a beautiful lake. The air is clean and clear, with a slight breeze blowing as he lies on the thick grass covered knoll. Next to him, Tina is also lying on her back and she is staring into the deep blue sky. He rolls over toward her, wraps his arm around her waist and pulls her into his body as he embraces her with a passionate kiss. Just then a man, whom David recognizes as Penny, walks up to them from behind and he shouts at the couple.

"He's a fraud; a drug junkie!'

David jumps up from the chair and is startled again at the image his mind has created. He is now sweating and feeling flushed, with a slightly reddish face and warm sensation penetrating his body. As he attempts to stand, he loses his balance and falls back into the comfort of the over-stuffed lounge chair. He sits for a couple minutes in stunned silence while breathing heavily. After a short pause David attempts to regain his composure. Several moments pass and he raises himself up from the chair and walks to the bathroom sink to douse his face with cold water and wake up from the crazed state that seems to have taken hold of his mind. He splashes cold water over his head and face a few times and turns to grab a towel from the rack to dry.

As he wipes his face dry, he wonders what could have caused those images to appear in his otherwise positive dream. He had experienced the dream before and it always appeared as a positive sign for him to continue following his passion to help others. Suddenly he has experienced something very different and wondered if it could be related to his withdrawal from drug use. Staring into the mirror for several minutes, he gathered himself and headed back into the suite to complete his work for the day. Whatever it was that caused those images to appear in his dream, it would not stop him from proceeding with his plan for a life transformation. He knew it would be challenging at times and there would be small hurdles to deal with, but David just needed to mentally set those distractions aside and refocus his attention. He did so by completing his daily reports and e-mails, then turned his attention to review the final chapter in the Lessons of the Mind.

He opened the book to the final lesson and began reading about the delicate balance between the conscious mind and subconscious mind. The lesson reads very straightforward; when dealing with the subconscious mind and its functions, the greater the conscious effort, the less the subconscious response. As he reads through the lesson, David begins to realize that changing his direction in life is actually easier than he thought it would be when he first embarked on this venture. The old saying "you're trying to hard" best applies to the chapter he has buried himself into. He realizes now that it is best to align all three aspects of his self, the body, mind, and spirit as he proceeds with his personal quest. When these parts are aligned, the thought energy we give to our personal goals starts to impact the physical, emotional, and spiritual parts and we begin to move in the direction of those personal goals. Once again, he also realized the words used in speech or thought can be critical because of the way the subconscious mind receives and perceives the messages directed toward it. The subconscious is the literal mind and it can easily interpret 'I am mad at something' to 'I am insane.'

David pauses to take in what he has just read and let it soak in for a moment. His understanding of the use of self-hypnosis and the critical nature of communicating to one's self or to others has become clearer since his work with Jefferson began. He closes the book after completing the final chapter and settles back into the soft lounge chair, leaning his head back against the pillowed rest. David closes his eyes and begins to drift into a comfortable state of relaxation and visualizes himself in a large home off the southern coast of Oregon. It's a beautiful ranch style home with green shrubs and colorful blooms of roses lining the walkways. The backyard is high on a cliff and presents the grandeur of the Pacific in a way that makes him want to pause in that moment to absorb the beautiful picturesque view. David sees himself relaxing on a teak lounge chair in the yard and then slowly the scene shifts to the interior of the home. The marble floors and counter tops are all done in fine imported Italian stone. The home is professionally decorated and exudes a simple yet refined look, with every detail covered. He senses a feeling of satisfaction and a level of comfort that he has never felt before. In his mind at this very moment is what success feels like to David and he is holding that feeling and those thoughts for what seems like an eternity, yet it was only moments, and quickly the next vision comes to his mind and his attention is diverted immediately.

David appears in his office, seated in his comfortable, custom, leatherback, executive chair. He is behind a rather large oak desk in the center of the room. His walls are lined with bookshelves and some classic pieces of art from the Renaissance period. The chair he is in faces outside to the large windowed doors going into the courtyard where a vine-covered lattice dome sits at the edge of the yard with another view overlooking the Pacific shoreline. David is just sitting there as he experiences the moment and takes in the view which has been framed by the edges of the glass window on the door. Books from various genres, including David's own novels line the bookshelves around the room.

Again the feeling of success surges through his body, mind, and soul as he continues into the relaxed state of meditation some might want to call a trance. David is extremely relaxed in every aspect of his being, however he is acutely aware of the visions he has created and lets them sit for his subconscious mind to absorb. This continues for fifteen to twenty minutes until David awakens to his conscious state and feels a sudden burst of energy as if he had just woke from an eight hour sleep. He takes a quick look around the room to survey the landscape and refocus his mind. Moments later he decides to take a quick shower before he prepares to head to the casino and possibly the café for a light dinner.

After the shower David quickly dresses and makes his way for the casino which is bustling for a Wednesday night. Then again, Las Vegas rarely has a slow night in the casinos or on the various gaming tables. He takes a short stroll around the casino floor and decides to play a few hands of blackjack before he eats dinner. Across the room is a beautiful Asian woman dealing cards at a five dollar table. Perfect, he thinks to himself before heading in her direction. She is a classic Japanese beauty with thick, silky jet black hair and pale white skin that gives her the appearance of a porcelain doll. Her lips are full and painted a luscious red, but not overbearing, they are just the right color. She is striking and David feels his pecker get stiff as he walks toward her. As he gets closer he smiles and introduces himself before sitting.

"Hi, I'm David. Do you have room at this table for another player?"

There are two others sitting at the table, drinking their free cocktails and losing stacks of chips, acting as if they have no concerns about it at all. They both pause to look up and greet David.

"Hi David, I'm Gary and this is my wife Janine."

It's obvious they have had too many cocktails and

David gives a quick nod in their direction not wanting to get into a deep conversation with a drunk and his wife. What he is most interested in is the dealer. He looks her directly in the eye and still smiling, sticks his hand out to shake hers and introduce himself again.

"No touching sir."

The command came from the pit boss standing just a few feet away from the dealer. She giggles and says hi to David.

"Hi David; yes we do have room. How much will you be playing with?"

"That's great Sakuri, thank you."

David glanced at her name badge and quickly shifted his eyes back on her face. He slaps down a hundred dollar bill while never taking his eyes off the beautiful woman that will soon be dealing him his cards. Sakuri counts out his chips and promptly slides them in front of him as she turns to check on the other two players at the table. Everyone is settled in and the bets are laid out in front of each player. Sakuri begins to the deal and shows a nine. Before she begins taking bets around the table, David flips over his blackjack. Gary, who is obviously intoxicated, blurts out loud.

"Oh my, we got a shark here."

Everyone laughs and Sakuri smiles at David as she lays down his winnings. After several hands over the course of ten minutes or so, David has compiled another one hundred dollars in winnings, on top of the original one hundred he started with. His is getting hungry, but the site of this beautiful woman dealing cards in front of him keeps him put. Several minutes passed and Sakuri's replacement shows up. He is a middle aged man with grey temples and a smile so perfect it may have been purchased. David quickly cashes out just before she can get off the table and collects his winnings. Sakuri then turns to the pit boss and waves her hands in the air for him and the players at the table to see. As she starts to walk off she turns and spots David checking on her direction. She turns back away from him and dropping her head she smiles. She knows for certain David is interested in her and she has a curiosity about him as well. The pathway to get in and out of the dealers area is congested and as Sakuri turns the corner to exit she spots David a few feet out in front and walking toward her. A smile breaks across her face and she greets David again, only this time she has time to talk.

"Hi there David, you did well tonight huh?"

David is taken by the warm, friendly energy this lady exuded as he grabs her right hand and gently pulls her in close.

"It's nice to meet you."

He is obviously joking as he referenced the no touching rule by slapping his own hand.

Sakuri giggles and maintains her brilliant, beautiful white smile for several seconds while David falls into a spell right in front of her eyes.

"You're so beautiful Sakuri. Where are you from, I know it can't be here?"

She points to the name badge that has the inscription 'Kyoto, Japan.' Immediately David feels foolish for missing the obvious display on her badge. The employees at all the casinos had name tags that gave the person's name and hometown, he should have known that when he got her name. She digs…

"How did you miss that one?"

"Okay, so I guess I'm not as good as I think."

David turns around and steps up right by Sakuri's side. Walking in stride alongside of her, he desperately thinks of what he could say when he decides to take a wild shot at inviting her to have dinner with him.

"I was just going to have some dinner, would you like to join me?"

"That's generous of you, but I am not allowed to stay in the casino. Employees have to leave the floor when they are off."

David wasn't going to let that stop him, so he presses further.

"We don't have to stay here. Let's go somewhere close by on the strip."

Sakuri was already exhausted from the long day on her feet and had some studying to do. She was a student in the Nursing School at the University. Sakuri had been in the country for the past five years and had been in school to become an emergency room nurse. She hoped to fill a position soon at the University Medical Center. She dealt cards in the evenings to pay the bills and cover her taste for nice clothes and jewelry. Actually, she considered keeping her dealers job a couple nights a week for the tips she earned. Las Vegas was a town where service jobs could provide a comfortable living because the tips were so good and she figured to keep that option open if the medical career didn't work out for her.

She paused to give thought to the dinner invite but after a brief moment she decided to offer to meet him for lunch the next day. That suited David just fine. He was taken by her charm and wanted to spend time with Sakuri to get to know her, so anytime would be fine with him.

"I'd like that Sakuri, do you want me to pick you up or should we meet somewhere?"

Sakuri wanted to keep it close to her home so she asked David if he wouldn't mind the drive to Summerlin in the northwest part of town.

"David, there are several restaurants in the Boca Park area. Do you know how to get there from the hotel your at?"

David was very familiar with the Las Vegas landscape and knew exactly where she was referring. He even suggested the location, and offered to meet her there.

"There is a PF Changs on the corner of Rampart and Charleston, can you meet me there at around noon?"

Sakuri lived in the area adjacent to the restaurant and was familiar with the location. She visibly portrayed her approval with two thumbs up.

"That would be nice David. I'll see you there tomorrow at noon."

David stepped forward to give Sakuri a short friendly hug, which caught her quite by surprise since the Japanese custom does not include much touching from strangers. For his part, David felt something stir inside him for this beautiful lady and he would not let it go until he played his hand, literally. The embrace was quick and they parted ways for the night, but each one knew they had just met someone that would become part of their life in a capacity they weren't quite certain of yet.

David headed for the café and a quick bite before going back up to his room. As he approached he spotted Alba through the large window cut-outs around the café. He walked up to the hostess and asked to be seated in her section. The hostess grabs a menu and leads David to a table in the rear of the café, to what had quickly become his and Jefferson's usual spot. It doesn't take long before Alba noticed David had taken a spot in her station. Having spotted him earlier on the casino floor with Sakuri, she thinks he must have struck out with the card dealer. She quickly heads for the table to say hi, get the dish on the dealer, and take his order.

"Hi David, how are you tonight? Will anyone be joining you, maybe the card dealer?"

Not bothered by the jab, David casually responds without acknowledgment of the fact he had been seen walking with Sakuri.

"Not tonight Alba. I'm eating alone tonight; care to join me."

He gestures to the seat across from him. Alba giggles and shakes her head.

"I'm working, if not I would join you."

She gives David one of those sultry smiles with her white teeth beaming off her golden brown skin. David grins back and places his order.

"All I want is a small dinner salad and a cup of your best chili."

"Thas easy."

She stated in her slightly pronounced accent.

"Sometheen to drink?"

"Tea is fine Alba, thanks."

Alba walks off in the direction of the kitchen. She stops at the terminal to the side of the entry and places David's order. When she finishes, she heads to the fountain and fills a tall glass with ice and a lemon wedge. She grabs a pitcher filled with tea and pours into the glass, filling it to the brim. She then takes both the glass and the pitcher in separate hands and spins on a dime without spilling a drop. She heads right back to David's table and sets the glass in front of him, to his right, and places the pitcher at the edge of the table.

"So what's new David?"

Alba starts the conversation and hopes to get to know this man that she met just a night before with her friend and former lover, Jefferson Paul. She wondered if Jefferson spoke to him about their history. Alba was very fond of Jefferson and knew their affection for one another would not lead to anything more than a torrid love affair. Even so, she had feelings for Jefferson and respected him for the help he provided her and friendship he offered.

"Well Alba, I guess I could go on about all the exciting new things going on with me or I could have you tell me about yourself."

He pauses with a smile.

"I prefer the later; to get to know you."

"Oh, well that may take all of a couple more trips back to your table for the entire story, or I could give you the reader's digest version."

Alba laughs, having picked up the cliché from a former customer. She smiles at David and asks him directly, without hesitation.

"So, did Jefferson share "our history" with you or was he a gentleman?"

She gestures "our history" with finger quote marks in the air.

"He told me you were a good friend who he helped with a few therapy sessions."

Alba gives him a shrug of her shoulders and throws her left hip out as she turns away from the table. She knows David had more details than he confessed and she is clearly flirting with him as well. David is intrigued but he is definitely not going to make any attempt at a romantic interlude with Alba. Even though she had a certain sex appeal that was engaging, she was off limits in his book. David understood the bond some men develop and since she was Jefferson's conquest at one time, he wasn't even going to consider going there with her. He smiles as she walks off and shakes his head, laughing softly. Moments later Alba returns with his salad and chili. He forgot to tell her salad first, and she sets both of them down in front of him. He takes the salad and slides it in front and pushes the chili back.

"Can I get you anything else David?"

He looks up with a smile across his face.

"This is fine Alba, thank you."

Alba senses he wants to be left alone so she doesn't hover to flirt with him any further. If nothing else, she is very perceptive and manages to read people well. Must have been a skill she developed over the years of serving folks in the casino's café and as a cocktail waitress earlier in her career when her body was athletic and taught like a tight rubber band. David devours the salad within minutes and turns to the chili, which was piping hot when she delivered it. So little time passed and it was still hot and delicious as he devoured it and washed everything down with a long swig of his ice tea. He sat and stared into the casino with his mind elsewhere and Alba spotted him from the counter where she stood. It was slower than usual for the night and she wished she could just take the night off and spend time talking with David, but it wasn't going to happen. He was somewhat tired from the long day even though he had taken a short nap and spent time in meditative trance. David looked ready to turn in when Alba reached his table.

"Can I get you anything else? Perhaps you would like a slice of pie?"

Alba remarked with an emphasis on her best sultry Latin accent. She played it up a bit, knowing David wasn't interested and would probably head to his room as soon as she provided him with his bill. She pulls out her pad and tears a piece of paper off, hands it to him and taps his shoulder as she starts to turn away.

"You're sweet David, have a wonderful night."

He knew she wanted to explore the possibility of

the two of them getting together and she wasn't going to let it go that easily. In the same way she teased him, he gives it back to her with an inviting look as he slides from the chair and table.

"I'll see you again lady."

He pauses and then adds.

"Real soon."

The sexual tension was obvious and they both knew this little scenario wasn't over yet. There would be more to this play than what they revealed tonight. For David, keeping the bond of his friendship with Jefferson was going to be hard to break and Alba knew that, but she was up to the game he seemed to want to play and would set it aside for another time. David stepped to her left and walked by on his way out of the café. He looked back when he entered the casino and caught her staring. She smiled and gave him a wink. He chuckles softly and turns away as headed for the hotel elevator and his suite.

Upon entering his room, David turns on the television set, sits back in the lounge chair and heaves a deep sigh that relaxes every part of his body with the long exhale. His isn't paying attention to the television, it only serves as background noise while he just sits there lost in thoughts about his life in the weeks since he met Jefferson. It has been different and he feels a change has definitely taken place. His demeanor, composure, confidence, and other aspects of his being are slowly developing, transforming him into the individual he had envisioned. There is no doubt in his mind the transformation process is underway.

His biggest challenge now is to be consistently aware of his thoughts and words, and to work diligently on his plans for a future that he envisions for himself. There is one way to ensure success in his plan for a new direction in life and David knows it is in mastering the techniques he has begun to work on with Jefferson as his mentor. He is excited at the prospect of their next meeting in which they will cover the final lesson on the list. And then two weeks later the training starts. He envisions his self being even more prepared to make significant strides forward after he completes the training and can't wait to get started. As he sits with all these thoughts flying in and out of his head, David closes his eyes and settles his mind by focusing on the visions he had earlier. Visions of the home on the cliff just off the coast of Oregon, the peaceful setting in the courtyard overlooking the Pacific enter his mind. He begins to relax his entire body again while the ample, limber feeling drapes his complete being and slowly takes over. David slips into a comfortable meditation and lets his mind relax further, further, until he finally allows himself to lose power of his thoughts and slips into a deep sleep for the duration of the night.

    Tomorrow's another day.

CHAPTER FIFTEEN

David awoke early the next morning, just before five forty-five. He felt refreshed even though he slept the night on the reclining lounge chair in his room. Since it was so early, he decided to take his shot at getting a massage, but not until after a light workout in the resort's exercise facility.

"It's a great morning at the Stardust Spa, how may I help you?"

"This is David Christian. I'm staying in room twelve thirty-six. I would like to schedule a massage this morning for around six."

"Let me see if we have any openings sir."

She slightly paused.

"Yes, we have a six thirty opening with Sharon; would you like to take that sir?"

"Yes, thank you. I will see you then."

David reconsiders the light workout and puts on his bathing trunks and robe and heads for the resort's spa and gym. When he arrives the place is virtually deserted. Most of the visitor's in Las Vegas are either still gambling from the erstwhile night or sleeping off the previous night's voluminous libations. He likes having the place practically to himself and strolls to the hot tub, drops the robe on a chair and climbs into the bubbling hot water. David settles into one corner of the tub and leans his head back on the edge, closes his eyes, and simply enjoys the soothing experience. So much that he falls asleep and is startled by a couple of vacationers that join him several minutes after he fell into a slumber. David checks the clock on the wall and it reads a quarter past six. He had been soaking for twenty minutes, lost track of the time when he slept and suddenly realized it was time to get to the massage center in the spa. In the back of his mind he hoped Sharon would be as good as Susan Hunter, both in her good looks and efficacy as a therapist. Only time would tell.

David entered the spa and as soon as he walked in a tall, red-headed woman with a curvy shaped body came from the back of the spa. She was surprised by him and quickly gathered herself before speaking.

"Hi, are you here for a massage?"

"Yes, I'm David Christian. I have an appointment for a six thirty massage with Sharon."

"Nice to meet you David, I'm Sharon."

David was pleased, but not as much as he would have had this been Susan Hunter. Sharon was pleasant looking and had green eyes to offset her thick red-orange hair. She pulled it back into a pony-tail and left bangs hung across her forehead. David takes her outstretched hand in his and squeezes softly.

"It's nice to meet you too Sharon."

She gestures for David to follow her into the area housing the private massage rooms. David steps inside and moves toward the table to the left side. She turns to face him and provide simple instructions for his massage preparation and get his request for work on any special areas or firmness of the massage.

"David is there any area you would like me to focus on today?"

"Not in particular, just looking too get some of the tension off the shoulders and neck primarily. I like a firm, deep rub."

Sharon smiles and finishes her instruction.

"Go ahead and disrobe to your comfort level and

I'll be with you in a couple minutes. We will start face down and go from there."

"Great Sharon, thank you."

The tall redhead spins away with a smile and closes the door gently behind her. Sharon is an experienced massage therapist and has worked the spa in the Stardust for six years. She has a steady following and picks up new clients whenever the opportunity presents itself. After a first look at David, she hopes to make him a regular when he's in town but she will have Susan Hunter to deal with if David decides to continue with consistently scheduling massages during his frequent business trips to Las Vegas. Susan is definitely his preference if she is available. David disrobes and places the damp pair of swim trunks on the towel bar that was installed in every room for expressively that purpose.

He lies his naked body down onto the linen lined massage table. His head fitting perfectly in the pad placed at the head of the table. Moments later Sharon re-enters the room and begins what will be the second best hour long massage David has ever experienced. Nonetheless, it would be exactly what he needed to get this day off to a great start. The hour passed quickly and throughout the entire massage, David was in a meditative comfort zone that left him feeling fully energized when the experience ended. He graciously thanked Sharon and would leave her a generous gratuity on the bill when he closed out at the front desk.

Back in his room David starts the shower and allows the water to warm up as he walks over to the desk and fires up the computer. A quick look at his Outlook mail and it appears to be a light morning which appeals to David. Today he would meet with Sakuri for lunch at noon, and he would rather not have any issues to deal with. A slow, comfortable workday will suit him just fine.

The water has run hot for a few minutes and the steam has covered the mirror as David steps into the bathroom. He adjusts the water and enters the shower. Today should be an enjoyable day he thinks to his self; he looks forward to the meetings he has planned with two of his newest friends, Jefferson and Sakuri, who he just met at the tables the previous night. Just the image of Sakuri as he takes the soap to lather, gives him a slight rise. She is a beautiful lady with a slightly submissive demeanor that would appeal to any gentleman, and it certainly did to David. He was smitten by her, but very curious to see if the feeling was real or just a passing infatuation. After a soothing warm shower David dresses in a casual pair of khaki slacks and button down, short sleeved, printed shirt. He won't be seeing customers, so it's casual dress, at least more casual than his usual. David runs through any urgent messages, which there wasn't many, prior to leaving the hotel room. He heads for the lobby and gives a quick thought to playing a hand of black-jack, but reconsiders and continues to the self-parking garage. He would grab a coffee and bagel before leaving the hotel and heading off the Boca Park for his meeting with Sakuri.

The day was cool and clear, with a bite in the air as the wind blew across the valley floor. It was a perfect winter day in the high desert and David was looking forward to spending at least the next couple hours with the beauty he had met at the blackjack table. Thoughts of her kept creeping into his head and he just couldn't shake them, even while attempting to exercise complete control and replace those thoughts with ones from his "go to" list. It was a futile exercise, so he went with the flow and let himself be taken by the parading images of Sakuri that would periodically take over his mind. Maybe it was a good thing for him to think of her, maybe not. He wondered if Jefferson would somehow learn of his meeting with Sakuri. If so, would he have concerns being they had discussed his commitment and focus prior to the start of his work with the master hypnotist.

To have a potential relationship as a distraction could lend itself to disaster if David wasn't able to manage all the changes taking place in his life. Add to that, Jefferson was already aware of Tina back in Baker. Another woman could spell failure if David wasn't equipped with the discipline to hold onto his purpose and maintain the diligence it was going to take for him to become the person he had begun to envision. He brushed away the thoughts as he pulled into the parking lot and quickly spotted an open space to pull into. His mind shifted to the one person he was headed to meet. The lady that had cast a spell the evening before was all he wanted to focus on for the next two hours.

David takes the long stroll from the parking lot to pathway that led to the front door. He's the first to arrive, a good thing. He was once advised to never keep a lady or a customer waiting. It may hurt your chances for winning either. David steps into the moderately filled restaurant and thinks the lunch crowd hasn't made it to their destinations yet. In the next fifteen to twenty minutes, PF Changs will be loud and crowded. He hoped not too loud and decided to ask for a table away from the bar so he and Sakuri could have a pleasant conversation without yelling above the noise or at each other to be heard. It was five minutes before the noon hour and a steady stream of people from all walks began filing in through the doors. The dining area began to fill quickly and as it did, David spotted Sakuri on the path to the front door. He jumped up and headed toward the entrance to greet her.

"Hi Sakuri."

David called out as she stepped inside from the cool breeze.

Sakuri was dressed in a classic black satin skirt with red silk top that almost matched her lips perfectly. If they were a shade off you couldn't tell. She broke into a beautiful smile and waved to David. As he approached, they each reached out to hug the other in a quick, friendly embrace. David steps back as his eyes gazed over Sakuri's perfect outfit. She was classy and elegant all at the same time and it was only noon! He wondered how elegant she might be had they decided on a five star for dinner. If lunch goes well he may get his wish to see.

"Hello David, I hope you were not waiting on me for too long."

"No, not at all; so tell me, are you enjoying your day off?"

Sakuri was in Boca Park enjoying the sights and window shopping at her usual spots. That was surely all the enjoyment she needed.

"Oh, very much David, thank you."

David gestures for her to lead the way to their table in the back corner of the dining room. He selected that spot intentionally and now realized her voice was softer than he remembered from the night before, so he was glad he did so. David does the gentleman's thing and pulls her chair when they arrive at the table. Sakuri smiles politely and sits as he pushes her seat forward to inch closer to the table. David takes his place to her right, not wanting to sit across the table and be further away from her. She smelled like a field of softly scented blooms at the Carlsbad Flower Fields. It was a heavenly scent and in David's mind she was heavenly sent. David settled into his chair and looks into her eyes.

"You're so beautiful. You do know that, right?"

"Oh stop it David; you're too kind. Please, tell me about yourself. What do like, where do you want to travel, tell me everything."

She brushed his compliment off with style and wasn't flustered at his focused attention. Sakuri was used to the attention; after all she was a very striking woman with taste and style in a town that had thousands of those types. Men would always hit on her in the casino and even at the local spots she would frequent in her personal life. Attention was nothing new to her. What mattered most to her was that this man she was about to have lunch with be a man of resource, character, and integrity. Sakuri wasn't out for a second stringer; she wanted a man who was confident of himself, a winner in life. Her selection for a committed life mate was serious business and she wouldn't settle for less than what she desired. First impressions of David were fine, but now she wanted to see if he would have substance to offer up for her to take him seriously.

"Alright, I'll tell you about myself as long as you are willing to do the same."

She nods at him with a smile and David gets started on his story. He tells her where he is from, family details, his schooling, and all of the other minor stuff she isn't interested in hearing. However, she listens with the patience of Job and puts up with this part of the conversation. She is more interested in what he does for a living and more importantly, what are his dreams. As they continue to discuss their upbringing and early lives, a waiter comes to the table to take their drink order and supply information on the daily specials the chef has decided to prepare. He finished the pitch, leaves them, and the discussion takes a quick turn with Sakuri at the lead. She doesn't want to waste too much time with a man of no potential and intends to dig for the information that is of most interest to her, so she starts her questioning by asking about his reason for being in Las Vegas.

"So David, what brings you to Las Vegas?"

"I work as a sales manager and Las Vegas is part of my region."

"What sort of sales are you in?"

"I sell bulk CO_2 systems and service for carbonation in food service establishments. The company I work for also produces various types of industrial gas products for a variety of uses and medical applications."

"Sounds interesting, how long have you been doing that?"

"Over fifteen years; and it seems as if it's been a quick fifteen years."

David smiles in reminiscence of the years and before she can get in another question, he shifts gears and quizzes her about her current situation.

"Sakuri, last night you said you had to study, what are you studying?"

She recoils from being the quizzer and pauses before answering his question. Just as she begins to explain the waiter stops by the table with their drinks and takes their lunch order. Both decide on a salad with seared tuna which made it easy and quick for the waiter. He saunters away and she gets back to their conversation and her current story.

"As I was about to say, I am in nursing school and plan to work as an emergency room nurse for at least a couple years. I may go back and get my license as a PA if the emergency room gig becomes a grind. Either way, I want to work in the medical field."

"I'm impressed, you manage to work full time and

go to nursing school, that can't be easy on you."

She skirts the compliment again and gets back to David. She likes him, but needs to know he isn't one of those womanizers that regularly travel into town on business trips only to prowl for a score in the casinos and strip joints.

"How often do you make it Las Vegas?"

David begins to feel a bit as if he is being interviewed for a position with a Fortune 500 Company but tolerates the barrage of questions and continues to answer with a smile. He wants to make the same assessment of Sakuri, so he sits comfortably and gets a few questions in himself for the next couple of hours. It was not as if the lunch was unpleasant; he was with a gorgeous lady, they laughed, and enjoyed each other's company. What could be better? The two hours he had hoped to spend with her flew by and before they knew it the clock was at two fifteen. David had to get back to the Stardust to meet with Jefferson in the café at three so he was forced to bring the conversation to a close for now. Sakuri was sorry to have to end it, but she was content for the time being with the information she obtained. If David wished to see her again she had already decided she would comply. He was an interesting man with still enough intrigue to keep her interested in seeing him again.

"I am not sure when I will be back to Las Vegas, but as soon as I know I would like to call you and make plans to see you again."

Sakuri was delighted that he wanted to see her again. She sort of expected it, but didn't want to appear to be too sure of herself. After all, David didn't hide his attraction to her, as was the case with most of the men she encountered on or off the job.

"That would be nice David."

She reaches into her red clutch purse and pulls out her card holder. She hands him her dealer's card and tells him to call her anytime, and not just for blackjack. David smiles and hands her his business card and lets her know he will be in touch. They walk out to the parking lot together and enjoy another quick embrace before they part ways. As he hugged her, David took a quick whiff of the perfumed scent and held it for a while. It could be weeks before he would see this beautiful woman again and he wanted to plant a reminder in his mind; one that was typically referred to as an anchor in the world of hypnotists. This anchor would conjure the image of the stunning beauty from the far away land in Asia he had just befriended.

CHAPTER SIXTEEN

David rushed over to the Stardust hotel and casino, pulled into the valet to have them park his car so he could get to the café before three. He didn't want to be late and actually preferred being first to arrive. Jefferson was a busy man and the last thing David wanted to do would be to make his friend wait. He arrived at the café and noticed Alba was serving in the back area, so it would be certain they would have her as their waitress. David just didn't want there to be an uncomfortable tension with them, Jefferson would easily detect it if there was. He walks into the café and approaches the front stand just as Alba comes from the kitchen area. She spots him and approaches the front of the café waving at him to follow her to their usual spot. David gives her a quick wave and hustles to follow close behind her. They reach the usual table and Alba turns to David with a flirtatious look.

"Hi David, what can I get you?"

She states with that lovely smile.

"I'll have my usual, ice tea with lemon wedge."

She gives him a coy look as he peeks behind her to see Jefferson. Alba begins to turn, but before she can complete it she is surprised by the good doctor, who approached from behind and placed his hand on her shoulder as he greeted the two of them. Alba's demeanor quickly changes and the flirting with David comes to an abrupt end.

"Ahh Jefferson, you startled me."

"You can make that two ice teas and I apologize for surprising you like that."

They chuckle and Alba leaves quickly to fetch

their drinks. She knows Jefferson, unlike David, is all business and doesn't like to waste his time. David is easily distracted by her flirting and that could be a problem for him later, when he is in hot pursuit of his life transformation. He would not have time for playing around, and would need to commit his focus and attention every step of the way. Tipping his weakness to Jefferson now could be enough for the mentor to halt any more private tutoring sessions. David takes a deep breath as Jefferson settles down and peers across the table at a pensive David.

"David, why are you so tight?"

Jefferson was the most intuitive man David had ever met and he was spot on with his assessment of David's demeanor. David wanted to discuss his earlier lunch meeting with Sakuri, but he knew it may bring Jefferson doubts that he could actually see his transformation through due to the distractions so he attempted to divert the subject.

"It's nothing, just a business deal I'm working on, it's weighing on my mind."

Throwing both his hands in the air, Jefferson questions once again.

"Care to share? I will listen."

"It's really nothing Jefferson, but I appreciate you inquiring and your offer to listen."

"OK, but if you need to get something off your chest, go right ahead."

Just then Alba arrives back at the table in short order with two tall glasses of ice tea and lemon wedges on a small plate. She pulls her pad from her apron even though she really doesn't need it as she takes their order. David has a side salad and nothing else, leaving Jefferson to wonder if he had a lunch meeting. Jefferson orders an iron skillet steak with grilled onions, sautéed mushrooms and a second side of steamed vegetables.

"David, are you sure that's all you want?"

"Yes, I had lunch earlier so I'll be fine with only the salad."

Alba gives him a quick piercing look that goes unnoticed by Jefferson. She suspects David had lunch with the blackjack dealer he was seen walking through the casino with. Alba doesn't miss much and although she didn't bring it up last night, she saw David making a play for the beautiful Asian lady before he entered the café. She jumps into the conversation without provocation from either David or Jefferson.

"So who did you meet with for lunch David?"

She knew she just put a noose around David's balls with that question and either he was going to have to come clean or Jefferson would definitely sense he was being disingenuous with his answer. She suspected it was the card dealer, but she was going to tighten the noose with another prying question and simply force him to explain his lunch meeting with her if she sensed he was in any way lying to them.

"I met a blackjack dealer last night and offered to buy her lunch today... okay? That's it."

He explains like a child avoiding his parent's wrath of inquisitive questions. David bows his head and loses eye contact with Jefferson and Alba as they look at each other and smile with shoulders shrugged. Alba decides to allow the men some privacy and walks away to place their food order. She's done her part and David is glad to see her leave. Jefferson leans back in his chair and sighs before he decides to dig a little deeper into the previous conversation. He felt he was entitled to ask since he was mentoring this individual at no cost, only his time, and he wasn't interested in wasting that.

"So David, tell me more about this card dealer you met last night."

"It's really nothing Jefferson. She's the pretty Asian in the blackjack pit."

Even though there was more than one female Asian blackjack dealer at the Stardust, Jefferson knew instinctively who David referred to.

"Ahh Sakuri. She is beautiful, isn't she?"

"God damn it Jefferson, do you know everyone in this city? Am I to be on notice or will I ever be able to get anything by you?"

Jefferson laughs out loud, causing Alba to look over from afar. She shakes her head and turns her attention back to the work in front of her. Back at the table Jefferson pries more and won't let David off the hook until he is certain David is not going to get off track. There would be no real guarantee, but Jefferson needed to have a level of comfort with his student or he would pull the plug and discontinue his personal mentoring. He looks David square in the eye.

"You know the nature of the game you have begun to play. It will take all your attention and focus to stop a drug habit and in the process pursue the type of life change you have in mind. What you are attempting to do is not easy. My goal is to help you be happy with your life and if I am going to continue with my help, I need to know your level of commitment. Does that sound fair enough for you?"

David is reluctant to discuss his early feelings for Sakuri, especially since he had already revealed another woman, Tina, and Jefferson had expressed his concerns for that situation. This new development would only make him more leery at the notion of competing with yet another woman for David's undivided attention and commitment. And it may possibly ruin the friendship they had developed over the recent weeks.

"Jefferson, I know you are concerned with my level of commitment, but let me assure you, my transformation is far beyond anything else I consider important now."

Jefferson looks into David's eyes without a blink or movement and responds candidly with little emotion.

"Your happiness in life is important David, but to get there you must realize it will take sequential steps, some hard work, and most importantly your focused diligence. You won't make it if you waiver. That's all I am going to state, other than I will quit this mentoring if I see we are getting nowhere because you are distracted with other persons or things in your life."

"That's fair enough, and thanks for not judging me. Let me prove myself to you."

"OK David, you got it."

Jefferson immediately moved to the subject they are meeting about.

"So did you study the last lesson?"

The two start their discussion on the final lesson but before they get too far into it, Alba returns with lunch. She places their plates on the table in front of each of them. With a smile she asks if there is anything else they would like. She detects tension from David and when she glances over he gives her a short, nasty glare to indicate he didn't appreciate her questions as they obviously opened Pandora's Box. He quickly quips.

"I'm fine, nothing else here."

David is clearly upset to the point Jefferson catches his negative energy as well. He looks at Alba and with a slight nod he motions for her to leave.

"You know David it doesn't help to take it out on Alba. You had the look of deceit on your face when I walked up so you would have been interrogated anyway."

They both smile and the tension in the air immediately dissipates.

"Was I that obvious?"

Jefferson shakes his head and softly chuckles as his student slumps in his chair and begins to pick at the salad he ordered as if now it wasn't enough. Jefferson observes his picking and motions to Alba. When she arrives, he looks at David and asks.

"Are you sure that's all you want. You're picking at it like you may want to sink your teeth into something a little more satisfying."

David laughs and smiles at Alba. He had put aside the thoughts he had earlier after Jefferson's little speech and Jefferson took note.

"Yeah, please bring me a chicken quesadilla."

"Oh David, you are a silly man."

Alba walks off to place the order and Jefferson immediately acknowledged David's ability to quickly change the thoughts in his mind, which he pointed out were emotionally conveyed with his obvious change in demeanor. It was the perfect teaching moment.

"Interesting David; if you didn't believe what I had taught you before, you just demonstrated how the thoughts you had earlier had been removed and replaced with something more soothing and positive. You're reaction to Alba tipped it off. I'm proud of you David. You seem to be using the lessons as instructed. Continue and it will definitely be to your benefit."

David realized Jefferson was right. He may have done it unconsciously, but his emotions changed with his thoughts. It was obvious and not only to him, but to the people physically closest to him. The positive energy could be felt by Jefferson and Alba as well, before she left to place his order. For David, it was an affirmation that he was on the right track and doing what he needed to make his change a lasting and positive experience. He suddenly realized the awareness of his thoughts would be prominent in the control of his emotions, and while this one time may have been inadvertent without the awareness he needed to regularly exercise, it was a perfect example too, of how the process works and a good one to learn from.

In between bites of his steak and vegetables Jefferson began to discuss the final lesson and questioned David. He was inquisitive and probed for the confirmation that David had learned the lesson.

"David, tell me what you know about the final lesson. Are there any questions you have that I may help you with?"

David felt confident he knew the lesson well and began to explain.

"I got a sense that the best approach for this process is to send messages to the subconscious and then get on with the business of the moment. In other words, there are times when we try too hard. If I understood the lesson correctly, and I think I did, the conscious effort we put into anything will reduce the subconscious response. It sort of implies we get things accomplished through the law of least effort."

"That's very perceptive David. Many folks don't understand that at all and work themselves to the bone but have no good results to show for it. Reason being, they are not making that connection of body, mind, and spirit. There is no involvement with the subconscious mind."

Jefferson pauses briefly before he continues.

'Remember, that is where it all starts. The thought that gets transported to the subconscious mind sets off a series of actions that take you in the direction of your goal. I am simplifying it, but if you understand the workings of the subconscious and how a repetitive thought can impress the actions or behaviors the subconscious produces, you are on your way to creating life and not just merely living it. That's the process of making change with self-hypnosis."

Jefferson finished his last bite of steak, sat back and took in the moment. He was proud of what David had accomplished so far, but he knew there was much more work to do and he would need a fully focused and committed pupil. The pleasure Jefferson derived from his help was to see an individual like David turn an idea or a dream into a reality. Not many people have that type of commitment and it's for that reason alone he kept his training classes small. Making money wasn't the issue for Jefferson. He was about providing help to those who were very serious about finding a method for creating life changes and realizing special accomplishments. He had the expertise in that method and if David followed his instruction, he would stand a much better chance of realizing the change he sought and executing the goals he had developed since their friendship began.

"So David, what else do you have lined up for the next day and a half?"

David sensed Jefferson had to leave early for the showroom and gave him an easy out.

"I actually have to stop and see a customer at the MGM corporate office when we're finished. Nothing real urgent, but they asked me to stop in before they leave."

Jefferson took the bait.

"Well then, I guess we better get going, huh?"

The two men shook hands and Jefferson turned to exit the café. David stayed behind to handle the check and say goodbye to Alba. As he walked ahead Jefferson realized David didn't follow him out and he turned around to wave at him and gave him a sign to call later. David wasn't sure why Jefferson wanted him to call later, but he would check with him before he left town. Alba spotted the table and saw Jefferson was no longer with David. This could be a ripe opportunity for her to delve a little deeper into the possibility of hooking the handsome young man for an afternoon fling. She smiled as he looked up to see her walking in his direction. There was indeed an attraction for each of them and she was bound to play this through, even though he resisted.

"Where did Jefferson go?"

"I sensed he had an early stage meeting and had to get outta here. I'll take care of the check."

Alba turned quickly to gather the check and left a trace of perfume in her wake as she breezed by David. He caught a whiff and it reminded him of Sakuri at lunch earlier. All these wonderful fragrances made his mind swirl. Alba came back inside of two minutes and handed David the tab.

"Where are you off to David?"

"I'm going to my room to wrap up the day and then I may play a little blackjack."

"Ohh, with your new sweetie?"

She couldn't resist the temptation and had to take another dig at him.

"She's just a friend Alba and we had lunch together, that's all."

"I'm your friend. Take me to lunch tomorrow, I am off work. Are you still here in Vegas?"

Alba was direct and had made her play for him

very obvious. As far as David was concerned, it would be difficult too. He really didn't want to do it, but to get it behind them he decided to take her to lunch or he wouldn't hear the end of it.

"Okay Alba, I'm here tomorrow. Where do you want to meet for lunch?"

Alba was shocked at his response and quickly searched her mind for a spot close to her condo in the northwest part of town. She too liked to spend time in Boca Park; it was the place to go for the lady's in town who liked to shop. Her mind fixed on the Cheesecake Factory and with a sly grin she asked.

"How about a little cheesecake baby?"

David broke out in laughter and she shined a broad smile as well. The sexual tension had not diminished, and if anything her comment just turned things up a notch. He would meet her there to avoid having to pick her up or even more dangerously, drop her off. He needed to keep an open exit to get out when the scene looked as if it might get a little too hot.

"Sounds good Alba; let's meet there around noon. I have to get out of town by two so it will give us a good couple of hours to eat and chat."

She wanted much more time than that, but took the invite anyway.

"I see you there at twelve David."

Alba smiles and is content for the moment. She turns away and leaves David to close out his ticket. He signs off the charge to his room and leaves her a cash tip and short note on the receipt.

It reads… 'See you tomorrow, cheesecake.'

CHAPTER SEVENTEEN

The next morning David woke up to a blustery, wind-swept day. The wind blew all night and with it brought cloud cover and a thin layer of dust, which inevitably would have him sneezing throughout the morning and early afternoon. This was a good day for him to leave Las Vegas, but David had the one appointment to deal with first. It wasn't even related to business. He had the lunch appointment he had reluctantly been cornered into by Alba. He actually didn't regret it. After all she was an attractive, friendly lady and to spend a little time with her to get better acquainted could be a good thing. He was just concerned about her expectations and how he would deal with those when the time came. She wanted him in a biblical sense, but what she didn't know was it was certain not to happen. David would surely resist her advances because of her past indiscretions with Jefferson. He saw her as an absolutely attractive woman, but he had the one hang-up and for that reason it would be lunch and only lunch. Obviously, she had something else in mind to keep him in Las Vegas for at least another night, but David had other plans.

As he went through his morning ritual, David started the shower to get the water warmed. He went back into the suite and fired up the computer on the desk. He wanted to clear any work issues before he got on the road, because once he left Vegas he wasn't going to be available while he drove to Baker. He sat several minutes in front of the screen and decided it was time to jump into the shower. After a thorough scrubbing, he steps out of the shower and grabs a pair of jeans and a Don Henley style shirt. Friday dress is casual, especially when he's planned to check out early to have lunch with Alba and then drive to Baker for dinner later that evening with Tina. David had no scheduled customer stops on his schedule, only time to contemplate his next move for the new business plan he was about to embark on. He thought to himself, this is the kind of day he dreamed about when he decided to commit himself to this personal transformation. He loved having complete control of his time and activity, but he knew he would have challenges along the way while he created this life for himself.

Building a business wasn't an easy venture, and he realized it even more in the past month that he had begun to work on it with Jefferson as his mentor. Over and over in his mind he kept hearing Jefferson's comments about commitment, focus, and diligence. He had begun a new path in life and while it was exciting, there were pensive moments too. Mastering the mind to a degree that directly impacts one's life is a noble pursuit, but not one without major challenges. For this reason he occasionally felt a slight preoccupation. He knew distractions would take him way off course and Alba presented that type of distraction to him. She was a wonderful lady, but he needed to keep her at arm's length. That wasn't going to be easy with the hot blooded Latin beauty. He anticipated her come-on at lunch and she would undoubtedly look the part too.

David completed the work he considered to be top priority and left a few minor tasks for later. Once done, he packed his bag and headed for the elevator. He walked across the casino floor and headed for the front desk to check out. It was eleven fifteen and he gave a quick thought to playing a hand or two at the blackjack table, but he didn't want to get hung up on a winning roll and have to cash out and leave. If he got started he would run out of time and potentially run late to his lunch with Alba at noon, and he certainly didn't want to leave her waiting. The young clerk at the front desk took care of his checkout expeditiously and he was out of the casino by eleven thirty.

The drive to Boca Park would take him most of the thirty minutes he had left himself being that he avoided the freeway and decided to take side streets. Traffic had picked up with people leaving offices and other retail businesses as they headed to their favorite lunch destination. Boca Park was typically a busy area during the day with all its shops and restaurants. Today would offer no change. The crowds were already out. It was Friday and some folks were already at their final destination for the remainder of the day. Heading back to the office was not going to be an option, especially after a few slugs of liquor or cold brews during lunch. David pulled into the section of the retail center where the Cheesecake Factory was located and the lot was filled enough so that he would have to go search and jockey with others for a decent space to park. When he entered the restaurant Alba was already there seated on the bench and waiting patiently.

"Alba, sorry if I've kept you long. All the traffic and getting a parking space, it's just crazy out there."

"It's OK David, I jus' arrived myself."

Alba stood and gave David a hug. He made it a quick one and then he stepped away and gestured for her to lead to the hostess counter to get them seated. As they approached a young attractive female of twenty something greeted them.

"Hello, will it be just the two of you?"

"Yes"

David responded frankly.

She grabbed two menus and came from around the counter to lead them to their table.

"Right this way please."

She sits them in the back area behind the bar, which suited David just fine. He really had a dislike for noise, crowds, and the occasional boisterous fool in a bar. David jumped in front of the hostess and slid the chair back for Alba. She settled in and he slid the chair forward a bit to close the gap from the table. Alba turns to him with a look of gratuity.

"Thank you David, you're such a gentleman."

David nods his head, smiles, and skirts around the table to take his seat across from her. He is not going to give her any indications this is anything but lunch.

"So Alba, is this one of your favorite spots in the Boca center?"

"I've been here a few times. It's a good menu with a lot of variety."

The two continue with their light conversation until the server comes to the table and introduces himself. He is a physically-fit, young man with a crop of blonde hair and tan that would make one think he is out of place and belonged on a surfboard at any beach with a surf break along the Southern California coast.

"Hi, my name is Trevor and I'll be your server today. Can I start you with a drink, maybe a cocktail from the bar?"

He spoke the script perfectly; so much so that he came across as having very little personality and almost robotic. Alba shoots David a look that makes him break out in a grin. He looks up at Trevor with the silly grin on his face, then turns back and defers to Alba and gestures for her to order first.

"I'll have a chardonnay please."

To Alba's dismay, David offered up an excuse to pass on the alcoholic beverage. She hoped to loosen him up a bit, but he would not comply.

"I have a long drive after lunch so I am going to skip the cocktail and have an ice tea."

Trevor gave them both the customary smile before he turned away.

"Great, let me get those drinks for you and I'll be right back to take your order."

As Trevor turned away from the table David placed his attention on Alba and searched for the best way to open the conversation and let her down easy. She had obviously conjured up different expectations for their get together and when David passed on the cocktail she knew things would not go as she had hoped. David, on the other hand wanted to make it clear up front he would not engage in anything more than a friendly lunch together. He was there to only spend a couple of hours with her and then he had to get out of town.

"Alba I know there is a physical attraction between us but you have to understand why I can't get involved with you."

She looked at him with both surprise and disappointment in her eyes as he continued.

"It has nothing to do with you; it's all on me and what I feel. Also, I have to focus on my work with Jefferson. I have big plans and I can't allow myself to get off course due to any distractions."

The look on Alba's face morphed into one of sadness and she became somewhat depressed with what she heard from David. She made one last attempt to guilt him and hoped to lead him to reconsider.

"Oh, so I am a distraction?"

She quickly continues before he can answer.

"You know Jefferson and me; we have nothing going on anymore. He helped me a long time ago and we are just friends. What I do is my business and it should be the same for you. Besides, you already got together with your lovely card dealer. So what David, am I just not good enough for you?"

She crossed over from friendly to smug with that last question and David also did not appreciate her insinuation that he and Sakuri 'got together.'

"Of course not Alba, you're a beautiful lady and anyone would be lucky to have you, but I just have other things in my life that need to take priority now. For you to assume I got together with Sakuri when you really don't know anything about it is really out of bounds for this conversation. I won't discuss that with you at all. We can be friends, period. End of story."

Just then Trevor arrived at the table with their drinks. It was very timely and for the moment, stopped what could have morphed into a conversation that may have ended their lunch before they even got started.

"I have a chardonnay for the lady, and ice tea for you sir."

As soon as he sets the drinks down in front of each of them, Trevor pulls a pad from the waiter's apron and glances back and forth, first at Alba, then to David.

"Have you decided on lunch?"

David raises his hand and gestures that they will need some more time.

"Can you give us a few more minutes?"

"Of course sir, take your time and I'll be back."

David immediately turns to Alba with a serious look on his face and starts in again.

"Alba, I don't want this to turn into something it

isn't. I surely do not want to have you upset every time I see you at the café, so we need to make things clear right now, before..."

Alba is a bit upset and her Latin blood is bubbling, but she contains herself as she cuts him off and states.

"Before what David? What are you talking about? This is nothing. We are just friends having lunch, that's all it is, right?"

"Yes, and I hope we can remain friends after today. I know this isn't what you want, but it has to be this way for now."

"Of course I can be your friend. What else you think I gonna do?"

She attempts to calm down and smiled at him which apparently began to ease the tension their initial conversation created. David smiled back and sipped his tea as Alba took an unusually large swig of her wine. She continued to drink it down quickly and has her first glass almost emptied by the time the waiter returned. As Trevor approached the table they both look up and then back down into their menus to make a quick selection so as to not have him go away and return again.

"Have you decided?"

David looked up at Alba.

"Go ahead Alba, what do you want?"

She basically decides by selecting the first thing she spots on the menu when she looks back down, Chinese Chicken salad. David orders the chopped Cobb salad. Trevor scribbles the order on his pad and before he leaves notices Alba's glass is close to empty.

"Would you like another wine miss?"

"Yes, of course, thank you."

She's still a little hot, but settling down with the effects of that first quick glass of vino. David lets out a slight laugh and she gives him a look as if she doesn't care what he thinks.

"What David, you don't think I should drink another glass of wine?"

"No, no, go ahead Alba. You're a big girl. You go ahead and do what you want."

"That's right and don you forget it."

Alba seemed to want to pick a fight, but David wasn't going to give her the pleasure. He does genuinely like her and is attracted to her fiery Latin demeanor, but he also had his reasons for wanting to keep a safe distance between them for now. Otherwise, he may have skipped the lunch and taken her back to her place for a raucous afternoon of sexual pleasure. He already knew she would go in a heartbeat and he sensed it could happen with one word, maybe two 'let's go.' David gives her a big grin and shakes his head while he states.

"Alba, I'm not going to give in and fight with you. You're my friend and I want it to stay that way, so let's just enjoy lunch and our time together."

"Oh David, you dunno what you are missing."

The two of them laugh at Alba's quip, and each seems to have a sense one day they will get together and when they do it will be all they had imagined in these moments. Trevor returns with Alba's wine and sets it down, taking away the empty glass without a word. Alba has begun to feel the effects of her first round and grabs the second glass of wine, raises it in front of her and gestures toward David.

"Toast to your future success David."

She doesn't wait for him to participate in his own toast and swigs from her goblet. David smiles, nods uncomfortably and gestures toward her with his hand.

"Thank you Alba."

He pauses and then adds.

"You're not being facetious now, are you?"

"Of course not David, don't be silly."

She gives him that sensual stare and sexy smile that he truly loved about her and in the moment all seemed well between them. A few minutes pass before Trevor arrives with their salads and sets them on the table placemats. He pulls the pepper grinder from his apron pocket and turned to Alba.

"Would you like some freshly ground pepper?"

Still with a lovely smile on her face, she responds.

"Yes darling, I love pepper."

She giggles as Trevor turns to David.

"And you sir?"

"Yes please, I'll have a few turns."

Before he begins to dig into his salad, David looks across the table and gets his eyes locked onto Alba's. She suddenly stopped fiddling with her fork and freezes with her eyes locked on him, thinking he may have had a change of heart.

"I do appreciate your friendship and support Alba. It's been a pleasure to meet you and I hope we continue our friendship for many years."

"Is that it David? I had hoped for a moment you would reconsider your early return home."

They both erupt in laughter and the mood definitely lightened another notch. Now David felt the way he had hoped he would when they initially planned lunch. He actually enjoyed her company and witty conversation. Alba had a good sense of humor and that helped her through her struggles earlier in her life. Over lunch she told David stories of her childhood in Brooklyn, New York. She was one of five children and had a father that struggled with a gambling problem. As a result of his irresponsibility toward his family, they didn't have any of the "luxuries" the so called rich kids had. Her mother was forced to work to make sure her kids were housed, clothed, and fed. No bicycles, scooters, or even board-games. As a child, Alba would amuse herself with her own imagination. She would create stories in her mind of the other families in the neighborhood and even dreamed she would one day become a writer and story teller for children's books.

David was amazed at the story he was hearing and let her go on for what seemed like hours without interruption. She told of the little disabled girl who lived next door to her as a child. Alba was the only girl in the neighborhood that would visit and befriend the poor crippled girl. Then one day while she was on a visit, she dreamed of spilling a magic pixie dust on her friend's legs and suddenly the little girl was able to walk. Having heard the miracle, all the other girls in the neighborhood now wanted to see the little girl and be her friend, but she wasn't interested in anyone but Alba. It was Alba who stood by her when she was in her chair and it was Alba who gave her the miracle of her legs. David sat in awe of the story coming out of Alba's mouth.

"Alba, have you ever pursued the dream you had as a young child... you know, to become a writer of children's books?"

"Never David, life goes on and before you know it you're serving cocktails to strangers in a lovely Las Vegas casino."

David chuckles but he goes right back to his earlier thought.

"Alba, I can see you have a talent for story-telling. You need to exercise that."

She looks at David with a quizzical look, not fully

understanding his last statement.

"What do you mean exercise?"

"You need to write Alba. You need to write those children's books. Tell your stories."

"Oh David, that dream is gone. I am too old and tired for that now."

She was actually aging her young forty year old self. Alba had cocktailed for many years and moved to the café so she would not have to deal with the heavy drinkers, and loud-mouthed gamblers. It was a miscalculation though. They come to the café after winning or losing on the casino floor and when they do it can be just as difficult serving them food instead of alcohol. Anyway, she felt as if her opportunity had passed and she was destined for a life in the café, or something like it for the remainder of her working years.

"My God Alba, you're a young vibrant woman, you need to start writing your books."

"Holy shit David, what got into you?"

Alba felt very loose now. She had just about finished her second glass of wine and was waving at Trevor to get another. David shook his head and lowered his brow.

"You just told me stories that blew me away. You have a knack for it, I can tell."

Alba suddenly realized he was not kidding. David was serious as he could be and encouraged her to follow her dream. Much in the same way he was. It was very clear now. She understood why he and Jefferson had continued to meet all those late nights, mornings, and afternoons at the café. Jefferson, in much the same way he had helped her to stop smoking was tutoring David in the use of hypnotherapy, or more specifically self-hypnosis. David wasn't just a friend of Jefferson's, he was a student too. He was being educated on the use of self-hypnosis to manifest his own dreams. She paused in thought and then suddenly became curious.

"So David, what is your dream? Is that what you and Jefferson meet at the café about?"

David laughed out loud and leaned back in his high back chair.

"Yes, of course Alba. I had an issue to resolve too. I also felt I was not on track with my life. I want to reach my highest potential. I mean what are we here for? I was tired of wasting my life and I have been in search of an effectual way to make significant changes. Jefferson has taught me the most effective method of doing that and now I want to do something that will impact other people in a positive way."

"What is that David, what do you plan to do?"

"I don't want to talk too much about it but I will tell you this, it's big. I am going for the gold ring Alba. I want to impact people's lives in a way that changes their perception of the world and especially of themselves and their own capabilities."

Alba stares at him with a stunned look on her face. David wasn't immediately sure if she had been affected by the surprise of his spoken words or the alcohol she had downed. He had such passion when he spoke about his dreams. It actually seemed to possess him and take over his being. She felt his incredible energy fly across the table toward her. She thought this must be the passion Jefferson talked about with her. He too encouraged her at one time, but Alba shrugged it off as inconsequential. Suddenly it was clear and she realized her passion to stop smoking was what Jefferson used to lead her to stop. If she could harness the same passion to write the children's stories she once dreamed of she may be able to create an opportunity for herself. Alba set her wine down and picked at her Chinese Chicken salad. She selected the best parts and left the rest. She was now absorbed with the preoccupation of thoughts that mulled through her mind. Thoughts of the conversation she just had with David as well the ones she had previously had with Jefferson some time ago. Had she missed her opportunity or could she rekindle the fire?

David devoured his chopped club and washed it down with a couple gulps of tea. Less than two hours had passed and they seemed to now enjoy each other's company in a way Alba never considered when she arrived earlier at the restaurant. Conversation had become stimulating and David had her in a psychological space she hadn't been in for quite a while, if ever. She could dream again, and more importantly she believed in herself. David brought the passion back for her in that moment, but then lunch would end and it would be entirely up to her to maintain it. For Alba, the test would be the same one David faced when he met Jefferson for the first time. He knew what she felt because he felt the same way and had to work it out for himself as well. She would have to maintain that focus and passion on her own if she was going to do anything with her dreams. He reassured her.

"Alba, don't give up on your dreams. I am just a phone call away if you ever need encouragement; just call me. I am in your corner Alba. I want you to dream big and to make those dreams come true for yourself."

She felt his passion and sensed his care for her was genuine. It made her want to hug him, but that wouldn't happen just yet. David checked his watch and realized he needed to get on the road if he was going to be in Baker in time for dinner with Tina. Alba didn't know the reason why, but she knew he wanted to leave so she let him off easy.

"Okay, Okay, I see you checking the time. I know you have to go."

He laughed and unconsciously stated out loud.

"I love you Alba."

"Be careful what you say David."

She paused and then shot back at him.

"I love you too."

The hug finally came in front of the restaurant. It was long embrace and not awkward at all. David squeezed Alba tight and she felt his positive energy. She would miss him, but she knew he would be back soon and when he returned they would have a new dimension to their friendship. One that might bring them closer and possibly move them in the direction she had hoped. For now she was content. David was her friend and he left her with a feeling of comfort she had not experienced in a long time. There was something about him that made her believe not only in him, but in herself as well. He had a way of making her feel an inner strength she had never imagined existed within her.

CHAPTER EIGHTEEN

Lunch with Alba turned out to be a success from David's point of view. When all commenced, he felt an energy boost from her company much in the same way she got from him. As he drove away from the restaurant he actually felt like he wanted to stay a little longer. Alba turned out to be a more interesting lady than he had initially taken her to be. He was intrigued by her sense of independence and her creative child-like imagination. David felt good to be in the presence of creative people. He fed off their energy like a radiant solar panel sucking in the suns bright rays. For him, Alba was that type of person. She was a confident, free spirit. An independent woman, who seemed to had given up sooner than she ought to in an attempt to realize her dream.

David thought to himself most people did that very same thing. They gave up on themselves just before their success was realized. They would fall into a pattern of making a living and then never realize their dreams for a life they would never experience. Even worse, some unfortunate individuals don't even make it to the point of being a productive citizen and regrettably end up being a nuisance or a burden to society. David's last thought saddened him and the emotion tied to the thought would serve as the anchor for the dramatic change he would embark on in his life. In that moment he further committed himself to be a person who once wanted to help himself but now realized it was better for his self to help others.

David now realized even deeper than ever before that all manifestations in the physical world are at first thoughts. Thoughts are in essence nothing but dreams. They are all mental illusions one conjures up in their conscious mind and everything that individual experiences in the physical world is keenly attributed to those thoughts. David would encounter skeptics without doubt, but the feeling he had in that moment was never stronger. His realization would carry him to another level of experience many people never reach in life. The 'ultimate joy of knowing' is a phrase you may get from an Indian guru. But to David it was just a process he learned with the help of a very skilled master hypnotist. It was a way to understand how to better control his thoughts and even further, what possibilities that level of awareness would raise for him in his life.

He stepped on the accelerator, entering onto the two-fifteen highway headed south from the Boca Park shopping area. He topped out at eighty miles an hour and soared around traffic in the first three lanes as he maneuvered to the far left lane. David grabbed his cell phone and dialed while dangerously speeding along in light to medium traffic. The phone on the other end rang but Tina was at work so he received her voice mail greeting and left a quick message.

"Hi Tina, I'm headed your way now. See you around six."

He pushed the red button to end the call. David looked forward to this visit with Tina. She seemed to have some of that creative fire that he liked to be in the presence of and he hoped it had not diminished since he last saw her. While he drove, David pondered Tina's situation and began to think of ways he might be able to help her get out of Baker so she could resume her search for a break in the theater or film industry. His thoughts would come back to the same solution over and over. He decided he would offer her a place to stay in his home for three to four months. It would get her away from the rut she was in and give her the time and opportunity she would need to land a job to support her monthly expenses and find a place of her own while she got her life back on track. Once she was set up in Southern California, she could start to spend time in search of gigs in commercials, community plays, or even a big break in television or movies. It was still going to be a tough road for Tina, but being geographically situated in the wheelhouse of entertainment would be a major advantage for her. She would no doubt take his offer, at least that's what David anticipated. If for nothing else, the two experienced a physical chemistry from the first time they met so she wasn't going to blow the opportunity to see if it was actually real even though that wasn't his intention. After he drove for what seemed an eternity but was only a little over an hour, David's phone rang. He grabbed it from the passenger's seat.

"Hello, this is David."

It was a habit he developed, always answering the phone with an announcement of his first name.

"Hi David; it's Tina."

Before he could answer she continued.

"I got your message. Do you remember how to get to my place?"

Just as the question came from her mouth she realized the size of the town she lived in and giggled out loud. David laughed along with her. "I'm glad you called me back, I might have gotten lost."

"Oh stop it. I'll be home before six, so you can come right over."

"Where else am I gonna go?"

He laughed again.

"Well, you know I won't be at the diner."

Tina seemed a little nervous on the call, almost as if she was meeting her prom date for the first time. It could have been her preoccupation with getting back to work or the fact she was anxious to see David again. She had just taken a quick break to return his call but had to head back in to finish her shift.

"I have to get back to work David. See you at my place around six. Drive safe."

"Okay, thanks Tina. See you then."

David hit the red button again and smiled as the call ended. He immediately envisioned of Tina in his mind that brought to him a sense of warmth. She was a simple girl, but not simple minded. Tina was resourceful in many ways. What she needed most was a small break and someone to help her believe in her talent again. He knew how she felt to be stuck in a mental frame of mind in which you have neither the resource of knowledge nor the money to help you create your life-long dream. In Tina's case she would need a little money to create a portfolio as well as take care of the needed expenditures she would incur going to casting calls, tryouts, and the sort. David sought to help her with the opportunity he was prepared to offer, the opportunity for her to move from the desolate town she had been left in. In doing so, he would give her the ability to pursue her dream. If she took his offer, she could find a living situation that would afford her the time she would need to pursue acting parts.

David drove for another half hour before he would come to the Baker exit. He pulled off the freeway and stopped at a convenience store at the onset of the road that led to the center of town. It was only ten minutes after five o'clock so he had plenty of time before he headed to Tina's. He considered a drive by the diner to see if she was still working, or possibly walking home, but quickly decided against it for not wanting to appear too anxious to see her. He was concerned that she might get the wrong impression if he showed up early and then over the course of dinner offered to have her move in with him. Though he was attracted to Tina, his intention was to keep their relationship strictly platonic… at least for the immediate and foreseeable future. He didn't want to tip her in any way that might otherwise indicate he had a romantic interest. David knew it could be disastrous if his offer to her was perceived as a play toward a romantic relationship and he wanted to take every precaution to be clear with what he was offering her. They each had dreams to pursue and he wasn't about to derail his own plans or stall hers any further with the start of a complicated relationship.

    At the convenience store, David pulled up to the island lined with gas dispensers so he could fill his gas tank prior to his departure later that night. He set the fill line into the gas receptacle of his car and left the hose inserted in the car's tank while he walked into the store and shopped for something he could bring with him to dinner. He was the type to always show up with something; bread, wine, flowers, he just didn't like to arrive at an invite empty handed. David spotted the wine section in the store and considered buying a bottle, but then reconsidered and decided against it due to his circumstances. He was on a quest to eliminate all his demons, so a drink was simply out of the question. Plus he still had at least a three hour drive to Oceanside ahead of him. He didn't plan to stay the night even though he knew Tina might offer him a respite, so he could rest before continuing the second leg of his road trip.

    Bringing a bottle of wine would not be the wise

choice to make at the time, so David searched the store further and spotted a stand with some beautiful plants and flower arrangements on it. He decided to bring Tina a desert plant for her home. It would be simple gesture and didn't portray any message other than his generosity, which was exactly what he wanted to convey, generosity and friendship. After making the purchase David walked back out to his car and completed the sale of fuel, collected his receipt and drove off. He still had over thirty minutes before Tina would expect him so he decided to take a short drive into the brush and cactus.

    The town consisted of a few gas stations, convenience stores and several food stops for passing travelers, as well as a small grocery store for the less than one thousand residents that lived in town. There wasn't much else to do or see other than driving to the outskirts of town to explore the surrounding desert. That's exactly what he decided to do. David slipped out of town on the road that would take travelers in the direction of Death Valley. A couple minutes on that road and suddenly there was nothing but a desert to look at. It was dusty, cactus occupied, barren desert. As desolate as it appeared, there was also magnificence to the landscape of the high desert. This was a place one could actually spend time in quiet solitude and connect with nature in all her natural beauty. David pulled over to park on the side of the road and got out of his car. He took a short stroll down a path into what appeared to be a forest of Joshua trees. As he looked around the immediate area, he recalled he had heard somewhere that it was unlawful to remove those trees from their natural habitat. If someone was caught doing so the fine would be significant and there was also the possibility of jail time. His initial thought was it seemed heavy handed, but then David realized the importance of allowing nature to dwell in its own place for everyone, or anyone to enjoy. This was after all, a very special place. It wasn't the bleak, austere town he had original thought it to be every time he passed through. The silence in the desert offered him a breathing space to clear his mind of the clutter that preoccupied most individual's thoughts. This was truly a place to connect with that force he knew existed inside of him.

The energy he felt in that moment was greater than anything he could have imagined he would experience in the town he once thought of as the armpit of California. The quiet stillness provided him a setting to enter into a hypnotic state that would be the gateway to his most insightful meditation ever. It was while in this quiet moment David further realized his quest for change would come in due time. He was so sure of the feeling that coursed through his body; he never wanted to let it go for fear of being unable to recapture it. In what seemed to be a long length of time in quiet solitude, David gathered his thoughts and placed his attention on the vision he had experienced in previous dreams. The one in which he spoke to a large number of audience members about the power of thought. In the vision, his confidence is portrayed with every word from his mouth as well as in the demeanor with which he presents the topic to his audience. The feeling at that very moment is so real; he is convinced he is seeing a vision of his destiny. The life he is in pursuit of creating unfolds before him in a series of mental pictures which race across his mind.

Moments later his mind clears and his senses are acute. David peers around the immediate area and takes in a long, deep breath. He exhales with vigor and seems to blow the toxins from his body with every bit of air leaving his lungs. He turns and walks to his car, ducks inside and starts the engine. David flips a U-turn and heads back into town in the direction of Tina's apartment building. His mission not yet complete, he will spend the evening in hope of paying it forward to his new friend just as he had promised Jefferson he would do. Although it wasn't exactly what Jefferson had in mind when he made the request, David's intention was still in the right place.

CHAPTER NINETEEN

The watch on his wrist read six o'clock when David arrived at Tina's front door. Before he could reach the door to knock Tina swung it open and invited him in.

"Hi there, I saw you drive up. Come on in."

Tina looked ravenous and the smells from the kitchen were very appealing too. Quite an appealing combination for David since his appetite had immediately perked up. He realized the salad at lunch was good, but not completely satisfying and he looked forward to the meal Tina had prepared for him.

"Smells great in here Tina, what are you cooking up for us?"

Tina smiled and was pleased he liked the aroma that came from the food she was preparing in the kitchen. Her mother had taught her to make some old world quick pasta sauces. She kept hold of those recipes for dishes she could make in a short amount of time and would be affordable on a tight budget. They were great for evenings like the one she had planned to enjoy with David.

"It's just a quick recipe for an anchovy sauce I put over linguine. I hope you like it. You're so funny David; most people don't go crazy for the smell of anchovies but I'm guessing you like them."

"Well I do like them and if the aroma is any indication, I am sure it will be great."

David hands her the plant he picked up at the convenience store.

"I wanted to bring a little something, and since I will be driving home later, wine wasn't the best choice so I brought you a house plant."

Tina hoped he would join her with a glass of wine, but thought 'oh well, it's a nice plant anyway.' She actually picked up a bottle of inexpensive red to enjoy with dinner. Maybe she would coax him to have a glass.

"It's beautiful David, thank you."

She paused for a moment and then asked.

"I did pick up a bottle of red wine for dinner; will you have a glass with me?"

David was concerned he would dampen the mood, but he had to level with her eventually and the present moment appeared to be the best time to do so.

"Tina there's something I have to tell you."

Tina looked at him with a concerned expression on her brow, questions in her mind, and anticipation of the worst outcome possible.

"Go ahead David, let me have it."

David started slowly and then let her have the full story of his drug addiction and the changes he sought to create in his life.

"I have a problem that I am dealing with and to make things even more difficult while at the same time I'm looking to change my entire pursuit in life."

"Well that sounds a bit complicated, so what is the problem... me?"

David chuckles softly and reaches out to place his hand on her shoulder. At first he struggles to locate the right words for fear of exposing his past indiscretions, but then he finds the inner strength to address the topic directly and honestly.

"No, no, of course not; it's actually me. I have been a drug abuser for quite a long time. I quit recently and I really need to stay away from alcohol too. It could possibly lead me to act compulsively, so it's best for me to just stay away from any mood altering substance whether it's drugs or alcohol. I hope you understand now why I can't drink with you."

She was actually relieved when he explained.

"David I'm sorry. I had no idea or I would never have…"

He raised his hand up and stopped her before she could finish her statement.

"Tina, you don't have to apologize for anything. This is my cross to bear and I'll get through it just fine. You couldn't have known, I didn't say anything before this because there was never a reason for me to tell you."

Tina stepped forward and reached her arms out to hug David. He smiled and advanced toward her in a warm embrace. They held each other tightly for a moment and then let go. They seemed to establish a unique bond in that moment. Tina's interest in David was now peeked even more than it had been in their two previous meetings. She was actually attracted to this vulnerable side of David. It was not evident in their previous meetings and the simple fact he felt comfortable to reveal that side of himself to Tina made him all the more attractive to her.

"David I know we just met but I'm your friend and you can count on me to support you in every way possible. Either drugs or alcohol, substance abuse is difficult to deal with and I want you lean on me if you ever find a need to do so."

David felt the genuine affection from Tina and he appreciated her concern for his struggle and well-being. He smiled and nodded then quickly changed the direction of the conversation to avoid getting to sappy.

"Now that that is behind us, it brings me to the other part of what I wanted to share with you. Do you remember when we first met?"

It was actually a rhetorical question and he didn't wait for Tina's response. He continued without hesitation.

"I was on my way back from seeing the 'Mind Bending Illusions' show in Las Vegas."

"Yes, I remember David."

David took a breath and blew out.

"Well I actually went to the show with the intention of meeting Doctor Jefferson Paul. He's the master hypnotist in the show."

Tina was now inquisitive and wondered where he was going with his story. She couldn't contain herself and had to ask.

"Why did you want to meet him David?"

"For quite some time I have been interested in what it is that makes us tick. You know; why are some people successful in life while others always seem to be in a consistent struggle."

Tina looked at him with an increased curiosity.

"That's interesting, but why would you so concern yourself with the topic of hypnosis and a desire to meet Jefferson Paul?"

"First of all, I wanted to make changes in my own life and it seemed to me this could possibly be accomplished with hypnosis. I saw an ad on television which pitched stop smoking with the help of hypnosis and it occurred to me if you can change a habit like smoking, couldn't you change any other type of behavior…maybe a drug habit or any other habitual behavior?"

Tina nods her head and keeps her eyes locked on him. She waits to hear more.

"Secondly, and this thought actually didn't occur until later. If I could be successful making changes in my own life with the use of self-hypnosis, I decided I would like to bring that formula to others so that they might be able to experience the same success, whether it be to kick a habit or to make a change of direction in their life that would be impactful."

"Wow David, that's pretty noble of you."

David continued on without acknowledgement of her compliment.

"Just think about this for a moment Tina. Most people miss out on their dreams in life because they don't have a clear understanding of the way their mind works or how to get what they truly desire."

David takes a slight pause to let Tina absorb his statement and then he continues.

"Anyway, I met Jefferson Paul and we have become friends. He is actually my mentor on the subject of self-hypnosis. I intend to create specific results in my life through the use of this tool."

Just then the water in the pot in which the pasta was cooking had bubbled over. Tina turned to the kitchen and hurried in to adjust the flame and bring the heat down. The dinner was close to being complete, so she put David on hold for the next few minutes while she finished preparing the pasta and tossed the salad she had planned for their meal.

"David, relax for a few minutes and let me finish preparing dinner. Then you can continue with your story. It's very interesting, I want to hear more."

David followed her into the kitchen.

"Is there anything I can help you with?"

"No, please sit down and relax. I have it all under control. I have some tea and diet soda in the fridge. Go ahead and help yourself."

David grabbed an ice tea from the top rack in the refrigerator and then sat down at the small table near the window of her tiny dining area. He watched quietly as

Tina finished preparing the meal they were about to enjoy together. As she worked in the small area of the kitchen, David couldn't help but think of how she appeared to be a domesticated housewife. He smiled as she placed the plates and salad bowls on the table along with the mismatched silverware she had been able to muster up from a friend in town. She gave a glance and smiled back at David.

"What... are you making fun of my mismatched silverware David?"

"No, it's all fine Tina. You're fine. I appreciate what you're doing for me."

"It's nothing special, a quick recipe from mom."

David knew it was a simple recipe, but what he really appreciated was the fact she took her time and the few resources she had to prepare him a meal. In her situation that meant everything to him. It wasn't as if she had plenty of money and time to spend on him, but she still made the effort to extend her generosity. He wondered how her former boyfriend could have treated her with such disdain and lack of appreciation for the type of person she appeared to be. David thought he must have been a real fool to not see the beauty Tina possessed, both inside and out. She was a special catch and he blew it when he mistreated and abandoned her.

Tina finished the preparation and served each of them a bowl of salad and plate filled with her special pasta and anchovy sauce. She joined him at the table and as they sat together to enjoy the meal she had prepared David could not help but think this would be a scenario they would play out many more times in the near future if she decided to take him up on his offer to move into his home in Oceanside. He smiled at her, looked down at the plate of food and took in a deep breath with the aroma filling the small dining area.

"It looks and smells wonderful Tina."

David raised his bottle of tea and toasted to their new friendship.

"I believe this just may be the first of many meals we share together."

Tina looked at him with surprise that quickly turned to pleasure. She would hope for the same, many meals and good times with her new friend.

"That would be very nice David. I hope we remain friends for a very long time."

"I think we will Tina....I do think we will."

She smiled and the two begin to dig into their hearty pasta meal. After several moments of quietly shoveling rolled up forks of pasta into their mouths, David breaks the silence.

"This is so good Tina. I think you nailed your mom's recipe. She would be proud."

"I'm glad you like it. Can I get you another tea or anything else?"

For some reason Tina still seemed a bit unsettled or nervous with the situation. It's as if she wasn't sure how to proceed with the conversation or the evening because she didn't understand David's intentions with regard to the two of them. She didn't want to be obvious and attempted to stem her anxiety from him the best she could. She thought how could she breach the topic with David and not create an uncomfortable feeling in the process. At that moment Tina began to speak, but David eased her tension by starting at the same time.

"David, I have..."

"Tina, there is one more..."

They both laughed nervously and David apologized for cutting her off.

"I'm sorry, you were going to say."

"Go ahead David, it was nothing. I have more pasta if you would like another helping."

She skirted the subject she really wanted to discuss with him and felt foolish with her awkward attempt to smoothly switch the topic. Luckily David took over the conversation for the moment and put her at ease.

"Oh no, thank you Tina, I am fine but there is one thing I want to discuss with you. I know you have struggled over the past couple years and had to put your lifelong dream of acting on hold due to the circumstances your former boyfriend left you in."

Tina stopped and stared into his eyes with wonder as to where he is going with the conversation. David continued after a brief pause.

"I want to help you Tina. I want to help you get your life back on track, so you can give yourself a chance to realize whatever it is you want to do in life."

Tina's mouth drops open and she is somewhat stunned at the words that have come from his mouth. She has a look of curiosity on her face and her brow has scrunched in a manner that would indicate she has questions. She had no idea how he could help her and certainly wanted to have him clarify exactly what he meant by his proposal.

"David, what are you talking about?"

"I want to offer you an opportunity to get the hell out of here Tina."

She is suddenly very quiet, looks downward and ponders the thought in her head. David continued to speak as she looked back up and stared at him with a shocked look on her face.

"You can move in with me for three or four months until you get yourself a job and a place of your own or with roommates to help defer the costs of living."

David paused and Tina, still a bit overwhelmed from what she had just heard, begins to tear up. She swipes across her eyes in an attempt to hide the tears and looks down again.

"I don't know what to say David."

He begins again, just to make sure she understands what it is he had just offered her.

"Tina this is not about you and me and romance. I want you to take the opportunity I offered and run with it. You'll owe me nothing; just go all out for what you want in life. You know you need to get out of Baker and move to the area where your chances to act will increase significantly. Come to the coast and plan your next move from there. You must do it for yourself... be selfish Tina. This is what you said you wanted, now prove it."

That last statement jolted her. If she took his offer to move he expected her to pursue her dreams with vigor. She would have to shed the excuse of her current living situation and prove to herself she could make it in the world of entertainment. She wondered briefly if she would be ready for the challenge that would come with the opportunity he offered. It didn't take long for her to realize this could be her last chance to pursue a dream she put behind her two years ago. She wouldn't let that dream go without a real attempt at success, so she decided to take the offer David put in front of her. With tears streaming down her pink cheeks she stood up and stepped toward David, grabbed him around the neck and hugged with all her strength.

"I don't know what to say, or how I will ever be able to thank you David."

"You will when you manifest the dream you possess in your mind. Make it come to life Tina."

She didn't want to let go, but he pushed her back slightly to look into her eyes. They were still welled with tears; she smiled, laughed, and then hugged him again.

"Thank you so much David."

She finally let go of her embrace and sat back down across from him. Her face still showed a look of shock and surprise, but now with a sprinkle of contentment. She breathed a heavy sigh and blew out hard, which released in her a relaxed state. Immediately she experienced a rush of thoughts in her mind; when would she move, she had to give notice to work and the apartment manager, how was she going to move her things, she didn't have many things.

David smiled at her, tilted his head left, and placed his hands with palms upward as if to ask her 'Do we have an agreement?'

"Well, what do you say Tina, are you in?"

Without hesitation she responded with exuberance and joy.

"Yes, yes, of course. I'm in."

"That's wonderful Tina, now let's finish this delicious meal you prepared for us and plan the details of your move."

They looked at each other, eyes twinkled, and both realized they were each in pursuit of their destiny. A new life loomed for each of them just beyond the horizon and for David, it was the first of many lives he would ultimately help transform.

CHAPTER TWENTY

The drive home from Baker seemed quicker than it ought to have taken and David attributed it to the state of mind he had when he left Tina. They both felt good about the decision he made to help her and her decision to accept his offer to temporarily move in with him. As he approached the exit for highway seventy-six that led to Oceanside, David thought about what Jefferson might say when he found out what he had done. He knew Jefferson wanted him to succeed and he also wanted David to pay it forward. He made that request when he began to mentor David, shortly after their initial meeting.

Maybe Jefferson would understand the arrangement he offered Tina was strictly on that basis, he intended to help her with her life-long dream of acting professionally. He would attempt to pay it forward just as Jefferson requested he do, by offering Tina an opportunity to move where she needed to be to have a chance. Living arrangements for attractive females was not in the agreement though and he knew he was treading dangerous waters. Tina was a beautiful young lady and David was very aware he would need to maintain a platonic relationship with her to make the arrangement work as he initially intended. David wondered if he should come right out and break the news to Jefferson about his offer to Tina or if he should sit on it and not reveal anything to him. It was after all his own life and he could do whatever he decided was appropriate for him in the circumstance.

The one concern would be to lose Jefferson's commitment to mentor him and that was something David really did not want to put at risk. He had established a trust with Jefferson and appreciated the time the doctor took to help David with his personal issue and quest for a significant life change. David decided it would be worth it to be open and honest. He would tell Jefferson, but he wasn't sure if he should breach the topic on their next phone conversation or in person. It's always best to see the reaction rather than guess, and he wanted to make sure Jefferson would be fine with the news he planned to share. He decided it could wait.

After a long night of dinner and celebration, without alcohol or drugs, David arrived home at two thirty in the morning. He was exhausted when he finally walked into his condo. The air was cool in Oceanside and David loved the breeze at night so he opened a couple windows to cool down the inside of the home, especially his bedroom. Sleeping was much easier for him in the cool night air and he was dead tired and ready to hit the pillow just moments after he unpacked his bags. David tossed and turned for thirty minutes or so. Unable to get to sleep, he finally got out of bed and walked down the hall to the living room. He headed for straight for the leather couch, grabbed the television remote from the end table and clicked the on switch as he dropped onto the cool, soft comfort. As he plopped down with a thud, he forcefully threw his head against the large pillowed arm of the couch. Thoughts of his earlier conversation with Tina came to mind and he was reminded again of how his living situation would be changed within two weeks.

David's mind began to race away from him. The next day Tina would make arrangements to leave her job and vacate the one bedroom apartment she rented. It was only a weekly rental so she planned to leave as soon as her two week notice to the diner was up. Would the arrangement be something David might regret? After she got moved in and settled into the beach style life, would she forgo her dream to act and decide to stick around and see if a serious relationship would develop between them? He wasn't sure he wanted that for himself or her for that matter. The questions came one after another. Questions he hadn't considered before he made the offer. It appeared to be a good gesture on the surface, but after he gave it more thought he wasn't as sure. He began to second guess his decision. The whole thing started to make little sense. He thought he may have been wrong to put himself in this situation, but it seemed too late to change now and he also did not want to disappoint Tina. She was so excited to have the opportunity to leave Baker and get back on track with her desire to act in theatre or hopefully on the big screen. David's hope now was for her to maintain that dream and keep focused. The last thing he would want to develop was a romantic affair with this lovely woman. That might be the one thing to derail both of them from pursuit of their life-long dreams.

    As he lay there with these thoughts running through his head and not paying any attention to the television monitor, he suddenly diverted his thoughts to the lessons of the mind and his meetings with Jefferson at the café. David had a challenge before him, one so large he needed to keep his focus and attention on the ball or he would definitely get drawn off course. In that moment David understood how real the lessons of the mind were and the impact they could have in such a sort amount of time. It was only hours earlier he and Tina had laughed and enjoyed an evening together as they talked about her move to Oceanside and how she would embark on her goal to act. He felt great, never better. Even earlier in the day, he had lunch with Alba and ironically had a similar moment in which he was 'passing it on' with the advice he provided her.

He encouraged her to begin to write again. Now it was the middle of the night, he could not sleep to save himself and worry was all over his face and in his heart. David sat there torn in pieces over the decision he made to invite Tina for a temporary stay. He was actually felt stressed and as if he wanted to indulge in his old pastime habit and forget everything or put it all on hold; but lucky for him the hour of night would prevent him from getting his old connection to stop by and slip back into that world of drug use and late night paranoia. He tussled with the idea of speaking to Jefferson about the decision he made. He even thought for a brief moment that he would just tell Tina he was wrong and they shouldn't go through with it. If he followed through and told her it would sure make things easier for him but he kept going back to the conversation he had with Jefferson and how he was asked to pay it forward. He spent the next fifteen minutes in a conversation with himself, within his own mind, and he finally convinced his self he would pass it forward.

David lay down on the couch and switched the channel on the television to watch a late-night classic movie, Casablanca. It was close to the end when the lead character puts his old lover on the plane to leave Casablanca. David was very tired and the film was close to the end so he shut his eyes and fell into a deep sleep on the couch and soon after slipped into a dream. He was in a romantic island setting and Tina was there. They seemed to be in an awkward moment and a bit uncomfortable with one another, much like the two old lovers in the film when she suddenly shows up in Casablanca with her husband. In the dream, David speaks and tells Tina they have to go their separate ways, the affair won't last under the current situation. She breaks into tears and begs him to stay with her and moves toward him to embrace. He steps back and holds her at bay. He won't allow her to get near him for his resistance to her is weak, but he knows he wants her and can't understand why he had pushed her away. David's feelings for Tina are evident in the dream. He is both in love and in conflict with how to handle the relationship because for him his primary love is what he is seeking to accomplish with a change in the course of his life. Always in the background are the words Jefferson spoke when they met at the café and David told him about Tina. Jefferson warned him about being distracted, especially with the challenges he would face while he attempted to eliminate his substance abuse. The last thing he needed was a relationship that might derail him from his plans.

    David was suddenly awakened by the noise from the newspaper hitting the front door. It was around five-thirty in the morning and he still took the weekend delivery of the local paper. When he jumped forward at the sound he heard, the dream was swiftly averted and he sat up in a confused state. He looked around the front room, unsure of where he was in that moment and then it came to him. He had left Tina's late Friday night and struggled with his sleep for the entire night. That's how he ended up on the couch. He turned his body on the couch and sat hunched over with his head dropped into his cupped hands and rubbed the sleep from his eyes. The dream he had the previous night or actually that morning, drifted back into this mind. He felt the stress of the situation all over again and his shoulders and gut tightened up immediately. This was going to be his first real challenge since he began his mentorship with Jefferson and he knew he would have to lean on Jefferson for support to get through it without losing focus on his single purpose; that being his intention to start his business of helping others through his newly found methods from the lessons of the mind.

He decided it would be best to reveal to Jefferson the decision to have Tina move in with him was in an effort to help her. He needed Jefferson to understand why he had made the offer to Tina and why it was important to him in his quest to become the person he intended to become. If he could convey the importance of what he intended to accomplish, then Jefferson might see it his way. Otherwise, he was going to have Jefferson question his motive and his commitment to the life he stated he wanted. That would be the last thing David wanted to deal with. He knew it was important to keep his friendship with Jefferson, and more importantly he would want to continue his work with the doctor as his personal mentor. Since their initial meeting, David had recognized many changes in his own being and he could attribute it all to the lessons he had learned and the guidance Jefferson had so generously provided. It was most important to maintain that momentum and continue the work he still needed to do for his own development. He keenly was aware of the possibility Tina could present a distraction, but it was going to happen at some point and he had better learn to control his thoughts, emotions, and actions now rather than later when he had more to lose.

David went to the front door and fetched the newspaper that had been thrown against the security door to create the noise that woke him. He headed for the kitchen and proceeded to make a half pot of coffee and then sat down at the kitchen table to read the news of the day. On the front page of the entertainment section was an article which caught his attention. The backdrop for the story was Las Vegas and the main character was Doctor

Jefferson Paul. As it turned out, David had come across an article that divulged things about Jefferson that he was not currently aware of. Jefferson Paul had been a clinical hypnotist for many years before he exclusively pursued his stage career and in those years he had helped many people with various personal issues.

It became apparent that Jefferson hadn't revealed his entire past, but then it wasn't something David had any concern with or even had the audacity to ask him about after he read the article. Jefferson's history was encapsulated in a two page article in which the author revealed his past work as a successful clinical hypnotherapist. Doctor Paul was an accomplished hypnotherapist with a large following of patients and people from various parts of the world who desired to gain his help or wisdom. He was well renowned in the world of hypnotherapy, and for quite some time he was a target for seekers in all socio-economic strata of life who sought his knowledge and expertise. Even the very wealthy, people dealing with the same demons as David, would seek the good doctor for his help in their efforts to overcome problems or issues they faced in their lives. It was in the article David had learned of Jefferson's past marital issues and eventual divorce. What he read came as a surprise to him and he could now see why Jefferson wanted his undivided attention and focus to be squarely on what he had stated his mission in life to be. Laid out in the article for everyone to read was the problem Jefferson Paul dealt with in having an alcoholic wife.

He loved her dearly and made many attempts to convince her to allow him to assist her with her affliction, but for some unknown reason she resisted. Ultimately the disease took her life several years after their divorce, but by then Jefferson had moved on to stage hypnosis to become the central figure on the Las Vegas Strips' Mind Bending Illusions. David sat at the table in deep thought, and wondered why Jefferson's wife would refuse help and possible life saving change from one of the masters in the world of self-control. He could not grasp the idea and now wanted to know more but was unsure of how he would broach the subject with Jefferson. The article was published for anyone to see, but would Jefferson be open to discuss it any further than what was divulged in the article. He would take a shot and find out the next time they spoke. The new knowledge gave David a different perspective and his energy changed in that moment. He was now certain that he would be doing the right thing with Tina; he just needed to make sure the arrangement would remain temporary and in the time she stayed with him, he could not allow them to have any romance. He had to mind his convictions and stay the course.

 A couple hours passed as David scanned the rest of the morning paper and drank his coffee. He felt hungry and decided to make himself some breakfast before he embarked on his 'to do' list for his day. David pulled eggs and bacon from the refrigerator. He peeled and sliced a potato and heated oil in a fry pan to get his potatoes started. He threw the bacon on an aluminum sheet covered pan and slid it into the oven which he heated to three fifty. As the potatoes and bacon cooked, he poured himself the last cup of coffee and walked over to the kitchen table once more to sit while his food cooked. He opened the sports section and browsed the results of the college basketball games before he moved back to the stovetop to check on his potatoes.

 He grabbed another smaller fry pan and placed it on a second stovetop burner, placed a dab of butter in the pan and when it was melted he cracked two eggs into the pan. Within minutes the entire breakfast came together and he sat at the table to devour it in less time than it took to cook. David cleaned the pans, plate, and coffee pot before he headed to the master bath to get his shower started. The day had taken a turn for the good and he felt much better about all that had transpired with Tina. He jumped into the cool shower and his body shivered. It brought a sensation that woke him and made him aware of his senses in the present moment. He made a mental note and acknowledged the fact he had begun to realize his mind drifted less and he was aware of the effort he exerted to stay in the present moment, which was key in his training with Jefferson. He felt sure Jefferson would be proud of his progress, but he did still have the one conversation pending; the one regarding Tina and it would take place soon. He wondered for a moment how the conversation with Jefferson would go; then he let the thought go.

CHAPTER TWENTY-ONE

David spent the better part of the early day on his business plan, but by mid-afternoon the long night caught up to him. He was exhausted and took a break from his work to lie down for a short rest. Just as he started to dose his phone rang. He wrestled with himself over whether to answer the call or let it go to voicemail. David rolled over to look at his phone and noticed it was Jefferson calling him, so he decided to answer.

"Hello Jefferson, how are you?"

Jefferson responded in his usual uplifting manner.

"I am excellent David. I am grateful as always to be alive, and to be able to do daily what I absolutely love to do."

"Well that sounds great Jefferson."

David quickly shifted the topic to the course he was scheduled to participate in soon.

"So we have training in a couple weeks. I am really looking forward to it."

Jefferson sensed David had something on his mind which he may have held from him. He would give David a little more time to gather the courage to bring it out as they continued with their conversation, until finally Jefferson asked a direct question that caught David by surprise and he couldn't dance around it.

"David, what's on your mind? You seem to be a bit pensive."

"What is it about you Jefferson; you're a mind reader aren't you?

The men laughed, but quickly refocused back on their conversation. David was hesitant at first but then decided to lay his cards out and see if Jefferson reacted.

"I have something to discuss with you and I want to start by reminding you of our first conversation when you asked me to pay it forward. I gather you wanted me to help others in the same way you're helping me."

Jefferson attempted to put David at ease before he could continue. He had a sense David was going to bring up Tina or even Alba, whom he had a short conversation with the previous night at the cafe.

"I do remember that conversation David and I will support you in your attempts to do so, in whatever it is you are doing."

"Really, you haven't heard yet, but you will support me?"

"Yes David, of course. The only way you develop as a person is to pursue big dreams, make mistakes, learn from life's experiences and grow. You won't always be correct in every decision and it's good to discuss these things to get clear on what you need to know as you're life plan evolves. This is advice even I must exercise in my own evolution."

David suddenly felt a level of comfort he hadn't felt over the past twenty-four hours as he struggled with the decision he made to discuss this matter with Jefferson. His friend just gave him the open door to breach the topic and he felt good to let Jefferson in on his plan for Tina.

"Jefferson, remember the young lady in Baker I told you about."

"Yes David, I do… Tina, wasn't it?"

"Yep, that's her… Well I made an offer to her."

Before he could continue, Jefferson jumped in to lighten the mood as David started with a concerned tone in his voice.

"A good offer I hope."

David smiled to himself and then continued.

"I know you want me to stay focused and warned me against the distractions that could take me off course; I want you to know I made this decision with that in mind."

"David, loosen up and tell me what have you done? I'm sure it isn't disastrous."

At that point David just blurted it out.

"I offered Tina a place to live for the next few months so she can get her own dream on track. She shared with me the fact she was on her way to pursue her goal to act professionally when her life took a dramatic turn."

"I do remember you mentioned that recently."

"Well you wanted me to pay it forward and I want to give her an opportunity to move to the area where she needs to be to pursue her dream."

"I get that David, but you must keep in mind something very important. When someone wants something bad enough in life, whether it's a change of career, a change in personal partner, kicking a bad habit, or any number of other things it is something they have to pursue on their own. The conviction needs to be evident in the individual who attempts to make the change. Otherwise, they stand a very good chance of failure."

Jefferson stopped to allow the statement to settle and then continued before David could respond.

"I know your intention is in the right place, but you must consider; if Tina really had a dream to act professionally, why did she give up on it so easily and allow herself to stay in Baker for over two years?"

"But Jefferson, you…"

Jefferson cuts him off before he can say anymore.

"David, I am not making a judgment about Tina; I am only asking a question based on information I have been told by you. She may well go on to succeed as an actress and attribute that to you, the one person who gave her the break she was in desperate need of and that's OK. Just understand, most people who accomplish the dreams they pursue in life, do so based solely on their own convictions. In other words, if she really had this dream to be an actor, I believe she would have worked to earn some money and found her way to Southern California two years ago. She would have done whatever she had to do within reason, in order to make that dream a reality. Do you get what I am telling you David?"

David was frustrated with what he heard from his mentor, but he had made a commitment that he had every intention of keeping.

"I understand Jefferson, but we all need help at one time or another, correct?"

"I'm not sure I agree with that totally. You see David, the dream is only one small piece of the sum of what one person needs to succeed in whatever it is they are pursuing. We talked about this, the thought is where the manifestation begins, but just as important or even more so is the plan, and the action that one takes to realize the thought, or dream as you put it. Tina had taken no action whatsoever in the last two years and so her dream is only a dream. It's the difference between daydreaming and actually living toward achieving your passion. Don't get confused with the two. Living your dream takes work, hard work in most cases, and she hadn't displayed that in the previous two years. She seemed to have settled and had been comfortable in her misery out there in that small shithole of a town. On the surface it appears as if you are bailing her out."

That last comment grabbed David's attention. He was surprised to hear such a derisive statement from Jefferson, who was usually very upbeat and positive. He paused a moment to give thought to what he was about to say, for he didn't want to upset Jefferson and potentially lose the friend he could least afford to lose at this time in his life. David pondered the thoughts rolling in and out of his head at that moment and realized Jefferson was correct. He reflected on his own situation and how he sought change. He did so by making a choice and the by taking each and every step along the way on his own. Nobody forced him or enabled him in any way.

He decided what he needed to do and pursued it on his own accord. Yes, Jefferson had become a friend, a mentor, and an enormous help in his quest, but it was still all his own choice and his own work that brought him to this point. And it would be his own work that would take him further if he was to stay focused to achieve his single purpose in life. He had a realization in that moment which might otherwise never had occurred if he avoided this conversation with Jefferson. He was glad he decided not to avoid the conversation and now felt thankful for the clarity that Jefferson brought to his life.

"Wow, I really don't know what to say Jefferson."

"David, before you say anything else, I want you to know I do understand what you hope to achieve by your offer of help to this young woman, but don't lose your focus in the process."

He stopped momentarily then continued.

"You must put the arrangement on a time bound period so it doesn't turn into something it was never intended to be. Help her, go ahead and help her, but make sure she knows it isn't timeless. She has to make it happen on her own at some point or the offer becomes fruitless and may inhibit you from your own work."

Jefferson had offered advice that was sound and brought clarity to the situation. For his part, David now knew how he would handle the situation and still enable himself to help Tina with a plan that would force her to take accountability for her own pursuit.

"Jefferson, I don't know how to thank you enough for the advice you have given me, not just today but all along this path we've been on together. I have a clear vision of what needs to be communicated to Tina and I will make this promise to you, she will definitely not become a distraction."

Jefferson was glad to hear David's commitment, but he also made sure David knew he was responsible to one person and one person only.

"You don't have to promise me anything David; it is your life. Promise yourself you will not allow anything or anyone to distract you from you life's work. If you allow that to happen, it is not me you would disappoint my friend, it's the man in the mirror."

David smiled again, and even though he couldn't see he sensed it and Jefferson smiled back at him. Jefferson wasted no time and moved on to the next topic. He immediately brought up Alba, and specifically the lunch she had with David the previous day. He met Alba in the café after his late show on Friday and he noticed she was bubbly and filled with confidence. She had told Jefferson how she was ready to take the literary world by storm with her new line of children's books. All this and yet she hadn't completed one book, let alone one chapter. Her story wasn't new to Jefferson. He had heard it all before and she never delivered on her promise to write. Alba was the perfect example for what Jefferson had just described in his reference to Tina, who had not taken any action in two years to pursue her so called dream.

"David I understand you had a nice lunch with Alba yesterday before you left town."

Unsure of where Jefferson was going with his comment David lay silent and allowed him to continue without response.

"She told me you inspired her to work on her dream; specifically the writing of her children's books."

"Yeah; I inspired her, so what now?"

"Oh David, you have been a busy little bee haven't you?"

"What does that mean Jefferson? I'm only doing what you asked me to do, pay it forward to help others like you have helped me."

Jefferson chuckled and then continued to give David an impromptu lesson on how to pay it forward.

"David, your genuine compassion for others is commendable but you still have a long way to go before you are able to really offer anyone legitimate advice on how they may impact their life. First of all, you haven't achieved anything for yourself yet, and please understand me when I say this; I know you may believe you have changed dramatically in the recent weeks, but the truth is your work has only begun. We have a long way to go my friend, which will become evident in the course you are signed up to take. It will help uncover specific things you are not even aware of yet. Don't be in such a hurry David; take your time and learn what you must before you embark on your mission to save others from themselves. In the long run, it will benefit you even more than you realize right now."

David felt a surge of anger wash over him as he perceived Jefferson to mock him for his attempts to help a couple friends. He started to react in a defensive mode but then backed away and let it go. After all, Jefferson was right; he was nowhere near the expert he hoped to someday be and he had a lot of work ahead him if he was to achieve his own goals. Before he could be a legitimate mentor for anyone else and provide advice on how to create a life, he would have to learn to create and be the master of his own.

"Jefferson, I only wanted to encourage her to pursue what she has been holding inside for so long. Had she ever shared her story with you? She has wasted her time and her talent for too long."

"Of course she had David. I do believe Alba is a very talented woman, but not unlike many others she is content with the easy way out. You see, most people are not willing to do the work needed to be done to realize their own dreams. It's hard work, but when you really understand the method of creating what you want in life, the work gets easier and easier, I guarantee it."

The conversation with Jefferson had been honest and straightforward and the messages contained therein had begun to resonate with David. He especially realized what he had done with Tina was to act as an enabler and he had not really been the person to pass it forward as Jefferson hoped he would be. He had good intentions, but it would ultimately be the work Tina did on her own that would decide whether she could make her dreams of acting professionally come true. As for Alba, she may have received a short jolt of motivation from David's encouragement during a lunch in which she consumed three or four glasses of wine and felt the typical rush one gets from stimulating conversation over a few alcoholic drinks. But again, it would be her own work that would determine if she would get anywhere with the dream of being a professional writer of children's books.

David quickly realized he could only be a conduit to the information he could provide for these woman, or anyone else for that matter, and the real work would always be the responsibility of the individual who sought the information to help themselves in an attempt to change their life. In the cases of Tina and Alba, neither sought information to make any significant changes, so the reality of their situations came full circle in the discussion he had with Jefferson. Both women stood a good chance of failure because all they were doing was following David's lead in hopes it would guide them to a better space than what they were currently in. The thought he could help either of them with the information he had obtained from his lessons with Jefferson would be far from what actually happens in that situation. He could only help if they came to him with the same resolve he had in his quest for significant change when he met and started his friendship with Jefferson. It is never the other way around and he realized that in the moment Jefferson spoke of Alba.

"Jefferson, I just had an awakening to the lesson you provided. I realize now it isn't what I do that matters, it's up to them and what they ultimately choose to do."

Jefferson beamed with pride on the other end of the call.

"You got it David, that's exactly right; and the fact that you initiated the action in both cases is an indication they are not really committed to their own dream; not anywhere near as committed as you are in your own mission to change your life."

David sighed and took a deep breath.

"So Alba is going to do whatever she decides to do, but what should I do about Tina?"

Jefferson laughed in his usual boisterous style and took a slight pause before he provided his good friend with some sound advice.

"You will soon figure it out David; you will soon

figure it out."

"That's it, that's all the great Doctor Jefferson Paul has to offer me?"

"David, this is your mess and I am sure you will find a way to clean it up. Take time to think it over and before you settle on anything I would be willing to listen and offer advice, but not until you have worked it out in your own mind."

Now sitting on the floor in the den of his townhome, David flops onto his back and lets out a deep sigh and hefty breath.

"I can't stop it now. I'll just have to give her a firm date of when she needs to have her own affairs in order, and that means a move-out date."

Jefferson stated frankly.

"If that is your plan, I would have to say it may be the best solution outside of calling it off all together."

David struggled with it in his mind but came up with no other ideas in the moment.

"I can't do that Jefferson. She made plans and gave notice at her job and apartment. If I call it off her life will be thrown into turmoil and it would all be on me."

"David, the key to what you just said is this…it is her life. You are not responsible for it and what she ultimately does is up to her, just like we discussed moments ago. But I will support you if you decide to let her live at your place for a specific period of time with a firm move-out date. It's not the ideal solution, but you must stick to the deadline for move-out. If not, she is going to stay as long as she can and may never leave based on how your relationship develops."

Jefferson knew he hit a nerve with his last quip, but he intended to drive home the idea that David needed to remain fully focused on himself or he would go down the same path as Alba and Tina, just a dreamer with no real results to show for the lack of ambition and work needed to realize ones dreams. David did feel the stick of a jab in Jefferson's last remark and was quick to respond with a passionate rebuttal of the possibility of a relationship blooming.

"It won't happen, Jefferson... It will not happen."

Jefferson chuckled softly but loud enough for David to hear.

"OK David, if you say so I have no reason to doubt you."

"Is that why you're laughing at me?"

"I'm sorry; I should have had more sense than to do that to you. I believe in you David, but you have a tough task ahead of you. Keep your head together and it will all work out fine."

David was tired and in real need of a long rest so he decided it was a good time to end the call with his trustworthy friend. But before letting him go, he had to ask one more question.

"Hey Jefferson, before I let you go and if you wouldn't mind, I have to ask you a personal question, is that OK with you?"

Jefferson, who was never fazed by any requests he had received, stated frankly.

"Go ahead David, but I may decline to answer."

Without hesitation David continued.

"You know I had lunch with Alba yesterday, and during our time together I got a sense she is quite the passionate woman. She made several passes at me and I didn't want to leave her feeling rejected, but I agree with you, I have to maintain my focus and not involve myself in any relationship that may take me away from my vision. With that said, I just need to know something, is

Alba as passionate a lover as I think she may be?"

Jefferson was caught a bit off guard by the question and laughed at the inquiry, but decided to give David an answer that would be just as intriguing as the question he asked.

"Let me just say this David, if she pursues her dream of writing and publishing children's books with the same passion she has as a lover, she will be a New York Times bestseller."

The two men laughed out loud, and all the while they both knew David may one day confirm what Jefferson had just stated. They quickly said their good-byes and ended their conversation for the time being. It would be two weeks before the hypnosis training, when they would see each other again. It couldn't be soon enough as far as David was concerned.

CHAPTER TWENTY-TWO

Less than one week after returning home from his business trip to Las Vegas, David was home in Oceanside working from his office. It was Wednesday morning and he had just returned from a short trip to Denver the previous night, in which he had met with two customers and closed current business opportunities he had pending with them. Everything on the job seemed to be move smoothly for him as the weeks passed since his friendship with Jefferson had begun. He used the principles in the lessons of the mind each and every day, and applied them to his regular work as well as to his true passion which was the development of his new business.

Two weeks prior, David had contacted a gentleman named Gene Bradley, whom he hoped would play an instrumental role in getting his products created and produced for the website he planned to launch at the onset of his business start-up. He was scheduled to meet with Gene on Thursday afternoon to review the details for the printed booklets he had developed. The plan was to feature the booklets on the website along with the recorded affirmations used in self-hypnosis. In the meeting, they would also confirm a schedule of dates to reserve studio time which David would need to record his affirmations for the compact discs he planned to sell.

David planned to drive back to Baker on Friday morning to help move Tina to his home in Oceanside. He felt excited to see her again, even if he had to keep a measured distance for the time being. The last time they spoke was brief; it was on Sunday after he had returned home from his Las Vegas trip. At the time she advised him she had already announced her plans to leave her job and move from her apartment, to both her manager at work and the apartment building owner. So it was apparent, the plan would move forward and there would be no change in course for the foreseeable future.

As David slipped into work mode at the onset of morning, he had begun to make customer calls and quickly lost track of time. The hours had dispatched quickly and before he realized, half the day had passed and he had begun to feel hunger pangs in his gut. He took a short pause and went to the kitchen to prepare a light meal for lunch and that's when the phone rang in his office. He walked briskly back into his home office and noticed it was Tina on the other end so he quickly picked up to answer before the call went to voice mail.

"Hey there Tina, what's new?"

Tina was glad that he answered her call; it was always good to hear his voice. She felt the joy rush over her when she thought to herself this would be her last day and night in Baker. She would be packed the next morning and easily gone by the next afternoon. Tina would soon be in Oceanside with a new lease on life.

"Hi David; I just wanted to say thank you again. I can't believe I am actually going to move to Oceanside tomorrow and will finally be out of this dusty little town."

David laughed softly and felt her joy come through the airwaves. However, he would take this opportunity to begin to convey the plan for the next two or three months.

"Well you have a lot of work ahead of you Tina. We'll talk more tomorrow on the ride back from Baker, but we need to get a game plan prepared for you. That way you can hit the streets hard and experience success early with your job and home searches, as well as your search for acting opportunities."

David's statement caused Tina to pause briefly to reflect. She looked forward to the move, but it seemed as if David was set to push her out already and he wanted her to become independent in a quicker time frame than they had previously discussed.

"Sounds like you want me to move out already. Are you sure this is what you want to do? David. I don't want this situation to be a problem for you, so if you have reconsidered your…"

David cut her off and reassured Tina.

"Don't be silly, I want you to succeed and in order for you to do that you must put a firm plan together with deadlines. It will keep you accountable, guide you in the right direction, and keep you in the right frame of mind."

"Geez David, you sound like a drill instructor."

David would not let up though. He knew what was at stake for both of them, and he would make sure he stayed on his own course even if it meant he had to push hard on Tina, he was prepared to do it.

"This is what you want Tina, don't let up now. If you want to live your dream, it is going to come with hard work. I don't want you to have any illusions about what it takes to create your life and to live in the manner you choose to live."

He didn't hesitate to use a part of Jefferson's quote from their previous conversation to reassure her of the direction she was on and how the work would become easier as time passed.

"It will be hard at first, but I promise you Tina, it gets easier and you will learn to bring things into your life in a way you never thought possible."

Tina knew David had worked with Jefferson Paul over the last few weeks and she was not surprised at the words he preached. She could realize the same benefit if she opted to listen and learn from David, who was getting mentored by the master. David expressed his views with passion and it was impressive to see and hear someone who believed in his vision and had the conviction David had acquired since his friendship with Jefferson developed. He was so passionate in his approach to convince Tina of the work she had ahead of her, it almost scared her into an announced halt of their plans to get her moved to the west coast. But she quickly let that thought go and decided she would go through with her move and continue with her desire to change her life by pursuit of her own dream to act professionally.

"David, I do trust you and I am committed to make this move work for me."

David was glad to hear Tina voice her commitment. He wanted her to be sure of the decision she had made because without her conviction she stood a solid chance to fail as Jefferson had pointed out when they last spoke.

"I am glad to hear that Tina. You must be committed to work hard on your plan or your dream to achieve success in the entertainment world will fall apart. Keep your focus and always work hard; there is no way you can fail if you do so."

Even though he sounded like he was a preacher on the pulpit Tina was inspired by what David had to say. He had spoken to her in the past about his life and the demons he struggled with so in her eyes his transformation was evidence that what he believed in was doing the job for him. She just needed to get more familiar with the methods he used so that she would be better equipped to make her own decision about their use and effectiveness in her own life. Tina quickly shifted the conversation to their plans for her move the next day. She wanted to confirm the plans so they could end their conversation and she could begin to pack her few personal belongings. Tina didn't have much to pack, but they would need a small U-Haul to move it all in one trip.

"So David, what time do you plan to arrive at my place tomorrow?"

Tina was filled with anxiety and excitement at the same time. Her head spun in circles every time she thought she was finally going to leave Baker and continue with her life-long dream. The dream she had arrived in Baker with when she first pulled into the old cowboy town over two years earlier with her ex-boyfriend. She continued on before David could respond.

"I just can't believe this David."

David responded before she could continue with her seemingly uncontrolled babble.

"I'll leave Oceanside by five o'clock in the morning. The drive to Baker is four hours or less, so probably around nine. I'll call you when I am about an hour away."

"That sounds good David. I'll let you go now; you must have lots of work to do."

Her comment wasn't really a jab at him for his earlier banter, but he did give it a second thought. After a slight pause he said good-bye and hit the red button to end the call.

David headed for the kitchen and prepared a salad with sliced cucumbers, tomatoes, and red onions. It was tossed in a light Italian dressing he prepared with red wine vinegar, imported olive oil, and several herbs and spices. It was one of his favorites and he often let it marinate for a day in the refrigerator before devouring it, but he was hungry and would dig in immediately. As he ate the salad and a side of warm sliced sour dough bread, David reflected on the training he would participate in with Jefferson in the coming weeks. The lessons of the mind set a very good foundation for David, but now he was ready to take the next step in his development with the actual hypnosis training course. Jefferson Paul had trained hundreds of students and many went on to successful professional careers in both stage hypnosis as well as clinical work.

 David's interest was neither, but if he had to define what he planned to do, it would clearly be more clinical in nature than the entertainment side of the craft. He wanted to bring his experience to the masses, to show people how they could impact their own lives. He wanted to offer them practical solutions for the issues most people face in life, as well as present a method and the tools they could put into place and use immediately to create their desired results. He would no longer play the game of life at the level he had grown accustomed to over the years. Instead, David would put into place a plan he created to bring his life to a level he had only dreamed of. For him, this would be a bold move to live big and impact lives, and possibly the world, as he would reveal the secrets to achieve all the desires any one person could have in this life.

 The phone rang out loud and broke his train of thought. He peered down at the screen to see who it was. Sakuri's name appeared on the screen and he smiled as he picked up the phone and pressed the green button to receive her call.

 "Well hello there lovely lady"

 Sakuri broke into a smile and giggled softly at David's greeting.

 "Hi David, how are you?"

"I'm great Sakuri, how are things going for you in Las Vegas?"

"It's been busy lately. I am looking forward to my vacation next month."

Sakuri had planned to visit her family in Japan. She was from the old capitol of Kyoto. It was a very beautiful majestic land filled with historic Buddhist temples and gorgeous, lush, green landscapes. After her move to the states she made it a point to visit every two or three years. With her aged parents, it was important for her to visit as frequently as possible. David was inquisitive and inquired without hesitation.

"Do you plan to travel anywhere or just take time to relax at home?"

"I'll return home for a couple of weeks David; I hope to see you before I leave."

David was delighted to hear she wanted to see him and made her aware of the same. He was fond of her and would like to spend more time with her if his schedule permitted when he returned for his training course with Jefferson.

"I hope to see you too Sakuri. I will be in Las Vegas in two weeks for a training course I have enrolled in with Jefferson Paul."

He paused a moment and then abruptly changed the subject back to her vacation.

"So where is home?"

"I'll be going to Kyoto, Japan."

David thought for a moment. He would love to be able to take that trip with her, even though her parents might not approve since they adhered to a very traditional Japanese culture. They were not pleased when she had decided to leave her homeland for the United States; it would certainly be difficult for them if she arrived on the arm of an American male while on her next trip home. Curious about the training course he would take with Jefferson, Sakuri changed the conversation back to David's plans.

"So David, what classes will you be taking with Jefferson Paul?"

She was aware of Jefferson Paul; it was hard to miss the billboards and banners around town and on the Las Vegas strip that advertised the Mind Bending Illusions. She considered his epic show and for a moment it seemed odd to her that David would take a course in hypnosis since he had told her of his work in an entirely different field.

"I will attend a three day course on hypnosis."

"That's interesting David; do you plan to become a hypnotist?"

"No, not at all, but I intend to use self-hypnosis in my own endeavors and I plan to build a business around the utilization of the skill to help people facilitate change in their own lives."

Sakuri was a bit dazzled at the response she heard from David. He never really shared these plans with her when they had lunch together. She was actually impressed to know he was even deeper than she had originally considered him to be.

"David, that's quite a noble plan. When did you first realize you wanted to help people in this manner?"

"I derived the idea through my initial meetings and friendship with Jefferson Paul."

Sakuri was now even more intrigued by this man on the other end of the phone. He had actually developed a friendship with one of the biggest names on the Las Vegas strip, but never let on that he knew Jefferson that well. Her curiosity heightened and now she wanted to know more.

"How long have you known Jefferson, and what were these meetings about?"

David let out a short laugh and then proceeded to tell her the story of how and when the two men met. He left out the part of his drug addiction for fear it might scare her away. He would leave that topic for another time when they would be together in person so he could more easily gauge her reaction rather than guess how it would be received over the phone. David concluded his story about the friendship that ensued after meeting Jefferson and that led to his reminder that he would be in Las Vegas in two weeks.

"So when I come back in a couple weeks for the training I plan to stay at least two extra days to take care of my regular business."

"That sounds good David; will we have time to see each other then?"

It was unusual for Sakuri to be so forward, but David had captured her attention and she was definitely intrigued by the depth he had displayed to her in this conversation. It was far more than he revealed to her in their first meeting and she wasn't about to let him go without further exploration of their potential for a serious relationship. David also felt the same; he was glad she came forward uninhibited with the question.

"I absolutely plan to see you, if only at the blackjack table, but I hope not just there."

A quick meet at the blackjack table would not work for Sakuri either and it certainly wasn't the setting she had planned to spend her time with David. If she needed to change her schedule, she was prepared to do it and make time to get to know him better.

"Let me know the exact days you'll be here prior

to your trip. I'll make sure I have at least one day free."

David perceived her interest in him had increased since their lunch together and he was delighted to know he would see her again.

"Okay, I'll contact you in a week or so and we'll make plans."

"Sounds good David; I'll speak with you then."

The two hung up and simultaneously smiled while thoughts of each other entered their minds. David mentally relived their last encounter. The smell of orchids that filled his senses when he gave her a quick hug before departing the last time he saw her suddenly filled him again. He envisioned her thick black mane, porcelain-like skin, slender body, and pursed red lips.

His mental vision of her, along with the sense of aroma that seemed so real in the moment, caused a spontaneous arousal. She was a beautiful woman, full of intrigue, and he would no doubt look forward to the day he would see her again. For a moment, the image he had conjured up in his mind was all he had and it would have to do.

CHAPTER TWENTY-THREE

Friday morning arrived and unlike the usual overcast coastal conditions, it was clear and beautiful. David was out the door shortly after five as he had advised Tina the day before when they spoke. He had picked up the small U-Haul truck the previous afternoon, so he would be able to get on the road early with no other stops to make. Traffic was light as he expected, and David arrived in Baker shortly after nine just as he planned. Tina anxiously waited. She was packed and ready to load up as soon as he showed at her door. She couldn't wait to get out of town as they worked fast and quickly moved her belongings into the back end of the truck. Less than an hour had passed and they were completely loaded, ready to set off on Highway #15 headed south.

As the two chatted while headed down the highway, David started again to tell Tina of the hard work that lay ahead for her. Less than an hour into the drive back from Baker, the mood turned pensive and clearly made the trip seem much longer than it actually was. In short due to the conversation David insisted on and continued to have with Tina. He had reiterated his wish to help her develop a plan which would be a guide in an effort to get her off to a fast start. She sat quietly and contemplated how the next couple of months would go if he kept the pressure on her in the manner he had begun to exercise. It occurred to her that she would have to find a home with roommates as quickly as possible so she could do the work that lay ahead of her without David's intense guidance. She appreciated his commitment to help her, but she needed space to work things out on her own and she could see the arrangement they had agreed to may have been somewhat premature and not well thought out. She needed his support, not his constant hovering and forceful demands. While she was still attracted to him, there was a side of David being revealed to her that she would need time to get used to. He seemed much more extreme with her when it regarded her career pursuit and he didn't appear to have any room for easing up on her. Tina was committed to work hard, but she wanted to make her way at her own pace without being constantly reminded of the hard work and time she would have to dedicate to be a success.

The final hour of the drive was spent in virtual silence with Tina and David each lost in their own thoughts of how the next couple of months would go. It was as if David wanted to see her succeed even more than Tina had displayed herself. His intensity seemed to overwhelm her and as they sat quietly for the remainder of the ride to Oceanside he searched for a way to let her know he only wanted to support her as best he could. He had made the commitment to Jefferson to pay it forward, but he seemed to forget the conversation they recently had in which Jefferson assured him it would be up to Tina to create her own path of success. He could only provide her with the tools, but she would have to do the work. However, in speaking with her David pressed too hard, but he didn't see it until Tina finally spoke.

"David, I know how badly you want to succeed and how you also want to see me do the same, but I just need you to allow me a little space to do this my way. I assure you, I want to learn from you, and I am committed to chase my lifetime dream, but you have to ease up on me a little."

With those words Tina seemed to wipe out the

tension that had crept up on them. David suddenly felt the weight lift from his shoulders and he displayed a look of relief on his face that wasn't apparent when he arrived in Baker earlier that morning.

"I'm glad you said that Tina. I am also sorry if I have pressed too hard. It's just…"

David paused for a slight moment to collect his thoughts and continued.

"When I started to work on my own issues with Jefferson, I made a commitment to him that I would help others in the same way he had helped me. I guess I just don't want to fail him or you… or myself for that matter."

"But David, you won't fail anyone if you just provide the way and let me do the work. Be my mentor just as Jefferson has been for you."

David looked into Tina's eyes with a warm smile on his face.

"OK, I'll ease up. But if you need anything from me to help you in anyway, don't hesitate to ask me. I'm here for you."

"I know you are David, you have already shown that when you provided me with this opportunity to move in with you."

David gave her a pat on the knee to reassure Tina he had confidence in her. They grinned at each other and David turned his attention exclusively back onto the road ahead. When they arrived in Oceanside the temperature was comfortable and the skies clear blue with a few puffy white clouds scattered about. They looked like large cotton balls in the sky. Tina stepped down from the cab of the truck and took in a long, deep breath of ocean air. She let it out along with all the tension that had built inside her for the past couple of years. As she looked around and took in the immediate surroundings her eyes welled up and a tear streamed down her cheek. Just then David came around the cab and walked up to her in time to notice her emotional reaction to their arrival at her new temporary home. She lunged forward and hugged him tight around the neck. She didn't want to let go, but he gently placed his hands on her waist and pushed back softly, slowly.

'What's the matter Tina?"

She sobbed and buried her head on his shoulder as she lost control of her emotions.

"Tina, are you Okay?"

She stepped back and detached herself from his hold around her waist, looked into his eyes with tears streaming down her cheeks and choked out a gratuitous thank you. He wasn't looking for her thanks or any type of payback. David wanted nothing more than to see Tina become what she had dreamed since she was a young girl.

"David, I don't know how I'm ever going to be able to thank you for what you're doing."

He laughed softly and smiled at her bowed head. David gently took her small, slightly pointed chin in his right hand and lifted her head. Looking into her eyes he made it clear the only thing she owed him was to give her new life the best effort she could possible provide. He knew that was all anyone could ever do and the rest would be up to the power of the universe to provide her with a result she would work so hard for.

"You will be a success Tina, and you will owe me nothing in return. Just live with a passion and go forward with a relentless desire for what you want to do with your life. That's all I want from you. Everything else will come together for you, I do believe that."

They embraced for a long moment, but then realized the work to get Tina unpacked and the return of the rental truck still waited them, so they got started without any more delay. Once they had her things moved into the guest room of his townhome, David set out to return the truck to the U-Haul facility. He left Tina behind to unpack her clothes and other personal belongings. She hung some of her better outfits in the closet and set everything else in the dresser drawers David had emptied for her to use while she stayed at his home. She set her favorite trinkets and two pictures out on the tops of the dresser and bedside tables. One of the pictures was of her parents and the other was of her mother holding her when she was just a small child.

    Once unpacked, Tina walked to the back patio and relaxed her tired body on one of the teakwood chairs set by the fountain David had installed. She took in the beautiful arrangements he had planted around the fountain and enjoyed the aromas from the various blend of flowers blooming in the hanging pots and wooded planters. Tina pressed into the high back of the Adirondack chair and closed her eyes. She drifted into a light slumber and felt more relaxed than she had in, well, the last two years of her life. She felt limp but had an acute awareness of her surroundings. It would be the feeling she would recapture many times over, but at this moment she wasn't yet aware this would be the state David would coax her into when he worked with her on the technique of self-hypnosis. It would be in this state of relaxation in which he would coach her to press on with her work to become the actress she had dreamed she would become for so many years. He would use this state of relaxation to guide her to a level of self-confidence she would not even recognize from the past situation she found herself in. Tina drifted into a deeper sleep until moments later she was startled with the noise of the door as it closed behind David when he walked in from the front door.

He spotted her on the patio from the entryway and headed in her direction. On his way out the French door which led to the patio, David hit a switch on the inside wall and the fountain turned on. He sat down next to Tina, who had a surprised look on her face from the water that had begun to stream down the waterfall on the face of the rock formation David had built onto the fountain. He dropped into the matching chair set next to her and let out a sigh of relief. The work of the day was done and it was time to relax. He leaned his head back and closed his eyes before he began to speak softly.

"I love the peace and serenity in this space."

Also very relaxed and with her eyes softy closed, Tina responded.

"It's even better now that you turned on the fountain. I think I can sleep here tonight."

David smiled with his eyes still shut. The two newly found friends quietly enjoyed the moment and nothing was said for the next twenty minutes or so. They just relaxed and enjoyed the sounds from the fountain's running falls and the quiet that surrounded them in the balance of the space they were in.

Twenty minutes into a restful and relaxed break, David's eyes popped open. He was disoriented and had forgotten where he was. Suddenly he turned to see Tina comfortably seated in the chair next to him with her eyes closed and he gathered his senses which had escaped him for a brief moment.

"Are you hungry?"

Not waiting for a reply from Tina, who appeared to have dozed off, he continued.

"How does dinner sound?"

Although she was tired from little sleep the

previous night and the short trip, Tina would oblige him. She also hadn't eaten anything since early that morning and felt a little hunger pang as well, so a good meal would definitely be welcomed. It would do them good to get out and enjoy a relaxed evening together.

"Sounds good David, but you have to let this be my treat tonight. You pick the location and I'll pay. I owe you at least that much."

Without hesitation David conceded and selected his favorite spot in the Harbor.

"There's a great little seafood café in the harbor, do you like seafood?"

Tina was a Texas girl who always preferred a steak or good cut of beef, but she would go along with his suggestion. Seafood in the Oceanside harbor had a nice sound to it.

"That works for me, let me clean up first; how about we leave in thirty minutes."

David smiled.

"That's fine; I can use a quick shower myself."

With that the two pulled themselves from the comfort of those Adirondack lounge chairs and headed into the house. They each took a short shower and dressed casually for an evening in the harbor. David wore his usual garb when not working, Kaki cotton blend shorts, a light blue polo shirt, and a pair of sandals that resembled something worn in biblical times. Tina wore a light, full length summer dress. It had a black and white vertical striped pattern on top and solid pink gown from just above the waist to the top of her ankles. She wore a pair of fashionable white sandals with pastel colored beads on the straps that appeared to be more for style than comfort. She pulled her dark, thick hair back in a ponytail and left her bangs dangling all about her forehead and brow.

David sat in the den with is head buried in a Newsweek magazine when she entered the room.

"Whatcha readin?"

He looked up, arched his brow and his mouth dropped open. Tina was a natural beauty and it was accentuated with her simple outfit and the plain way in which she wore her hair. Everything seemed to work just right. For a brief moment he was at a loss for words. She looked even better than she had in all the times he had seen her before, which were few. But it was enough for him to see the stress had come away from her features. She appeared more relaxed than he could remember any time prior, and a beautiful energy flowed from her that was never evident in their previous meetings. David suddenly realized he was taken by this lovely young woman's presence and her natural beauty; the next few months just might be tougher than he initially considered. Just then a thought flashed across his mind, 'oh no Jefferson was right!'

"Uhh, it's just an article in Newsweek on the crisis in the middle-east. What else is new?"

Tina smiled and his knees weakened. For a minute he worried he wouldn't be able to make it to his feet. David struggled to find words to begin.

"Tina, you look uhh... different; like something has changed."

Tina softly giggled, threw her arms out to her sides and retorted.

"Yeah, I showered and cleaned up."

David not sure of what he wanted to say, stood up, turned and began to approach her.

"No, something about you is different Tina. You seem at ease and... well, I just can't put my finger on it, but something about you has changed."

She shook her head while she laughed, grabbed his hand and pulled him toward her.

"Come on David, we need to get some food in you before you lose your mind."

Tina turned and they both headed toward the front door. David opened it and stepped back to allow her to proceed out onto the outdoor walkway. He locked the door behind them and caught up to her as they strolled side by side down the walkway to his car which was parked in a space directly in front of the townhome. David's townhome was a few minutes away from the harbor and traffic was light after the late afternoon rush. Friday evening in the harbor would be a bit crowded but they had gotten an early start and would have no problem with a wait at the café. It was a cozy little place right on the waterfront walk. David and Tina elected to sit outside on the patio and enjoy the early evening breeze in the harbor. It was middle of March so the temperature was still a bit cool, but a very welcomed change for Tina who had been stuck in a virtual hell hole for the past two years. The harbor in Oceanside was a wonderful attraction; a place she had never thought she would be just one month earlier when she and David had first met. Now here she was, and it all seemed like a dream. In a sense it was. She had received a break from someone who cared enough to help her dream again and she wanted nothing more than to make that dream come true. David got her here, now it would be up to her to carry the baton and finish the race for the life she desired.

Tina sat back in her less than comfortable patio chair, but was not bothered by it as she took in the many sights, sounds, and smells of the harbor. It had been a long time since she had been to the coast. The last time was in the gulf, at least three years ago when she lived in

Texas. She missed the cool coastal air and smell of the sea. It seemed to breathe life into her as well as everyone else she took notice of in the harbor. It was apparent; the passers-by all seemed to enjoy the moment as she locked onto their smiles and playful interactions. Couples and families with kids smothered the boardwalk.

"This is perfect David, just perfect."

David smiled at her and nodded his head in agreement. He was relaxed and would let his worrisome thoughts go for the balance of the night. He wanted to just enjoy Tina's company.

"Yes it is. I love to come here whenever I can. It's one of my favorite spots and the food is excellent. I'm sure you will enjoy it."

David still somewhat distracted with Tina's presence, seemed to miss the point she had attempted to make. Tina actually referred to the moment they were in and not necessarily to the café as being perfect. She was absorbed in the whole setting, the ambiance of the harbor and the people that surrounded them from every direction as they populated the walkway. She wasn't going to say anything to David though and politely acknowledged his last comment.

"Yes, I am sure I will. What do you recommend?"

Just then it seemed as if a light went on in his head and David suddenly realized what she meant when she had referred to the moment as perfect. He looked up from the menu in which he had his head buried and took a long gaze at the sparkle of the emerald green that surrounded the dark black pupils in the center of her eyes. For a moment David was lost in the abyss, but found a way out before he appeared to be in a deep daydream of his own. His mind cleared and just then a broad smile came across his face as he spoke.

"It is perfect Tina, absolutely perfect."

They each understood this would be the start of a beautiful friendship and the look each gave to the other indicated as much. Tina smiled and her nod of the head confirmed to David that he had understood exactly what she had meant with her earlier comment. What David didn't realize was Tina would be a quick study and she had the insight to take the lessons he learned from Jefferson and apply them to herself with ease. She had read materials previously, about being in the present moment and her comment was an indication of what she understood to be the key to a successful life. Tina's awareness of how to live in the present, along with the new information David could provide, would be all the tools she needed to set her in the right direction and excel in any endeavor she decided to pursue.

"So, what do you recommend David?"

David shifted his attention back to the menu and selected a couple of the specialties.

"The Cioppino is excellent if you like a combination of seafood and shellfish, or if you want to share we can do the clambake, which is a large bucket of clams, mussels, shrimp, crab legs, and various pieces of whitefish, with potatoes and pieces of corn on the cob."

Tina was in the mood to share and the mess they could create with a bucket of seafood sounded like it might be fun to enjoy together.

"Let's share the bucket David; that sounds good and it will be fun too. Is that okay with you?"

"That sounds great; the clam bake it is."

Just then a waiter approached their table.

"Hello, my name is Jeremy and I'll be your server this evening. Can we get started with a cocktail or glass of wine from our wine list?"

Tina, well aware of David's issue with substance abuse, elected to support his effort and ordered an ice tea with lemon wedge. David took the same. They placed their order for the clam bake and Jeremy scurried off to fetch their drinks.

"You know you could have ordered a glass of wine Tina, I really don't mind."

"I know; I would rather not though. I'll have an ice tea and support my best friend."

David was struck by her act of solidarity and the fact she referred to him as her best friend. He felt a warm glow in his chest and was glad she was there with him. It had been a long time since he had female companionship and Tina displayed a genuine compassion for him and showed consideration for his battle with substance abuse. In a flash David experienced a brief thought of the times he and Laura had enjoyed in the harbor, but the spark whipped through his mind and it was not for long as the thought left him as quickly as it popped into his head. His focus would stay on Tina for the rest of the evening.

He was exactly where he wanted to be and she was everything he needed at that moment. And likewise, it was he that she needed as well. The newfound friends enjoyed their dinner together and the conversation seemed to flow naturally without hesitation or a loss for what to say to each other. Tina was more relaxed than she had been for quite some time and physically displayed her contentment with the moment. David sensed the change in her earlier, but it became more evident as the evening went along. He suggested they walk the harbor after dinner and Tina jumped at the idea. She was in a new world with new beginnings and wanted to absorb every bit of it for fear she may awaken and come to realize it was all a dream.

"It is a beautiful evening in the harbor David. I would love to walk with you. A very long walk would be perfect after that bucket full of delicious seafood."

David was pleased and felt a positive rush of energy emanate from her, and he too, wanted to absorb what he felt in the moment and store it in his memory for future use. The boardwalk around the harbor was dense with people in some parts, but as they drifted away from the shops and restaurants and toward the outer docks, the crowd thinned considerably. They walked in silence for what appeared to be a long time, considering the conversation had not ceased during their dinner. But it was comfortable and not at all awkward. Tina and David had created a bond from the start, and in the short time they had known each other it seemed as if they were very comfortable in each other's company. There was no pressure between them; the time they had spent together was always at ease. As they walked along the outer docks in the harbor they began to take notice of the names on the yachts and smaller water craft. One in particular got the attention of both and when she spotted it, Tina turned to David who had eyed it at almost the very same moment. They looked at each other with gleaming smiles across their faces.

It read in big blue letters with gold leaf trim:
Sea You at the Top

The clever play on words struck accord with Tina and David as they both broke out into loud laughter. David quickly took the moment and used it to incent both of them to take action and work on their plans for a successful future.

"So what do you think Tina?"

Without hesitation Tina responded gleefully.

"Sounds good to me sweetie, I will see you at the top one day soon."

David couldn't resist any longer. He took Tina by the hand and pulled her in close.

"We will arrive there soon Tina, you and I... we will arrive."

With that, David gave her a tight, meaningful hug and then cautiously turned away to continue their walk together. Tina was somewhat startled at his behavior, but felt a comfort in his arms as he hugged her. Especially after the talk they had earlier, while on their drive into town. She knew he would ease up and guide her with the lessons he learned from Jefferson, which he would begin to offer her in the days, weeks, and months ahead. David would give her what he had learned as well as what he was about to learn. All the while, he would provide her with the space she needed to pursue her dreams on her own terms.

CHAPTER TWENTY-FOUR

The days would pass quickly while David looked forward to the hypnosis training he had scheduled with Jefferson. In that time, he mentally prepared for the rigorous lessons he anticipated Jefferson would have in store for him. Prior to his trip back to Las Vegas, he worked with Tina as much as he could on her own development. David gave her the book, "Lessons of the Mind," and she devoured the information in a manner he had hoped she would. Tina was intrigued with the subject and took advantage of every moment David had to spend with her. In much the same manner as he and Jefferson had done. Tina and he would spend long periods of time in conversation. Tina would ask numerous questions of David to learn everything she could about the subject of self-hypnosis.

David was encouraged by her commitment to study and learn how the skill of self-hypnosis could be applied to help her gain direction in her life. He was a good teacher and she the good student, just as the roles would reverse with him and Jefferson. David was patient and attentive; he addressed every question Tina had as well as he could with all the knowledge as he had obtained thus far from his work with Jefferson. She was thankful to him for the individual attention and passion he brought to every conversation they had on the subject. David seemed to be in his element as he taught her everything he had learned to that point in his own education of the subject. It was as if he took Tina under his wing and though he agreed to ease up on her, he would not let her fail under his tutelage. Since his friendship with Jefferson began, David had developed a unique passion for life and he would look for it in Tina as well. It pleased him to see the spark she displayed while he mentored her on the finer points of the subject of hypnosis. She would be his protégé and he gently pressed her with an intention to see Tina take the information he conveyed in their conversations and put it to good use.

It was Wednesday morning, two days before the weekend David would be in Las Vegas for his training when Jefferson called to catch up with him. David was in his office immersed in the work he had attended to for the website he would launch with the start of his new business. The loud ring of the phone broke his concentration from the work he was lost in. It was Jefferson on the other end of the line. When David answered slowly, and still a bit preoccupied with the work in front of him, Jefferson didn't wait for a greeting before he spoke.

"David, how are you?"

"Uhh, I'm good Jefferson."

David still a bit distracted, cleared his head before he continued.

"To what do I owe this pleasure?"

Jefferson paused briefly, and then continued to explain the situation.

"Well David, I have had a couple of cancellations for the scheduled hypnosis training and it appears as if you are the sole student in the upcoming course. I wanted to advise you so you could make a decision to either continue with the classes as scheduled or we can postpone until the next training in three months which will include four students as well as yourself."

The news was not going to detract David from what he intended to do. In fact it was actually good news to him. He would have the master all to his self. David was firm in his commitment as he responded without a second thought to what he wanted.

"Jefferson, I would actually relish the opportunity to advance in the training as the only student. If you're OK with it, I want to continue this weekend."

"That sounds wonderful David. It will be a great experience for you, but there will be a session or two in which we may have to adjust the itinerary since you will be the only student. Normally, I would guide the students in a session where they would actually hypnotize each other, but we will do something a bit different and focus on self-hypnosis since that's your main objective for this training. We'll sort of customize it for you."

"Sounds great Jefferson, I am excited to see you and get started."

David hoped Jefferson would not bring up the topic that seemed to sit like an elephant in the room, but he didn't get his wish. Jefferson would not let him off the hook that easily and moved to ask frankly.

"So tell me David, how are things going with you and Tina?"

"I guess I should have expected you to bring up that topic."

"Well of course I was going to bring it up. I am interested in how the two of you are getting along, especially you and your focus."

Jefferson paused to let his statement settle with David before he continued.

"I want you to know David I will only bring it up as a show of support and nothing else. If you need help with anything, I am here to provide it."

David silently questioned Jefferson's motives, but he answered anyway, with as little information as he could get away with. He wanted to end the call quickly and deal with this matter another time.

"Things are good Jefferson. Tina has worked hard to find a job, as well as suitable living conditions. It's been less than two weeks and she has a lead for a good job that would help her get started on her own. She's actually on her last interview today."

"That's good to hear David, and how are you doing with the situation?"

David knew what information Jefferson pried for and he wasn't going to give him any unnecessary details about the situation between him and Tina. Jefferson wanted confirmation that David was not distracted with any romantic notions and his focus was still intact. David stated as much.

"No worries Jefferson, I am fully focused on my intentions. No distractions here."

"I'm glad to hear it David."

Jefferson smiled as he acknowledged David's comment. Though he had never seen Tina to witness her subtle beauty for himself, he knew it wasn't going to be easy for his good friend to have an attractive female live with him while he attempted to take on the enormous challenge he would soon embark on.

"You must be busy David, so I'll let you go for now. I look forward to your arrival tomorrow night."

David understood that comment as a suggestion they would meet Thursday night after Jefferson's show.

"Jefferson, did you want to meet at the café after your nine o'clock show?"

"That would be nice, let's say a few minutes after eleven. We'll make it a short visit; we have an intense weekend of training that begins Friday morning."

"I'll see you at the café Doctor."

Jefferson chuckled as he hung up from the call. David paused in thought and reflected on the conversation that just took place. It occurred to him, he could have asked Jefferson if Tina could join them since the two students who previously scheduled had to cancel. That thought quickly passed through his mind though without any further consideration. He had planned to spend time with Sakuri on this trip and to have Tina there with him would only create an uncomfortable situation for him that he simply wanted to avoid.

David would spend the remainder of the day in his office focused on the design work he needed to complete for the pages of his website. The products he planned to launch were in the early stages of development and he intended to complete the set of booklets and CD's soon after he trained with Jefferson. He looked forward to the wealth of information they planned to study in the training sessions and David knew it would provide the knowledge he needed to compile effective tools for others to use in their own development. For now he would execute the design of each page of the website and when the tools were complete he would work with his web builder to create the website for his business launch.

Late in the afternoon, around four o'clock, David heard the front door open and close. He walked out to the entryway where he greeted Tina. She stood in front of him with a big smile on her face that could hardly be contained.

"Hey Tina, looks like you had a pretty good day by that smile on your face."

Tina did feel good and it was displayed in her relaxed, confident demeanor. She walked up to David and gave him a big hug which caught him by surprise.

"I got the job David, I got the job!"

Tina was excited to share her good news and her enthusiasm seemed to circulate in the room as David reciprocated with a tight hug around her lower back and congratulated her.

"That's wonderful news Tina and I wish I had time to celebrate with you, but I have a trip to plan and pack for. I leave early tomorrow afternoon"

She was a little disappointed that David opted not to celebrate, but Tina's enthusiasm would not be diminished. She was on an emotional high and would not allow anything or anyone to deflect her from her desire to maintain the momentum she had established, and that included David as well.

"It's OK David; we can celebrate when you get back from your hypnosis training. We'll have one more thing to celebrate."

David sensed he may have been too quick in his response and wanted to reassure Tina he was not only happy for her but very proud that she had shown real initiative in the short time since she made the move.

"I am so proud of you Tina. You have worked hard for the past couple weeks and I promise we will go out for a wonderful celebration dinner when I get back."

In her heightened enthusiastic moment, Tina slipped and let out a comment that could have been mistaken for an unconscious thought… or maybe it was what she truly felt.

"Oh David, I love you."

David looked into her eyes and smiled uncomfortably. Not knowing how to respond he just turned and walked back into his office. But there it was out in the open, the line he certainly wanted to avoid and definitely did not want to cross. Tina realized what she had said and shrugged her shoulders, grinned and let it go for the moment. It was a simple subliminal slip of the tongue. She knew the topic would resurface again; she just didn't know when.

CHAPTER TWENTY-FIVE

The next morning David spent a few hours at his desk as he handled the day to day activities from his regular work. He was at a point with his job in which he knew he needed the income to support his lifestyle, but he truly felt less motivated to do the work he had spent the better part of fifteen years at to advance his career. David's attention would often be distracted and his focus would shift regularly to the dream he had created in his mind and to the work he had begun to develop for his start up business. His intention was solid and the course work he would embark on over the weekend which lay ahead would expand the foundation he had begun to put down, with Jefferson's help, in an effort to create the significant change in his life that he desperately wanted.

As he worked half-heartedly on his duties, his thoughts continued to drift and he would catch himself in moments in which he visualized his future. At times without pause the same scene from his previous dreams seemed to reoccur over and over in his mind. It would simply pop into his head, even without an attempt to enter into a meditative state. He pictured himself on a lit stage in front of a large audience. As he stepped along the edge of the wood planked floor, he spoke with the confidence of a man who possessed the keen knowledge that he knew could impact the lives of those who took his words and applied the techniques he taught with such clarity. It was in these moments David felt secure about the decision he had made with regard to the direction which he intended to steer his life. For those precious few who clearly envisioned their destiny in this life and understood how to pursue it with conviction, the end result always offered an abundance of all that any one person could want or even imagine they could have. For David, it meant taking on a responsibility that he could not have imagined just a short three months ago when he settled into the recliner in his den and watched a New Year's celebration on television while in a cocaine induced, drunken haze. He would use that wretched image of himself as a motivator to stay firmly on course in his quest to make the significant change he sought in his life, as well as to help others avoid the pitfalls he had faced or to overcome the obstacles they regularly dealt with in their own lives.

After he dealt with the most pressing issues of the early day, David decided to take a short break and eat lunch before he packed up his car and readied himself for the short trip across the high desert and into Las Vegas. Tina was home and in her room doing some reading of her own. She was actually given to read the "Lessons of the Mind" a second time so the concepts would resonate clearly in her mind. She was absolutely committed to her pursuits and used the visualization and self-hypnosis techniques David had taught her each day as she advanced her own agenda to make the change in her life she had dreamed of as a young adolescent. The door to her room was open, but David knocked anyway and it broke her concentration from the book.

"Hey Tina; how are you doing?"

Tina looked up from the pages of the lessons she had been focused on and smiled at David as he breached the entry to her room.

"Hi David; I'm good. What time do you plan to hit the road?"

"I figure early afternoon; a little before two o'clock so I can get in front of the rush going up through the Cajon Pass. I'm meeting Jefferson tonight after his late show, but I'd like to check in and relax for a while before I see him."

Tina jumped up off her bed and stepped toward David as he blocked the doorway. He stepped back with a surprised look on his face and turned sideways to allow her to pass through to the hallway.

"Don't worry David I'm not going to attack you."

Tina joked as she walked by him, into the hallway and headed for the kitchen. She knew David wanted to keep his distance while the two stayed on track with their career work in progress and she loved to kid with him every chance she had the opportunity to do so. She was attracted to David, as he was to her, but she knew it was all for not at this time and felt comfortable to tease him about the attraction they both knew existed.

"Let's have some lunch before you have to leave."

David, still in the doorway started down the hall and followed Tina to the kitchen. She opened the kitchen cupboard and grabbed a bag of wheat rolls, turned to David and suggested a simple menu for lunch.

"How about we make sandwiches with the left-over roast beef?"

"Sounds good to me; what can I do to help?"

David actually felt very comfortable with Tina in the house. She took control of meal preparation and completed most of the domestic chores which suited him just fine. Tina was the ideal partner for him, but he knew she would eventually leave and he would be left to fend for himself again. But while it lasted, it was good for both of them and David knew it. Tina reached into the refrigerator, pulled out the plate with the left-over mound of roast beef, and handed it to David.

"Slice the meat big guy; thin please."

She gives him a wry smile and David returns the look. They work quickly to pull lunch together and settle down at the kitchen table to enjoy the benefits of their combined efforts. After they each devour an extra-large roast beef sandwich, side of mixed fruit salad, and chips, David suggests they sit outside at the fountain and relax for a bit before he completes his last minute chores and packs up for the road trip ahead. He switched the fountain setting to on as he stepped out into the patio and took his familiar spot in the Adirondack chair positioned next to the edge of the fountain. Tina followed him outside and took her spot in the chair opposite his and nestled into a comfortable position with a Newsweek magazine she grabbed on the way out. The two of them sat in silence for several minutes as Tina read her magazine and David just sat quietly and enjoyed the solitude of the moment with his eyes closed before he broke the silence.

"I was about to ask Jefferson if I could bring you along for the class, but I didn't want to be presumptuous, since I had not checked with you first."

Tina turned to David with a look that indicated she had been taken by surprise that he would even want her to join them in a hypnosis training course she had not prepared herself for.

"David, I think it's best you do this course on your own without me there to interfere."

"Interfere, what are you talking about?"

David looked at her with a curious arch to his brow. He sensed Tina had a suspicion he would be in the company of someone else while on his trip to Las Vegas. It was as if she had a sixth sense about the matter and she was accurate in her assumption.

"Well, you know, this is your deal with Jefferson and you may have someone else you'll want to see while you're in Las Vegas."

David now had a look on his face which indicated he had been caught in deception, but he attempted to recover and clear the air.

"It's nobody special Tina, she's just a friend who deals blackjack at the Stardust."

"It's no big deal David; this is after all only a temporary arrangement, correct? You do whatever you want to do. There is nothing going on between us."

"Yeah, that's correct... nothing."

David knew he had just opened Pandora's Box and now he would have to divulge the story if he didn't want Tina to constantly tease him when he returned. He wondered if there was a bit of jealousy as well, but quickly let it go because the situation between he and either of the two women was strictly platonic. There was nothing for her to be jealous of.

"Her name is Sakuri and I met her while on one of my business trips to Las Vegas. We have only recently become friends, nothing else. Heck, I barely know her."

Tina reassured him, but in reality she loved to see him squirm.

"David, you really don't have to explain anything to me."

David felt tense for some reason, but couldn't identify it. He decided he would close the discussion as he rose from the table, turned to leave the kitchen an answered as he walked away.

"Yeah, I know I don't have to explain."

Tina smiled and giggled low enough so he couldn't hear her.

In his office, David sorted the business items he would need to take with him on the trip. He packed his digital devices as well as his personal computer since he had scheduled two appointments to conduct business in Las Vegas after the hypnosis training and prior to his return home. He also went to his bedroom and checked his garment bag to make sure nothing was missed. As he perused the contents he recognized a strange feel of remorse had come over him.

For some unknown reason he felt uncomfortable with the discussion he and Tina had just had and he wondered why that emotion of guilt had come over him. David was in a crisis situation and he really didn't even realize the magnitude of the problem he had created for himself. The situation he had engaged in with Tina seemed fine on the surface but in the course of, as well as in the aftermath of their brief conversation, he had begun to realize the emotions and feelings he had for Tina were even deeper than he initially considered them to be. It was in that moment David decided he had to make a firm decision as to what degree his relationship with Tina would elevate to. For some unknown reason he felt compelled to explain to Tina his plan to meet with Sakuri but he couldn't understand why, until that very moment when he pondered how he truly felt about her. For the second time it occurred to David, he may have crossed the line Jefferson had warned him about. As that thought remained stuck in his head David gathered his bags and hauled everything into the garage which was attached to his townhome, and he loaded up the trunk of his car before he would head off for Las Vegas.

Before he left David walked back into the kitchen to let Tina know he was ready to leave and caught her as she cleaned up the left-over mess from lunch. He felt a warm glow come over him as he watched her perform the domestic chores without her notice of his presence. He stared for a minute in silence and then surprised her when he spoke.

"Thank you very much for cleaning up Tina. I appreciate everything you do around here more than you'll ever know."

Tina was caught a bit off guard by his sudden appearance and comment. She looked up at him with a startled look on her face.

"Hey you, you snuck up on me."

David repeated his thanks.

"I just wanted to say thanks for your help."

"Oh stop it David, this is the least I can do for the guy who helped me get my life back on track. Besides, I enjoy the chores around here."

She smiled and turned back to the dishes in the sink. As she grabbed hold of a plate and began to wash it off with the foam scrubber, David stepped toward her, leaned in and gave her a peck on her cheek. It wasn't expected and Tina actually felt somewhat uncomfortable with what had just occurred. She paused, unable to know how to react and just stopped to turn and face him. She sensed something had unexpectedly preoccupied David's thoughts, but she wasn't sure what it was.

"What was that for David? Are you OK?"

David realized he had just reacted without hesitation or thought and tried to divert the attention his action had caused.

"Oh that... it was just a little thank you peck on the cheek."

Tina furrowed her brow and turned her head slightly to the left.

"OK, mister. You drive careful and I'll see you in a few days."

They both knew something happened in that moment but neither was ready to elaborate on it now.

David had to get on the road and Tina needed time to think about what he had just done. It was just a small peck on the cheek, but it meant so much more than he had alluded to in his brief explanation and they each knew it.

"OK, see you next Tuesday night. I should be back late, around nine or ten at night."

"I'll see you then David. Be safe."

Just as David turned away to head into the garage his phone rang. He checked the screen as he proceeded to the garage and saw it was Jefferson.

"Doctor Paul, how are you?"

Jefferson was his usual steady self.

"David I am wonderful and you?"

"Well, I am on my way out the door as we speak. Should be in Las Vegas around seven this evening. Are we still on for tonight?"

"That's exactly why I called. Yes, we are on and I will see you no later than eleven fifteen in the café. Until then… drive safe my friend."

David responded but Jefferson had already begun to hang up the call and didn't hear him.

"See you then."

CHAPTER TWENTY-SIX

David arrived at the hotel earlier than expected and he attended to the important details of work prior to his close of the day. He rested for a couple hours and it was fast approaching ten at night so decided to go down early and check the casino floor to see if Sakuri would be at one of the blackjack tables. He was due to meet with Jefferson in a little over an hour, but wanted to touch base with Sakuri and firm up plans to meet with her while he would be in town. As he walked through the casino he spotted her at a table and she seemed to spot him in the exact same moment. She smiled at him and quickly turned her attention back to the game in process on the table. There were two older men seated at her table and it was apparent why they would decide to play at Sakuri's station. She usually attracted the old perverts and loners who thought they had a chance at an impromptu night with the lovely dealer. David knew better and grinned when he noticed the two men hard at work on her and the hands they played. He walked up as if he was the subject in Sade's hit song, 'Smooth Operator.'

"Hey there, how are you doing tonight?"

Sakuri giggled softly and nodded her head.

"I'm good David; are you going to play?"

The two old timers give David the once-over and turn back to Sakuri as she collects the cards from the previous deal. One of them quips impatiently.

"Just deal 'em sweetie."

The pit boss was close by and within earshot. He looked toward the table and glared at the man to let him know the comment was inappropriate and uninvited. The man put his head down and then decided to close out and move on. David sat down opposite the remaining old timer and put a hundred dollar bill down. Sakuri closed out the player with the smart comment and then turned to count out David's chips before she included him in the next deal. As she dealt the cards, David asked.

"Did I interfere in his game?"

"Don't be silly David."

Sakuri dealt the next hand and David turned a blackjack out of the gate. The old man that remained couldn't believe his eyes and gawked at David and Sakuri, thinking there may be a sting on. He took a card and busted with a twenty-three.

"I'm outta here."

Sakuri counted out David's win and laid the chips on the table. The old timer collected his chips and moved on from her table. David grinned, shook his head and laughed after the man had walked away far enough that he wouldn't hear.

"Sorry, I didn't mean to clear the table."

Sakuri smiled, shrugged without an emotional reaction and responded.

"They come and go… no big deal."

Her demeanor was cool and calculated as she continued to deal cards with only David left on her table. She spoke softly as the pit boss leaned in and attempted to bug in on her conversation.

"So how long will you be in town David?"

David looked over his cards and signaled for another with a swipe of the table back to fro.

"I'll be in my hypnosis training for the next three days and then regular business Monday and Tuesday. Are you free at all while I am here?"

Sakuri smiled and reminded him he had forgotten

to call her prior to his arrival. She looked forward to his visit though and made arrangements anyway to be free on both Monday and Tuesday.

"Yes, I'm off Monday and Tuesday. You forgot to call me, but I scheduled the days off anyway. I work the weekend though."

"I'm sorry, I just completely forgot about that call, but it worked out well. The weekend is when you make your money, isn't it?"

David was a bit naïve with regard to the gaming business in Las Vegas. This wasn't a town that thrived on weekends; there was money to be made every day. Sakuri didn't correct him though and just shook her head, smiled and agreed.

"Yes, it will be fine David. Let's plan to meet Monday when you get free."

David stared at Sakuri as she spoke and dealt the next hand. He was captivated by her beauty, but as he pulled his hand up to look at his cards, his mind shifted to the thought of Tina back at home. He suddenly felt conflicted and knew he would have to work this situation out before it became the distraction Jefferson warned him about. Those thoughts lingered as he played for another forty minutes before Sakuri was moved off the table for her break. She gave him a signal and mouthed "call me" as she walked away from the table. David responded.

"I will."

The prevailing thoughts in his head were not enough to distract him from blackjack and when Sakuri left the table he was up two hundred dollars. He decided it would be a good time to quit so he closed out and took his cash out before he would head for the café.

CHAPTER TWENTY-SEVEN

David sat on the bench seat in front of the café while he waited to greet his friend. Jefferson spotted him from a short distance away and waved as he strolled up to the entrance of the café. He extended his hand, David stood and they shook hands.

"Well, shall we get our table in the rear of the dining room?"

David smiled and nodded in agreement as he responded. Jefferson seemed to be in great spirits, but that was the norm for him. As he thought about it, David couldn't recollect a time he had ever seen or spoken with Jefferson in which he wasn't in a good mood. He was one of the most even keeled people David knew and it wasn't by accident either. David also knew that.

"Sure, let's grab our spot."

The two men were led to the rear of the cafe by the hostess and as they walked through the restaurant, David noticed Alba was on and worked the station in which they would be seated. Alba noticed them and looked at David with that smile on her face as he waved to her. She came to the table as soon as they were seated. With emphasis on her lovely accent she greeted David.

"Well hello there stranger. How are you? We all miss you so much?"

She alluded to Jefferson with a nod as she made her last comment.

"Is that right Jefferson?"

"Yes, of course Alba."

Jefferson played along but he was more interested in food and drinks at the moment.

"Please bring us a couple of ice teas while we decide on food."

Alba sensed he didn't have the time, nor desire to engage in small talk so she obliged him and scurried off to grab the drinks. She gave David a wink before she turned away from the table and he just smiled and laughed softly as he grabbed the menu to take a look at what he might want to snack on. It was late and a big meal didn't appeal to him so he decided to order an appetizer of potato skins. Jefferson decided on a dinner salad and turkey sandwich. When Alba returned with the drinks they gave her their order and she was gone within seconds. It was exactly what Jefferson preferred as he was intent to set the tone for the training course and wanted no distractions, only complete focus from his prodigy.

"So how was the drive in David?"

"Not bad at all, traffic was fairly light. I arrived around seven this evening."

"So what have you been up to since then... playing blackjack?"

David knew he was in for these types of questions from Jefferson. The training they had scheduled would be rigorous and there wasn't much time to get all the information in, so it would take his complete focus all weekend. If Jefferson sensed he wasn't there mentally, he would end it without hesitation. David needed him to know he was still just as committed to this venture as he ever was.

"Yes, I played a few hands. But I am now entirely focused for the weekend training."

"David, it's not just a weekend of training. This is a life change you have decided on and are in the process of creating. You need to view it that way, and with that, start to measure your actions. Focus on what it is that you want to accomplish and do so without distractions. That is the only way you will be able to establish positive behavior patterns and more importantly the only way you will stay on course and not break those patterns."

David already sensed a heightened level of urgency from Jefferson and felt the increase of tension throughout his body as he sat back in his chair.

"I know Jefferson. I know this will be hard work."

"Only if you make it hard; it can actually be very easy if your approach and execution are flawless. I'll continue to remind you David, because I want nothing more than for you to realize the success you're about to embark on."

"I appreciate that Jefferson."

Alba showed up at the table with their food and attempted to get David into a discussion as she set the potato skins down in front of him.

"Here you go David. How long are you in town?"

Jefferson looked at him with an unemotional stare across his face.

"I'll be very busy Alba."

"Okay, Okay… I was jus asking."

She took David's brief answer as a snub to her inquiry and turned away as the two began to eat. Alba returned with a pitcher of ice tea and gave them refills, but didn't say a thing until she was ready to leave again.

"Will there be anything else?"

"We're good."

Jefferson responded as he looked directly at Alba. She got the message, actually felt it, and immediately turned to walk away; she only returned once more with their check.

"She's a nice lady David but that's exactly what can derail you if you do not keep your focus on the important things in your life."

David knew he was right and laughed as he shoved a bite of the cheesy potato skin into his mouth. Jefferson wasn't finished with his inquiry though and continued to question David.

"So how are things at home with Tina? Has she found a new home yet?"

David knew he would eventually have to deal with this situation, but it wasn't something he wanted to enter into a lengthy discussion about at the moment.

"She has worked hard to find a job and hasn't found a new home or roommates yet, but it is on her list of priorities."

That certainly wasn't the answer Jefferson wanted to hear, but he would let it go for now. It was late and they needed to wrap up and get ready for the early start Jefferson had planned for them. He took the check and signed off on it and left cash for Alba's tip. Jefferson slid a card across the table toward David.

"The address on that card is where we will meet for the training. Let's get started at eight and go as long as we can. We only have three days and there is a lot of information to review and discuss. We will take breaks as needed, but I would like to get a good, full day in for the next three days. Does that work for you?"

David looked at the card and then up at Jefferson.

"It works."

"See you in the morning at eight David. Get a good night's rest."

Jefferson slid away from the table and rose up from his seat. As he stood, he extended his hand and David took it again. The men shook hands and Jefferson took one last dig before he turned around and walked off.

"No more blackjack tonight."

David just smiled at Jefferson and sat for a moment. As he pondered the work he had ahead of him for the weekend, his train of thought was broke when Alba returned to the table.

"Where did your friend go?"

"We have a busy schedule this weekend Alba. We start early in the morning and he wants to get a good night's sleep."

Alba wanted to get together with David before he left town and made another attempt to see what his schedule would permit.

"So do you have time for lunch or dinner while you're in town?"

"I really don't think so Alba. I'm sorry, but maybe next time."

She graced a sad smile on her beautifully tanned face and walked away. Alba knew David would be on to bigger things after his training with Jefferson and they would most likely never have the opportunity to spend any time together again. It left her to wonder if Jefferson had told David to avoid her. She still had her dream to write children's books, but for now it would stay put on the shelf.

CHAPTER TWENTY-EIGHT

David woke up to a beautiful spring morning and felt refreshed after the good night's sleep he had gotten. David had looked forward to the training he was about to embark on ever since the day Jefferson had mentioned it to him a couple months prior. After a quick shower and light continental breakfast, David headed for the address of the office building Jefferson had provided on the business card he left him at the café. The building was in the Howard Hughes Center not far from the Stardust where David stayed. The drive over took less than the ten minutes he needed to find his car in the parking structure and David arrived five minutes before eight and was greeted at the front desk by a lovely young female receptionist. She directed him to the seventh floor office that Jefferson had reserved for the training and being that everyone in town knew Jefferson she figured David may be a client in need of some sort of help.

Jefferson was in the office already seated at the table and sorting materials they would use in the class when David walked in unannounced.

"Good morning Doctor Paul."

Jefferson was focused on the work at hand and he didn't even look up initially.

David entered the room with a broad smile on his face and when Jefferson finally glanced up at him, he had a look that indicated he was ready to get started and dive right into the material. There was a lot to cover in their three days and Jefferson wanted the experience to be the best he could provide so David would get the full benefit of the training. He knew if David learned the material well and applied the techniques he would be exposed to, he would become efficient as a skilled hypnotist and could regularly execute hypnosis on either himself or others as he desired.

"Good morning David. Glad to see you are full of energy and ready to get started."

The large table in the room was oval shaped and David sat opposite Jefferson as the doctor handed him several items including two binders filled with information and notes, as well as a book on self-hypnosis that would become the focal point for the section of the course David was most interested in exploring. As Jefferson shuttled the material toward David he spoke.

"David, we will review the material in the binders but first I would like to discuss the specifics of what hypnosis is and just as important, what it is not. That will lay a foundation for the entire course and when we get to the point of actually putting into practice what I teach you, you will then know exactly what to expect from the standpoint of how it feels to be hypnotized."

David appeared to be the eager student and listened intently to what Jefferson offered.

"It sounds good to me Doctor, let's get started."

Jefferson nodded in agreement and continued.

"Up to this time we have talked about the lessons of the mind and you have a good foundation of how the mind works based on your study and our discussion of those lessons. What we will get into deeper while in this training is the actual techniques which you can incorporate in either hypnotizing yourself or others. I imagine up to now you have done some meditation to help you improve your focus on the change you seek to make in your life and in some respects that seems to have worked to this point. What I want to teach you in this weekend session is how to bring your meditation to a level in which you actually change the beliefs that reside in your subconscious mind. That's where change takes place permanently."

David stared at Jefferson as he had begun the lesson on the definition of hypnosis and the various stages a person will enter into while they are being hypnotized. One of the facts he found to be most interested in is the fact intelligent people are actually easier to hypnotize. That point is based on the fact intelligent people do not have the fears an ignorant person would have with regard to a subject that is taboo with many who are uninformed.

They continued to review and discuss the myths of hypnosis and cleared up any questions David had with regard to whether it is a practice that could affect someone's moral will or mental health. Jefferson assured him the use of hypnosis is healthy and in some cases even more practical than other means to attempt to change behaviors or bad habits. For virtually everyone in their daily routines, hypnosis is a way of life. In whatever it is that one person does, whether they drive, type at work, or even dance, they operate at a level in which the subconscious mind is directing them. So in that regard, hypnosis is not dangerous at all and is actually more prevalent than most people know about or would even realize. Jefferson was passionate about this subject which he loved so much and continued his tutorial.

"One thing I mentioned to you previously was that all hypnosis is self-hypnosis and that stands to be true. The only difference is in what we refer to as hetero-hypnosis; which is when the hypnotist guides your thoughts, whereas in self-hypnosis, you guide your own thoughts. This is done through a process we will cover in more detail later in the session. For now, let's delve further into the topic of 'the state of hyper-suggestibility' and how we get to that point in our consciousness."

David listened intently as Jefferson paused to acknowledge his questions, but David had none so he continued with his explanation as David followed along and took notes on the pad Jefferson provided for the classroom lectures.

"I believe we may have spoken briefly about the critical faculty, which is our power of evaluation and discernment."

David interjected at this point.

"Yea, I remember you spoke about that in one of our meetings at the cafe."

"Well then David, you may recall when we are in hypnosis and thus in a relaxed state of mind, the critical faculty is not operative and suggestions made to the subconscious mind are accepted literally. That is the very simple version of how we can create or replace a behavior we wish to change or eliminate."

Jefferson paused briefly to allow David to absorb the information he methodically doled out.

"The subconscious mind does not have a critical faculty and therefore it accepts the information we feed it as reality. Many well informed authorities on this subject actually believe the subconscious mind has a feedback mechanism. This mechanism, when information is fed into the subconscious mind, will in turn feed that information back into your conscious life and have a profound impact on the individual's experience or reality. This happens because the information we feed our subconscious mind actually becomes our reality. Keep in mind, early in our lives there are others who play a significant role in what kind of information is fed to the subconscious mind, provided we accept what they say to or about us."

Jefferson paused again as David had a confused look on his face and stopped him to ask a question.

"So if we do not accept what is said to us or about us, we are not affected?"

"That is correct David. We control our own stream of thought. So while parents, teachers, coaches, and clergy, all may have played a role in our development, it is important for each and every one of us to understand this concept because at some point in our lives we must take responsibility for our own actions based on what we think of ourselves. The affect each and every one of us creates in our life depends on it."

David sat and was blown away by the information that Jefferson shared throughout their initial session. He knew when they had met months ago, Jefferson had a special understanding of life and how it worked. Even more importantly, he knew what each person could do to make it work for them. He fully understood and applied the techniques he taught David. It was no secret to Jefferson what it took to create whatever one wished for or wanted to achieve in life. The steps were actually very simple, but few in life have the conviction to execute because it isn't easy at the start. Jefferson knew though, once you set a course and push yourself through the toughest period, it becomes easier and easier to fulfill the destiny one sets for himself. Good things come to those who set good habits. It really is that simple and he was a living example of what he believed. It was not long ago Jefferson was homeless and found himself in a situation that would have driven most to either, give up and live on the street or worse yet take their own life. But it was in this time of perceived desperation that he was inspired to live in accordance with what he had come to believe. As a result of his conviction and diligence, he was now the star of the biggest show on Las Vegas Boulevard in a town known as the entertainment capital of the world. And for David, he was fortunate to have had the opportunity to meet this man that would help him change his life forever, in the same way he changed his own.

The day passed quickly and the information Jefferson shared with David would be the cornerstone of the business he envisioned to create. As he sat and absorbed each detail, David thought of how he would not only apply the techniques and concepts to his own life, but even further how he would package and present it for an abundant audience to learn from. David was certainly inspired and had a feel of warmth and comfort inside. He was convinced he had made a sound decision to go forward with a business that would impact other's lives and he almost couldn't wait to get started. But he knew there would be much more to learn over the next two days and the commitment to work through the tough times would be exactly what he would have to bear if he was going to push ahead and create the life he envisioned for himself... his future.

The clock showed it was a quarter to five and Jefferson would have to wind down the first day of training to prepare for his Friday night shows. He and David had worked hard and put in the time required to complete the initial lessons which would lay the foundation for the next two days. The training course would now shift from theory to practice and David would soon get a clear understanding of teachings Jefferson had laid out, by actually practicing what he was being trained to do.

"Well David, this has been a productive day and we are at a perfect spot to end our session. Not to mention, I have to prepare for my shows tonight."

David was exhausted, but he felt a heightened energy within like he had never felt before. The valuable information conveyed throughout the day provided him with a confidence which he seemed to outwardly demonstrate. At this point David had no idea how far that confidence would surge, but he was excited to get on with the balance of the training Jefferson had in store for him.

"Jefferson, thanks for the time and valuable information today. I look forward to tomorrow when we begin to put these concepts into practice."

"Ah yes, tomorrow will be a good day. I had scheduled to have a couple of people come in at different times to help us in our practical applications of the material. It will be good practice and interesting to see how well you apply the technical information."

David had a surprised look on his face.

"Am I getting my first chance to hypnotize someone?"

"Yes David, you are. For that reason, I would like you to study your scripts tonight. It will be important to deliver them with a steady flow to your patter; so the better you know them, the better the results will be when you work with the subjects I have asked to come in."

Jefferson smiled and gave David a pat on the shoulder. He collected his books and binders, turned toward the door and before he exited the room, left David with one last thought.

"Commit yourself, study hard, and stay off the blackjack table."

David laughed but he knew Jefferson was dead serious. If he didn't apply himself to the homework Jefferson assigned for the night, it would show in his work the next day.

"Gotcha Doctor, I'll stay in and study."

With that, the two men exited the room. The ride down the elevator was quiet. In the lobby they shook hands and each went in an opposite direction.

CHAPTER TWENTY-NINE

Upon his return to the hotel, David had decided he would order room service and stay in for the night to study the material as Jefferson had advised. Before he headed to his room though, he would make his way to the blackjack tables to see if Sakuri had started work yet. As he approached the area where blackjack tables were set-up, David noticed she was at a table but had no players at the time. It would be perfect for him to get a few minutes with her before he headed to his room for the night. She spotted him as he strode across the casino floor toward her and his infectious smile broke across her face too. She thought she would acquire her first player for the shift, but wasn't aware David would have to pass on blackjack for the night. He would have loved to sit and play awhile, but he knew he had more important work to do and would have to forgo the opportunity to spend time with Sakuri, even though it was work for her.

"Hey David, I just started my shift. How did your class go today?"

David was glad to see her, but torn over whether he should stay for a few hands. He thought of the commitment he made to Jefferson, but didn't realize at the time, it would be this difficult to keep it. He really wanted to stay, but knew it wasn't the correct thing for him to do. If he got started, the play could go on all night and it was best for him to avoid the temptation all together. David had resigned to the fact there would be no blackjack for the night.

"The class was great; we covered quite a bit of information today. It was all theory and concepts today, but tomorrow starts the real hypnosis training."

"Wow, it sounds interesting David."

She jokingly asked.

"Are you going to hypnotize me when you're finished with the class?"

David just shrugged his shoulders and grinned as he stared into her eyes. He wasn't sure if she was serious or just poked fun at him. Sakuri gestured to the table with a wave of her hand, as if she was one of the models on a game show, and asked in her sultry tone.

"Would you like to play David?"

The look she gave him as she asked was so inviting and for a moment David realized why she made such good tips at the table. He would love to have played but David had to show restraint. It pained him to have to tell her no, but after a slight pause he would. Without her knowledge of it, Sakuri had actually helped David in that moment. The temptation to play with her as the dealer would be a test of his commitment. He didn't even realize it at the time however his decision to not play would serve as a foundation of the focus he had developed. It would be a display of the seriousness he had acquired toward the change of life he had set out to accomplish.

"I would like to Sakuri, but I have too much work to do tonight. Tomorrow will be a test of not just what I have learned, but how well I apply it."

Sakuri was slightly disappointed and displayed it with a pout of her full pursed lips, though she knew David was on a mission with much to accomplish and she definitely did not want to be the one distraction that would derail him. The look on her face quickly changed back to the brilliant smile she had when she greeted him.

"I understand David."

It wasn't just a hollow statement either. She really

did understand, being that she would also have to forgo personal desires to accomplish what she was in pursuit of as well. She was very aware of the study time needed to get through difficult courses. Sakuri had to deal with the same temptations at times and had to make the tough choices to realize her career dream of becoming an emergency room nurse. David acknowledged it as well.

"I knew if anyone could understand it would definitely be you."

They smiled at each other and David made her a promise before he left.

"I promise you I'm all yours on Monday after my morning appointments."

She looked forward to their time together. David was certainly an interesting fellow that she wanted to learn more about. Sakuri would be patient and wait until Monday when David would give her his undivided attention, or at least that is what she anticipated.

"I'll see you then David. Study hard and do well in the course. I'm sure Jefferson will be proud to call you one of his prized students."

David knew the work ahead would be difficult and he hoped to be one of the best students Jefferson ever mentored. His decision to work rather than play blackjack was a move in that direction, so he decided to get up to his room and begin the work that awaited him there.

"I'll be in touch before Monday to plan our time together. Until then, have a great night."

Sakuri pursed her lips in a thin smile without display of her pearl white teeth and waved with an open hand as if she was in a holiday parade. David slowly turned and walked away.

CHAPTER THIRTY

The class began promptly at eight the next morning with Jefferson providing a brief summary of the previous day's material and a recap of what would be in store for the remainder of the course. He had scheduled to have two participants arrive in intervals over the next two days so that David could get exposed to using at least one of the hypnotic scripts he provided, in a practical setting. The two subjects were clients Jefferson had spoken with in regard to scheduling previous sessions before he had ended his clinical practice. They each had a smoking habit they sought to overcome and neither had found an effective solution to their problem as of yet.

When Jefferson reached out to them, he was pleased to find they each would be available for the weekend course. Jefferson had approached them with a free offer if they would agree to work with him in a classroom setting. Most clients knew of Jefferson Paul and his level of expertise, so to get them to work with him and his students in this type of setting for free would be very easy. Jim Haustell and Candy Switzer had each lived in the city of Las Vegas for several years. They would be the two clients for the Saturday and Sunday afternoon sessions. Jim was scheduled for one o'clock on each day and Candy would come in later, at three o'clock.

Jim was a construction foreman and made very good money during the boom building years in town. Business was still pretty steady and he currently had a couple crews he oversaw on different construction projects. Jim had smoked for twenty-four years and his wife constantly nagged him to quit, if for nothing else but his health. She hated the habit and disliked the smell it left on his clothes, their furniture, and in their automobiles. It was just a disgusting habit to her. Jim wanted to quit but every method he tried seemed to be a temporary solution and he would ultimately go back to his old habit, so he reached out to Jefferson when he heard the efficacy of stop smoking with hypnosis was far above any other treatment. He, as well as his wife, would be very happy he pursued this method to quit and he would get the treatment for free too.

Candy was a stripper at the Palomino, one of the city's oldest and most prestigious gentlemen's clubs. She was an attractive twenty-eight year old blonde who took advantage of her taught body and good looks to make her money seducing men with her smooth moves and sensual teasing on stage. Candy, like many of the women in the industry, was a habitual smoker when she was not on stage. She also had a strong desire to eliminate the dirty impulse she had developed since that first smoke in her early teens and sought Jefferson's help, only to be disappointed to learn he had closed down his clinical practice. When he contacted her to inquire, she was very pleased and happy to accept the free offer in lieu of her participation in the class.

Jefferson had scheduled to have the two participants come in at different times for the afternoon sessions, so he and David would have the mornings to practice with each other. David was anxious at first, but looked forward to the time he would apply the scripts and techniques that he had learned in real-life situations. Until then, Jefferson and he would take turns at hypnotizing each other. In reality, David was unsure of what he was doing and Jefferson had actually wanted him to practice the scripts live, so when he worked with actual clients, his delivery would be smooth and uninterrupted. Delivery would be very important when he worked with actual clients in the afternoon. They would have to be convinced he knew how to work with hypnosis and would be able to help them with their objectives. Jefferson schooled David.

"Okay David, let's take this one step at a time. First, we will work with two smokers who seek to end their bad smoking habit. I have had conversations with the two clients and they are both very committed to end their habits. You will recall from our study, commitment or conviction is imperative to the process of creating a change in behavior."

David watched Jefferson intently as he lectured.

"Remember the facts we have discussed. All hypnosis is self-hypnosis. They will become hypnotized if they are convinced you will hypnotize them, so you must be smooth and confident in your delivery."

David, suddenly now more than ever, felt anxious and unsure of himself.

"How will I know if it has worked?"

"You will see a slight flutter in their eye lids, they will become very relaxed and physically limp, and finally their eyes will almost always close."

Jefferson paused then continued to explain.

"Remember David, you are just a guide for them to reach a state of trance. Once they are in that state it becomes easy to plant suggestions in their subconscious mind because their critical faculty has been diminished to a point in which they no longer consciously evaluate your suggestions. Their process of evaluation is virtually eliminated with the loss of their critical faculty and they will accept whatever you say as true; remember what I told you, it becomes their reality."

For the first time in the course David had a look

on his face that depicted his lack of self-confidence. He knew he was at a crossroads and his performance would lead him into the next phase of his development in the field of hypnosis.

"I'm a little nervous Jefferson. Are you sure this is going to work?"

Jefferson had been through this before with other students and David was no different. He had begun to question himself and Jefferson had to convey the importance of keeping his composure, confidence, and professionalism. If the client perceived these qualities in David, the practice of hypnosis would come easily. This was a practice that involved the client's ability to be hypnotized through their own belief in the hypnotist's skills, and an expert such as Jefferson knew that to be the truth. He knew he would not have had success in his own practice, or in his shows, if his clients and participants didn't believe in his ability to perform for them. He knew it would be paramount for David to develop the same demeanor that required his client's believe in his skill as well. Otherwise, David would be in for a tough time with his new ambition.

"Take a deep breath and relax David. We are going to practice the stop smoking script and you will be fine when you deliver it to your clients this afternoon."

"Okay, if you say so."

Jefferson grinned and let out a slight chuckle as the two went to work for the next three and a half hours until they finally decided to stop and have lunch. Over lunch Jefferson assured David he was ready for his first session and encouraged him to believe in himself as well. As much as David felt some insecurities Jefferson knew if he could get David to outwardly expose the confidence he had portrayed the previous day before they had left, he would be fine when the actual sessions got underway, so he went to work on David over lunch.

He knew from his own experience that David's self-confidence would naturally carry over to the client's belief in his ability to hypnotize them. That's all he needed to have a successful session and Jefferson worked to re-establish the confidence he saw in David the previous day.

"You will be fine David. This is going to be a great start to your new ambition in life. Keep that positive thought in mind and you will perform very well. Remember to always maintain your confidence before, and especially during the process of hypnotizing your subject. I guarantee you, when the client senses your self-assurance they will oblige you with their own belief in your ability and that leads them into the trance you seek to facilitate."

David seemed to gain more of his self-confidence from Jefferson's encouragement and felt much better going into the afternoon sessions than he did earlier that morning. The conversation over lunch had helped to put him at ease and when they returned to the room for a final review before the actual sessions would begin, David felt very good about his newfound confidence. He was suddenly excited to get started and wanted to display not only himself, but to his mentor that he had everything it would take to be a success in the field he had chosen to pursue his big dream of assisting others with their lives.

CHAPTER THIRTY-ONE

Jefferson had previously arranged to have a lounge recliner sent up to their classroom for the hypnosis sessions he had scheduled over the course of the two days that remained. When they returned from lunch, it had already been delivered to the room and was positioned in the back corner away from the main table. At a couple minutes before one o'clock a burly, middle-aged man entered the room and introduced himself.

"Hello there guys, I'm Jim Haustell."

He immediately recognized Jefferson, approached him and extended his hand to shake. Jefferson greeted Jim, took his hand and then turned to introduce David.

"Jim, it's a pleasure to meet you. This is David Christian. He is a student of mine and he will be a participant in your sessions over the next two days."

Jim nodded and shook David's hand.

"Hi David, it's nice to meet you."

David grabbed Jim's hand in a firm grip and as they shook hands he spoke confidently.

"It's good to meet you Jim. I look forward to our work together."

Jefferson jumped in to explain how he had planned to proceed with Jim's sessions and laid out the objectives for the next two days. He explained that he would actually be sidelined as an observer and would allow David to take the lead role in both sessions. He assured Jim of David's skill, which helped to build Jim's confidence in David, and also alluded to the fact he was not a novice but someone who had trained for quite some time with the master. He added, additional refresher courses where not uncommon and David was in town to further enhance his skill in both clinical and stage work. Jefferson knew exactly what he was doing and the information he conveyed not only left Jim with the confidence he would have a good session with David, it also continued to build up David's confidence in himself as well. Jefferson was truly a master at communication and he knew the subtleties of how to make his students successful in their own right, while he let the client know the objective remained the same either with or without his direct participation.

"Jim, you will get the benefit of the treatment just as if I was the therapist. David is very adept and excellent with these types of treatments. I suspect you will be a non-smoker when he is through with you."

Jim nodded in agreement with Jefferson and then turned toward David who sat next to the lounge chair Jim would soon be comfortably seated in.

"Well David, shall we get to work?"

"Absolutely Jim, please have a seat, recline a bit and get comfortable. We will start with a few of my own comments in regards to the objectives I have for the sessions we will conduct and then a few questions I have for you with regard to what your expectations are in terms of the results you seek to accomplish."

David wanted to set the stage as Jefferson had instructed him to do. It was absolutely critical, in a clinical setting, to establish the client's objectives and thus measure the depth of commitment they had to resolve the issue they would address in their therapy. The client's level of commitment would be the best indicator of whether or not this method of therapy would work. Before they even began with the hypnosis, David would ask several questions to determine the length of time Jim had smoked, how often he smoked, and in what conditions he felt compelled to smoke. He also wanted to uncover how Jim felt when he smoked. It would be important to uncover all those very important tidbits of information so that when they began the process to introduce new behaviors, David would be able to do it in a way in which he would introduce positive substitute behavior patterns for the old behaviors that led Jim to habitually smoke.

As the session got underway, David felt a surge of confidence he recognized he had missed earlier in the day. The brief explanation Jefferson had provided earlier did more for his sense of assuredness than he had realized up to that moment. David got started in a manner which would indicate to the client he had all the skill and experience his mentor possessed, which would allow him to deliver similar results. Jefferson actually observed with a slight surprise at how adept David was in this new skill he worked so hard to acquire in such a brief period of time. It was quickly evident, in all the time they had spent in review and discussion of the topic of hypnosis at the café, as well as in the first session of the course training, David had seemed to learn it well. His confidence appeared to grow as the session continued and it would be a test for him when they actually reached the point in which he would practice hypnosis.

"Jim, I would like to begin our session and take you into a state of hypnosis. Are you comfortable and ready for the session to start?"

Jim stretched back in the lounge chair and conveyed his confidence as he relaxed and gave David an indication with a slight nod that he was prepared to begin. David started slowly.

"Jim, I want you to lay back and begin to let your

whole body relax. Let's start with your toes and work our way up to the top of your head. Start with your toes and let yourself relax in a manner you have never experienced before. Let that feeling move up into your legs and now your torso. Let your entire body drift into a limp, relaxed state, that's right…"

With those words David Christian had begun his venture into a world that would forever change his life. He had started his first session of hypnosis and it would be the start of his quest to reach others with an objective he had only dreamed of up to this point. At the end of the session, Jefferson consulted with Jim and led him out the door into the hallway. They spoke briefly in regards to the session just completed and the expectations for the session the next day. Jim was pleased with the way it went and he felt David had done a fine job.

Jefferson returned to the room and provided David with a brief recap of how he perceived David's first hypnosis session had gone.

"Good job David. You had a steady flow to your patter; the rhythm you established was smooth and you did a nice job to set a tranquil mood for your client. Overall, I believe you did a very nice job for your first time as a practitioner."

David was very pleased to get the positive feedback from Jefferson and it increased his confidence to an even higher level than he had prior to the start of the session. He now felt sure of himself and exuded confidence in his facial expressions and physical demeanor. He was no longer anxious and looked forward to the next session with Candy, which would present a different sort of challenge that he was not aware of until she arrived.

Candy was a stunning blonde and unlike many of

the women in her occupation, she was a natural beauty. In her years of work as an exotic dancer, she had never undergone any cosmetic surgery and possessed a very unique look that attracted many customers, both male and female, to her nightly performances. Her one downside was the bad habit she had wanted dearly to rid herself of, and that was her smoking habit. Candy started as a late teen and found it difficult to quit, especially in the environment she had worked in. In her discussion with Jefferson, she had convinced him of her commitment to quit and he had remembered her when he sought clients for the course he scheduled with David. There was also an alternative reason for his selection of Candy and David became aware of it the moment she entered the room in which the training was held.

When she walked in, David was caught off guard by the natural beauty of the stunning blonde as she introduced herself to Jefferson.

"Hi Jefferson, I'm Candy; we spoke on the phone a couple of times."

And Candy she is Jefferson thought as he looked up from the table.

"Yes we did Candy, how are you today?"

Jefferson knew from their conversations what Candy did for her livelihood and assumed she was going to be attractive, but he had no idea she was the expected beauty she turned out to be. His intention was to bring someone in that would present David with an unusual challenge to his attention and focus. Now that she was present, Jefferson knew he made the correct choice and she would be the ideal candidate. She was the type of woman Jefferson would barter with when he helped so many of them stop smoking. He noticed the manner in which David sized her up when she walked into the room.

There was no doubt the physical attraction was present and the session would provide Jefferson with what he wanted to see. If David could set aside his lustful infatuation and perform his duties as a competent professional, he would convince Jefferson of his increased focus and attention to what would be most important in his new pursuit. Jefferson took hold of Candy's extended hand and turned to David for their introduction.

"Candy, I want you to meet David Christian. He has worked with me for quite some time and he will conduct the initial session today if that is okay with you."

Candy was aware of the situation and felt fine with the move Jefferson had proposed. She had only one concern and that would be to stop smoking. If she could accomplish that objective with David as the hypnotist, it would be just fine with her.

"Hello David. It's a pleasure to meet you."

David felt a slight swell in his trousers and quickly set aside the nasty thoughts which pervaded his mind, regained his composure and took her hand.

"The pleasure is mine Candy. I'm certain we can help you with your objective today."

Jefferson stepped into the conversation and described the details as he had been informed by Candy in their earlier discussions. As he spoke directly with David and provided periodic glances to Candy, he watched closely for any reactions from David which might indicate he was not ready for the unique session he would soon begin. Jefferson had a tremendous amount of experience in his work with this type of client and he wanted to be sure David could handle it in a manner that was above board and maintained a high degree of professionalism. Candy was the kind of client that presented the type of distraction which could derail David, and Jefferson would certainly want to make sure his protégé could handle the challenge.

"So Candy, David will conduct the session from start to finish. You and I will have a brief conversation afterward to make sure you're happy with the results of the session and want to continue tomorrow with your next appointment. How does that sound?"

"That works for me Jefferson."

Candy turned to David and smiled. David smiled back and stated.

"Well then, shall we get started?"

Candy acknowledged his request with a nod and David motioned toward the recliner.

"Please have a seat Candy, lean back a bit and allow yourself to get comfortable."

David described the steps he would follow in their initial session. He began in the same manner as his previous session with Jim. The conversation and questions flowed smoothly and David had reached the point where he would begin to hypnotize Candy. She laid back in the recliner and closed her eyes gently. Ironically David no longer viewed her as a sexual object and he proceeded as the professional Jefferson hoped he would be. He spoke with a soft, relaxed tone but it was loud enough for her to hear him clearly.

"Candy, I want you to relax and let your body release any tension you may have felt prior to our session today. Allow yourself to become limp from head to toe. Start at the tips of your toes and feel the tension leave your body, that's right. Now in a moment you will begin to feel relaxed, even more relaxed than you have felt in a long, long time…"

Moments later Candy was in a deep trance and David proceeded to follow the script to a tee. He took her through the detail in which he would suggest new behaviors to replace her old habitual reactions based on her answers to his earlier questions. The session stretched for thirty minutes, but when she awakened she felt as if she had had a long restful sleep, much longer than the short time the session had actually lasted. Jefferson greeted Candy at the conclusion of the session and led her to the door and into the hallway where he conducted the brief recap he had described earlier. She had reacted with positive feedback and again Jefferson was pleased with the work David had done and took pride in the fact his protégé had done as well as he had.

When he returned to the room, Jefferson spoke with David for a few minutes in regards to the two different hypnosis sessions and the unique challenges each one had presented. He highlighted the positives and gave David a couple of points to consider for his future work with these clients, as well as other similar types he might come in contact with. In general, Jefferson was pleased with David's initial attempts at hypnosis and he was sure David could continue to excel in this line of work if he decided to commit to it long term. David had other ideas though of how he would use the skills he acquired and would now work on those plans he had begun to develop. It wouldn't be long before he would launch the business he had dreamed of for the last few months. After a brief discussion of the day's work, the two men left and would meet the next morning at eight for David's final course and two more hypnosis sessions.

Before they left, Jefferson asked him to continue with his commitment to study the material and work on the scripts even more. He wanted to make sure David maintained his focus and didn't waiver in light of his recent success with Jim and Candy. If he did waiver, the success would surely be short lived and that was certainly what Jefferson wanted to avoid with his star pupil. It would be critical for David to build on the initial success with two more exceedingly good sessions the next day. He knew the importance of spending more time with the scripts and additional study of the material, and how it would be the way to the success they both sought. With those thoughts in mind, he committed to spend the night doing as much.

CHAPTER THIRTY-TWO

David spent the night in his room and studied the scripts as Jefferson had asked him to do. Although he wanted desperately to see Sakuri, he was pleased with his own determination to work on the material and his choice to stay in his room to study all night. When the next morning arrived, he was clear headed and excited to get started again with Jefferson. David showed up early at the classroom and again Jefferson was already there ahead of him, seated at the large table centered in the room. He looked up at David and greeted him in his usual good natured way with a poking gesture.

"David, it's good to see you this morning. I thought you would have given this a second thought and headed to the Palomino last night for a closer look at our lovely volunteer, Candy."

The two men laughed at Jefferson's jab, and for a brief moment David reflected on what it must be like to see Candy's beautiful body in the nude. He quickly let the vision go and turned his attention back to Jefferson with a seriousness that had taken him over. In a strange way, David had found it easier now more than ever, to erase thoughts he chose to eliminate and move on to another in a matter of seconds. It was all part of the process to master one's own mind.

"Nothing will stop me Jefferson. I am committed now more than I ever was."

"Well I am very happy to hear that David. You did a fine job yesterday and if you continue to practice with diligence, I am sure you could become a very competent hypnotist if that is your desire."

David beamed with confidence at the encouragement Jefferson provided, but had no idea of the impact it had on him subconsciously. Jefferson took every opportunity he could to place suggestions and positive anchors with those he truly cared for, and David would be the recipient of many of these messages without knowledge of it. The session Jefferson had planned for the day would be very similar to the previous except for one critical element; he would focus his attention on the practice of hypnosis for one's own self use. This was the area David would be most interested in since it would be the foundation for the business he had planned to pursue. Jefferson began the discussion with a basic outline of the steps toward a positive experience.

"David, let's get into the area of this subject that I believe most appeals to you and will be most important to what you intend to do with your future plans."

David acknowledged Jefferson with a slight nod of his head and the doctor continued.

"Typically, the quickest and easiest way to achieve success with self-hypnosis is to engage a qualified hypnotist to work with you for several sessions until you become efficient with the practice. Since we do not have that luxury, I am going to delve deep into the process for the first half of our session today and it will be up to you to develop a method that works best for you. You will understand more as we get deeper into the subject matter."

"Sounds good Jefferson."

David stared intently as Jefferson began with some basic lessons on attitude, time management, and practice schedules. Then he started to discuss the actual tools with which an individual works to achieve the state of hypnosis on their own. These include suggestion and imagination and the methods one uses to become hypnotized and thus suggestible. He provided David with examples of suggestion tests in an effort to determine the best method for him.

"When we get into the area of self-hypnosis, we travel the road of suggestion, but the vehicle in which we travel is imagination. Remember David, everyone is suggestible and could therefore be hypnotized. The key is to find the manner in which you respond best to suggestion and that is where your imagination comes into play. We have several tests which we could utilize to determine the most effective for you; to get you into a state that increases your ability to respond to suggestion."

Jefferson took David through the various suggestibility tests to get him exposed to the methods he could use in his own practice of self-hypnosis. He also wanted David to understand each test so he could convey the information in a way that would be useful to those he would market his information to. In most cases they would use the affirmation recordings he planned to create, but in the event he had a client that wanted to explore other avenues of self-hypnosis, it would be very helpful for David to know the information and processes so that he could effectively coach them toward positive results. The second step in that process would be to create the hypnotic formulas that could be used to create whatever change in behavior or action an individual sought. Jefferson continued to counsel with regard to the next step, which would be hypnotic formulas.

"There are essentially two ways to use the hypnotic formulas, and those are either in recordings or in just thinking them. If you choose the recorded version it literally makes you the hypnotist in your own session."

David had a quizzical look on his face and held his

hand up to stop Jefferson.

"So I can use my own recordings as a means to hypnotize myself?"

"Yes, that is correct David. It's basically what you plan to do for others who will buy your recorded affirmations. They will listen to the recordings which will induce them into a hypnotized state and then you will have a suggestion on the recording which will serve their desired outcome, whatever that might be. One thing I must point out before we go on. In the live sessions we did yesterday and you will do again later this afternoon with Jim and Candy, notice the suggestion is to 'breathe in clean air' and not to 'stop smoking.' You never want to use a negative statement as your suggestion because the subconscious mind cannot distinguish the negative word 'stop' and therefore will recognize the suggestion as continue smoking."

David nodded his head, but still had a look on his face that indicated he would need more time to absorb this information to fully grasp the concept and understand the process. Jefferson continued with his initial lecture about the two ways to use hypnotic formulas for self-hypnosis.

"Now then David, when you make a recording to listen to yourself, you have become your own hypnotist and that is a form of self-hypnosis."

The look on David's face changed as if a light went on in his head.

"Keep in mind however, you would need a compact disc player with you everywhere you went in order to execute this manner of hypnosis. On the other hand, I would highly suggest you learn the hypnotic formula for whatever you want to achieve and know it so you don't have to listen to a recording, but can achieve the same result by thinking it. Don't ever forget David, this is a process that is affected by thought, so you don't have to listen to anything; just think it repeatedly as you enter into the state of hypnosis and the subconscious mind accepts it as reality. That my friend is true self-hypnosis."

Jefferson stared ahead at David for a moment to see if his pupil had any questions or comments and then he continued with more.

"It is exactly why I encouraged you to learn the scripts, so you would be able to deliver them with ease and in a manner that helped induce the two clients you worked with yesterday. The process of self-hypnosis is essentially the same. Know the script for whatever it is you want to accomplish, and just think it; you don't have to hear it in your voice or anybody else's voice; it's in the voice nestled in your mind."

Suddenly David had a smile that bannered across his face. For the past few weeks, since he and Jefferson had met, David had used meditation as a means to change his behavior. He really lacked the understanding of the tool, but used visualization and saw pictures in his mind of the results he sought to achieve. In some ways it was effective, but he realized over the long term, he would need an effective method to impact true, lasting change in his behavior. In the moment Jefferson spoke, he realized he now had something that would be even more powerful than the meditation he had begun to practice. He immediately understood the power he could harness within himself if he could create scripts for essentially anything he desired. If he learned them thoroughly and practiced the process Jefferson had just described, he could finally create a world wherein he could be in total control of his behaviors and ultimately his life. In the same moment, Jefferson realized it too.

"Something just happened to you David. I see it in

your expression."

"I get it Jefferson. I believe I just had a moment of realization and the pieces have all come together in a way that I now understand."

Jefferson sat back in his high-backed chair and took the moment in. He then spoke with firm direction as he stared into David's eyes with purpose.

"You must practice this process each and every day; and preferably at the same time every day. Set a schedule for when you will practice this technique and stick to the schedule. Don't overwhelm yourself with too many suggestions all at once. Work on one thing at a time. Don't move on until you have achieved the result you sought and experience the behavioral shift and marked change as a result of it. David, you must understand how critical it is that you focus on one singular purpose at a time and only one; otherwise you will become frustrated at the lack of accomplishment due to too many suggestions with very little focus and repetition on any of them. It's those two factors, focus and repetition; they will be key factors to every challenge you set yourself in the pursuit of. If you develop the skill to focus sharply on one thing at a time and stay consistent with the behavior, meaning do the self-hypnosis every day and at the same time if possible, I guarantee you will blow yourself away with what is possible in your life."

David had never seen Jefferson animate in the manner he had just displayed. It was as if he had suddenly become overwhelmed or possessed with an outside force that drove him. He obviously believed in the utilization of self-hypnosis and for the first time since they had met, David realized the passion he had for the subject and the desire he had for David to realize success in his own endeavors. Jefferson continued to explain the principles of effective suggestion all the while emphasizing the two keys he had just passionately conveyed.

"Let's take the topic of effective suggestion and break it into pieces, or principles, that will help you develop effective suggestions for yourself and for those who will use your material for their own benefit. These principles are in the material I have provided you with and you should study them and be aware of them when you work with others, develop scripts for your recordings, or create your own suggestions for use in self-hypnosis."

David, the ever intuitive student, stopped Jefferson to ask a question.

"Why would any suggestion be ineffective? I mean, if you are in hypnosis, doesn't the subconscious mind accept whatever your feeding it as reality?"

"Remember what I said earlier David; if a suggestion is not worded correctly then all you have done is taken yourself, or a client, into a state of physical and mental relaxation, but no behavioral change will occur because the structure of the suggestion is not worded properly and conveyed in the correct manner. It's important to understand this and apply it, especially when performing self-hypnosis, because you know what emotions motivate you."

David slipped back into his quizzical look and rubbed his forehead as Jefferson proceeded further with his explanation.

"You see David, when you work with a client the first step you take is you question them in an attempt to uncover their emotional motivators, moral convictions, and other details that will enable you to word your suggestion in a way that will be most effective in each session that you conduct with them. You did that with Jim and Candy and didn't even realize it when you did it."

"Yeah, I guess I did now that you mention it."

"Yes, you did. As an observer, I saw its effectiveness and you will notice it today."

Jefferson continued with his explanation of the principles of effective suggestion.

"Since you're already aware of what motivates you in terms of emotions, as well as the extent of your moral compass, it is easy to create suggestions that will be effective in any self- hypnotic session in which you desire to create a change in your behavior."

David nodded and responded before Jefferson could continue.

"Okay, I see how that makes perfect sense."

"One very important principle David is the principle of reversed effect. This is the principle I mentioned earlier. It goes like this, when you create your suggestion, be sure to make it a positive statement. Again, notice the script you rehearsed and used with Jim and Candy. It wasn't a negative suggestion. You never once said "stop smoking," but rather made positive suggestions such as "take deep breaths of fresh air." You want to be sure to always use positive suggestions because a negative suggestion only creates a negative vacuum in the mind."

Jefferson paused, took a shallow breath and continued as David scrunched his brow.

"It is very important to understand this principle, because if you do not exercise the principle in the correct manner, you leave the subconscious mind without a positive suggestion or direction to take. An example is if you state "you will stop smoking;" you haven't replaced the negative behavioral statement with a positive substitute behavioral statement. In effect, you have only reinforced the negative behavior by making it the predominant factor in your thought or statement, whichever the case may be, and it will become the focus for the behavior to continue."

Jefferson stopped and sat back again. He took several moments and watched David's reaction to the information he had delivered before he asked.

"Does this make sense David? I want to make sure you understand these concepts thoroughly before you attempt to proceed with the use of them on yourself or anyone else for that matter. If you have questions, let's address them now."

David grinned.

"But Jefferson, you let me conduct the sessions with Jim and Candy."

"Yes I did; but do understand, those sessions, as well as the ones you will conduct today are done under my supervision and I wrote the scripts you used. I'm present and can bail you out if need be. However, if you don't understand what you're doing when I am not around, you will only become frustrated and will not see positive results to your desired outcomes."

David still had the grin on his face.

"I get it Jefferson. I really do understand."

"Okay, fine; let's break for a quick lunch and come back for our afternoon session with Jim and Candy. I would also like to meet tonight at the café, just to recap a few important items before you return home and begin pursuit of your business plan. You need to be absolutely sure of what it is you're doing in the business of hypnotic transformation or self-realization before you start, so I'll help you with that too."

David wasn't too sure what he meant by that last statement, but he always looked forward to the opportunity to learn more from the master when he had the chance.

"That sounds great Jefferson. I want as much as you can fill my head with. Every bit of information you believe could be helpful will be graciously accepted."

Jefferson retorted.

"Come on, let's grab some lunch."

He stood and pawed at David's shoulder and turned him toward the door. The two men headed for the building cafeteria and a much needed lunch break.

CHAPTER THIRTY-THREE

Moments after David and Jefferson returned from lunch, Jim Haustell arrived and walked into the room as the two of them were in a discussion about the details of the afternoon sessions.

"Good afternoon guys I hope I haven't intruded in your conversation."

Jefferson looked up to notice Jim with his hand extended out. The men shook hands and Jim turned to David and shook his hand as David spoke.

"No, no you haven't at all. Good to see you Jim. How has your day gone so far?"

"Good David, not one instance where I had a desire to smoke."

Jefferson quickly chimed in since this was new ground for David.

"Jim, while that's great news we want to continue with the hypnosis sessions and get the behavior change planted firmly into your subconscious mind. The whole process usually takes anywhere from twenty-one to thirty days. For some it could take longer, but I have a good feeling for the way you have responded to the first session. We will continue for a few more sessions after David has returned home and I will take over for him."

Jim was only slightly concerned that he might react adversely to a change in hypnotist.

"Is there any possibility I can regress with a change in hypnotists?"

Jefferson quickly snuffed that notion and put him at ease.

"I am confident we will have no issues whatsoever

Jim; you are in good hands. Shall we get started with your second session?

"Jefferson turned to David.

"David, are you ready?"

David approached the reclining chair and sat down on the stool next to it.

"Yes I am; Jim, please take a seat on the recliner and get settled and comfortable."

Jim sat down and reclined back on the lounge chair as David began the session.

"Jim, today we will bypass the questions and get right into the hypnosis, so lean back and allow yourself to begin to feel loose and relaxed, that's it… "

David went on to conduct another successful session in which Jim showed definite signs of being hypnotized and responded in kind to the repeated suggestion David had planted.

In his second appointment with Candy, David seemed to have prevailed in the same manner and she too had a successful session in which he skillfully guided her through the same repeated suggestion that she seemed to fully embrace. Jefferson observed on the sideline again and was very pleased at the two sessions he oversaw. He felt as if David had been one of his fastest learners and could possibly experience a great deal of success in the field of hypnosis if he continued down the path of continued practice and persistence the two had discussed earlier that morning.

The afternoon sessions ended with success and prior to their departure, Jefferson had informed both Jim and Candy that he would take the lead role for the next four sessions, since David would return home to Oceanside. They would be fine with the transition and ultimately, both would end their cigarette habits as a result of the hypnosis-therapy they each had experienced. Jefferson was not in the business of therapy any longer, but the sessions he performed for Jim and Candy proved to be good for him as well. It was not long ago he used to help folks overcome the issues they had with hypnosis therapy and the level of satisfaction he felt with Jim's and Candy's success reminded him of the start he had in the world of hypnosis. Though he was satisfied with their results, it wouldn't be enough for him to change his direction and slide away from the spotlight of his hit Las Vegas stage show.

In the end, Jefferson knew he wanted to be an entertainer and that was precisely where he would stay. However, in David Christian, he knew had a protégé he could mentor and develop. Jefferson intended to fully assist David in his effort to create a successful self-help business and turn his vision into a reality. In a strange sort of way, helping David would allow Jefferson to live vicariously through his new friend's business and achievements. If they managed to develop the vision David had conveyed to him, the business could go on to have a tremendous positive impact on people all over the world and that appealed to Jefferson in a way he couldn't express to David.

Secretly, it was a vision Jefferson had had for himself quite a long time ago, but he decided entertainment would suit him better and he left the thought of being the self-help guru behind him. That is until he met David Christian. Now he had the opportunity to play a significant role in an attempt to indirectly impact people all over the globe. His old dream may have gone dormant for a time, but it could possibly be realized soon through David.

With the afternoon course successfully completed

the two men agreed to meet later that night at the café. It would be their last meeting for the weekend and David decided it best to forgo the plan he had to surprise Sakuri with a night out after her shift ended, and go along with Jefferson's request to meet in the café after his late show.

"David, you did extremely well in the course and I am pleased with the manner in which you handled the two clients I brought in. As some might say, you're ahead of the game and it's due to the commitment you made to work on the material I provided. I'm proud of you."

David felt good with the compliment he received and though he knew there would be so much more to accomplish, he still acknowledged his mentor.

"I owe it all to you Jefferson. I would never have been able to accomplish what I have so far if not for the opportunity to work with the best... the master. I have you to thank for that."

"Well, that's nice of you to say David."

Jefferson paused and then continued in a matter of fact way.

"Let's plan to meet after my late show tonight, say no later than eleven thirty at the café."

David nodded and agreed to meet. He knew it would benefit him in some way. How? He wasn't exactly sure, but it would be revealed soon enough.

"I'll see you there."

They shook hands and each departed, heading their separate ways.

CHAPTER THIRTY-FOUR

In his room, David contemplated his plans for the evening. He decided he would take a couple hours before his rendezvous with Jefferson, to see Sakuri at the blackjack tables. When he arrived on the casino floor, the crowd bustled and he sauntered toward the blackjack area only to notice Sakuri had a table full of participants. She caught a quick glimpse of him from a short distance and winked at him. None of the players noticed, but David did and he smiled back at her. He decided to hover for a few moments to see if a chair would open on her table. Fortunately, within ten minutes of his arrival one of the players rose, collected his chips, and headed toward the craps tables. David quickly moved in to take the seat and when he got comfortably settled he laid out a hundred dollar bill. As Sakuri counted out his chips, she greeted him with a warm smile.

"Good evening David. How are you?"

Before he could answer, the player to his right chimed in without an invite.

"Whadda we got here, a regular?"

He was a middle aged gentleman, appeared to be in his early fifties with grayed temples and lines around the mouth from years of inhaling cigarettes. David thought to himself, he should have been at the class over the weekend and he could have taken care of that bad habit. As David turned to address the strangers comment, Sakuri diffused the potential confrontation and handled it for him.

"Oh David is just a good friend that plays here occasionally. Now, shall we continue gentleman, please place your bets."

David held his tongue and threw out a small wager of ten dollars. He was there for the opportunity to spend a little time with Sakuri, not necessarily to win big money at blackjack. It wasn't the ideal situation, but it would have to do until they could be alone the next day. As she dealt the hand, Sakuri asked David about his weekend hypnosis training.

"So David, how did the training classes go over the weekend?"

"It was very helpful. I'll tell you more tomorrow when we get together."

David felt a bit apprehensive to discuss the course in the presence of the other players, so he put it off for later and changed the subject.

"I have a few things to manage in the morning and then I'll be free for lunch and the rest of the day. Are we still on?"

Before she answered, Sakuri glimpsed the gentleman that made the previous comment. He shook his head and commented again as he rolled his cards to display a bust.

"I should have known. I'll cash out here sweetie."

Sakuri took his cards and finished the play before she turned toward David.

"Yes, we are David. I look forward to it."

The two other players on the table decided to roll up and leave as well. One of them felt as though they were intruders in a lover's rendezvous and took the opportunity to comment.

"We'll leave you two alone so you can plan your get-away."

Sakuri just smiled and did not respond as she turned to David with a nod and gestured toward the card deck. David responded.

"Let's play. This is what I had hoped for anyway. I'm sorry if I ran your players off."

"Oh David, don't worry about it. People come and go. It's all in a nights work."

They both grinned at each other and Sakuri continued to deal the cards as the conversation flowed. The two firmed up their plans to meet for lunch in the Boca Park area again. Sakuri loved to spend her down time in that area amongst the great gift shops, clothing stores, and restaurants, not to mention the mall that housed all the major department store retailers. They decided to meet at the Kona Grill which featured a varied menu sure to appeal to most tastes. The card game continued for the next forty-five minutes until a new dealer arrived and the traditional trade-off occurred prior to Sakuri's final break for the night. Before she departed, she gave David another wink of her eye.

"I'll see you tomorrow, noon at the Kona Grill."

David acknowledged their plans.

"I look forward to it. Have a great night Sakuri."

She smiled, turned away and walked off into the crowd that mingled all about the casino floor. It was still a bit early and David, not able to accompany her to the employee lounge, decided he would take a short walk along the strip before he would return to meet with Jefferson. As he walked, David began to reflect on the last encounter he had with Tina. For some strange reason, that image of her settled into his mind and would make harbor there for the rest of the night. He walked among the crowd of tourists on the strip and wondered if he had created the problem Jefferson had warned him about. If so, David would eventually have to deal with it and he wasn't sure what he wanted to do so. He had realized his desire to pursue a deeper relationship with Tina, but also had an interest to learn more about the exotic beauty from the Orient that had recently come into this life. Either way, David moreover realized the importance to maintain his focus on the dream he envisioned for himself and he knew the relationships could not become a distraction or the whole thing would end up in a huge disappointment to him and his mentor. He felt the weight of obligation toward Jefferson for the help he had provided and David didn't want to let him down.

He walked for another thirty minutes while numerous thoughts lingered and flowed swiftly in and out of his head. It was time to meet Jefferson, so he returned to the Stardust and headed for the café.

CHAPTER THIRTY-FIVE

Jefferson waited at the entrance of the café when he saw David had not arrived yet. He spotted him about thirty yards away and waved as the two caught each other's eye. A rush of nervous tension seemed to envelope David's body as he approached. The chill left him with an uncomfortable feeling all about himself and he wondered if he should bring up the topic with regard to the women. He was concerned about Jefferson's reaction, so he decided to just let it lie and deal with it on his own, but Jefferson had an intuition that seemed to pierce through any armor David could put up to mask his concerns. Jefferson would inevitably bring up the topic.

"David, how was the blackjack tonight?"

There it was. Jefferson knew David wouldn't stay away from the table and an opportunity to see Sakuri. He measured David with the comment to see what kind of reaction he would get. The doctor wanted to know if David would be straight with him or if he would attempt to get around the subject they both knew existed like an elephant in the room.

"Okay Jefferson; yes, I went to play a few hands of blackjack and see Sakuri. We plan to meet tomorrow for lunch."

"Well I hope you at least won."

David let out a heavy sigh and responded to Jefferson's quip.

"Is that it, that's all you've got to say?"

"Oh David, settle down. I'm just ribbin' you a little bit."

"I did come out ahead so I'll buy."

Jefferson chuckled and David paused momentarily before he decided to continue with the topic he had earlier thought he would keep to himself. As they proceeded toward their table David started slowly.

"Jefferson, I do want to discuss something else with you."

"Sounds serious David, what is it?"

"I am a bit conflicted about my current situation."

David realized it would be a benefit to get the matter out in the open and solicit his good friend's advice. He held the details until they reached their usual table. They sat down and just as David was about to continue, Alba showed up.

"Well hello there, how are you two this evening?"

Jefferson gave her a quick response, ordered drinks, and turned to David to continue the conversation he had started.

"We're good Alba. Please bring us the usual ice teas and put a lemon wedge in mine."

David chimed in.

"I'll have lemon as well. Thank you."

Alba realized she had just received the brush off and walked away with a hurt look on her face. She turned to get a quick glimpse of David, but his attention was already diverted back to Jefferson as the two continued their discussion.

"So David, what is the situation that has you so conflicted you need to get it off your chest?"

"I should have listened to you Jefferson. I didn't think I would get into a spot where I would feel the way I do about Tina."

Jefferson just stared, without emotion, into David's eyes as he spoke.

"To make things worse, I am interested in Sakuri

too. I just can't get either one of them out of my mind."

Jefferson finally smiled, which actually surprised David. He fully expected his mentor to scold him for not adhering to the advice he provided, but Jefferson's reaction was total opposite of what he anticipated. He did have his say though. Jefferson laid out a response that David should have known would come when he brought up the topic.

"You know you created this hornet's nest and now you must deal with it. You have worked hard to learn the information I provided and now you have a grasp of the techniques to help you succeed in your venture, but all you did was to make things more complicated and certainly more difficult for yourself."

Jefferson sounded part advisor, part father, part pissed off friend. He wanted David to experience all that would come with the development of the skills which would bring him true control of his life, but David had made the matter more difficult with the situation he had created. Jefferson knew he could still move his life in the direction of his dreams, but it would be difficult while he dealt with the relationships he currently seemed to place himself in. To David's surprise, Jefferson continued to provide him constructive advice, but he wasn't going to help David solve the problem he had created for himself. It was his issue alone as far as Jefferson was concerned.

"Look David, that's all I'm going to say about this. You have my support, but it is a situation you will ultimately have to work out on your own. Nobody can do that for you. I am here to help and be a sounding board for you if need be, but the matter is yours to work out."

Jefferson took a brief moment to allow David an opportunity to say his piece before he continued with his counsel. David had no response, so he continued.

"I do want you to know, it is going to be critical for you to keep your vision in front of you as you do work through the relationships with these two women. Otherwise, you could easily get sidetracked and loose the intention you have displayed over the course of the past few months since we have become friends."

David sat with a blank look on his face. He knew he would have to deal with the matter in the best way he could and hoped he would not hurt either Tina or Sakuri in the process. He had grown fond of each and didn't want them to feel the hurt he had felt when Laura had departed from their relationship a couple years ago. Though he wasn't as deep into a relationship with ether woman, he knew all too well the hurt one felt when a bond with someone was broke due to one's recklessness. In this case, David felt he had moved with a bit of recklessness and should have maintained control before it got to this point.

"I'm sorry I didn't take your advice when you offered it Jefferson. I do want you to know though, I will continue to work hard and stay focused on my goal. I have come too far to let my plans blow up on me now."

Jefferson sat stoic and nodded his head.

"Good David. I am glad to hear that. Now if you're done, let's discuss the reason I wanted to meet with you in the first place."

Before he could start Alba returned with the ice teas and set them down on the table in front of each. She had a subdued look to her and flatly asked.

"Will you gentlemen be eating tonight?"

Jefferson looked across the table at David who had already eaten. He waved no, so Jefferson quickly answered and dismissed her.

"No thank you Alba, drinks will be fine."

"Okay, thank you."

Alba was gloom in her response. She was obviously disappointed David had not taken at least a few minutes to chat with her. She turned in a somber manner and left the table with her head pointed down. He knew what she felt, but David had to press on with the important exchange he had come to meet Jefferson for. Time was short and he wanted to be sure to leave town with everything Jefferson had to offer that may help him launch his business at a pace which would bring him quick, positive results. In the coming months, David would begin a mission that would ultimately end his current employment and launch his new career as a self-help entrepreneur specializing in self-hypnosis. He would need all the help Jefferson had to offer and was ready to provide him with.

As Alba walked away, Jefferson directed his attention toward David and began to explain the details of why he wanted to meet. He started by explaining to David his past experiences when he initially began his career as a hypnotist.

"David, as you know I used to have a regular practice of hypnotic therapy. As part of that practice, I had a similar dream as the one you possess. At the time, my intention was to create a business in which I could help people with the issues they deal with in everyday life. As a result I created affirmations that I could sell via a website business, much like what you have described to me in our conversations."

David listened intently, but now broke in to ask.

"Why did you stop?"

Jefferson held up his hand and gestured, he had more to explain and he continued to do so before David could ask more questions.

"I was also at the start of my venture into stage hypnosis which was another passion of mine. As I progressed with my stage act I found it was truly the area of hypnosis I wanted to pursue as a long term career. Being that it was, I decided to give up my practice and the thought I had to create the website and market products that would help people with certain needs."

Jefferson paused and took a sip of his tea before he continued. As soon as he paused though, David piped up and asked another question.

"So why would you give it up? Wasn't it something you could have done at the same time your stage career took off?"

"That may have been, but time was limited and I decided the stage was where I wanted to be. It provided me with the personal satisfaction I wanted. Not that I wasn't interested in seeing people benefit from my work as a therapist, but I had to make a decision on where to spend the time needed to be successful and stage is what I chose. It was best for me to commit fully to one or the other and I enjoy the entertainment experience too much to give it up. Besides, in a strange sort of way it is therapeutic for my audience, so I get the benefit of giving them a good time when they see me perform."

David sat quietly and stared at Jefferson as he spoke. He had begun to wonder why the doctor wanted to meet and explain this to him.

"So why are you telling me this? What does it have to do with me Jefferson?"

"I was getting to that. You see, I have all the tools you need to create your business. All you need is the exposure to gain speaking engagements and seminars, as well as build a website. I can give you all the materials on the topic, the recordings for your affirmation's and even some written works for manuals, pamphlets and possibly books if you decide to take it in that direction. If you would like to use my material, I will provide it at no cost so you can start quickly to build your business and not have to spend unnecessary time in product development."

David's eyes opened wide as he realized the amount of time and work Jefferson would save him and the impact his generous offer to help would have on his business launch.

"Seriously, you'll give me all your material?"

"Yes David. I would never use it otherwise and you have shown me that you are committed to your venture. Because you have displayed a serious commitment to change and create a new path for yourself, I would like to help you reach your dream. In some strange way, by doing so, I can live vicariously through you in your effort to help others as you have described you want to do."

"Ahhh, I get it Jefferson. You can still experience a portion of your initial dream by assisting me with the material you have already created."

Jefferson smiled.

"Yes, I guess you can say that."

David was grateful for his friend's generous offer and made sure Jefferson understood.

"Jefferson, you have been so generous with me already. I don't know how I can thank you for all you have done."

"Just continue with what you have started and stay the course David. Become the person I know you now want to become."

That was all Jefferson had to say to him. David would leave that evening with a newfound energy and when he returned home from Las Vegas he would dedicate everything he had, all his energy and focus, to fulfilling what he now believed was his life's purpose. But before he would leave town there was still the matter of the one person he had to meet, Sakuri, and he knew it would not be easy.

CHAPTER THIRTY-SIX

Sakuri arrived at the Kona Grill just before noon. She sat out on the patio and waited just a few minutes until David arrived. He spotted her as he walked through the parking lot toward the entrance and cut through the gate that led to the patio dining area.

"Hi Sakuri, it's good to see you. How are you?"

Sakuri stood up to greet David and they embraced in a short, friendly hug.

"I'm good David. How are you?"

"I'm very good, thanks. It's especially nice to see you outside of the casino. I know I won't be losing any money to you."

They both laughed at David's jest as they sat back down. The hostess approached them at the table to inquire if they wanted to stay on the patio or move to a table inside the dining room. It was a cool, clear day so they decided to remain on the patio and take in the pleasant afternoon outside while they would enjoy their lunch as well as each other's company.

"So David, you have to tell me all about your weekend courses with Jefferson Paul."

David sat back in his chair and took a deep breath before he started to describe the weekend to her. As he began to speak, Sakuri leaned forward which indicated to David she had a genuine interest in the venture he was about to describe.

"It was a thorough examination of hypnosis, everything from theory to execution. I even had the opportunity to hypnotize the two clients Jefferson brought in especially for the weekend classes."

"That must have been exciting. Did you get to actually hypnotize them?"

"Yes, it was unbelievable and I did have success with the hypnosis sessions which made me feel good about the direction I have decided to take with regard to my career. The weekend gave me the confidence to know I can do this."

Sakuri smiled and nodded at David as she reassured him.

"Of course you can do it David. You have put in the hard work and you're mentored by the best in the business, right?"

David agreed with her and responded firmly.

"He certainly is the best Sakuri. Jefferson is the master as far as I am concerned. He executes with such ease and he is an exceptional instructor. I couldn't be in better hands. He has also offered to help me accelerate the launch of my business by providing many of the tools he developed years ago when he considered pursuing a similar path."

"Wow, that's wonderful news David. I am sure you will be a great success with his help."

David sat up and leaned forward to place emphasis on his comment.

"I will as long as I maintain my focus, work diligently, and pay attention to the details."

He paused and took a deep breath, but before he could continue the waitress arrived at their table to take the couple's lunch order. Rather than order separate meals, they decided to share a selection of appetizers. Sakuri ordered a glass of Chablis and David, although tempted to join her, decided to have his usual ice tea with lemon wedge. When the server left the table, David continued with his last thought.

"Sakuri, uh... there is something I have to share with you."

Before he could go on, Sakuri interjected.

"David, you're acting so serious? Is there something wrong?"

"No, there isn't, not really. I just want to be honest and up front with you."

David paused and looked into her eyes.

"I have to admit Sakuri, I am attracted to you and would love to see you as often as possible; that is if you felt the same way. I'm torn because I just don't know how fast I will be able to grow my business. If it goes well and I am able to leave my current job, I'm not sure how often I would be able to see you being that my job is the reason why I come to Las Vegas as often as I do."

A blank look spread across Sakuri's face as she attempted to disguise the disappointment she felt as David advised her of his dilemma. She did have an attraction to David and had hoped they would develop a closer relationship as time passed and he continued with his regular business trips to Las Vegas. The news he just delivered had indicated otherwise though.

"I understand David. I do feel as you do, but you must continue to chase your dreams. I don't want to see you give up a passion you have for my sake. It wouldn't be fair for either one of us. If it is destined to be, time will bring us together again when it's right."

David smiled, but he didn't feel what his face tried to express. He was actually sad to share the news he had just shared with Sakuri, but if he didn't do it he would be headed down a difficult path just as he and Jefferson spoke about. The time was right for a clean break from the possible direction he would otherwise take and he knew it had to be done. Before he could continue with the conversation the waitress returned with their drinks. She set them on the table and turned away without a word spoken to either. She seemed to sense the couple was engaged in a difficult conversation and sped away to provide them with their privacy, at least as much privacy as their place on the patio could provide. David began to speak again.

"I don't want this to sound like I won't stay in touch or see you again. When I do come to Las Vegas, I will let you know ahead of time so we can plan to get together if that's something you also want to do."

Sakuri went along with the idea, but she knew in her heart David was going to be very busy with his business and would have limited time to see her.

"That would be nice David. I would like to stay in touch if you have the time, but I know you will be very busy with your new venture."

David shook his head as he looked at her across the table with a half-hearted smile pasted on his face. He also knew in his heart, it would be difficult for the two of them to maintain, let alone grow their close friendship with the possibility of an exclusive relationship. He didn't want it to end this way, but it was inevitable and he had to make the tough choice. His business plan would have to take precedence if he wanted to experience the success he had envisioned for himself. The two sat quietly for a moment and stared into the distance. The lunch had taken a turn and not developed into what either had hoped it would be when they planned it.

Just then the waitress arrived carrying a tray filled with the selection of appetizers they had chosen for lunch. It now seemed as if neither had the appetite for the food they ordered and they just picked at it while the conversation stalled and finally waned. It was apparent the time had come to end the lunch date and part ways, at least for the time being anyway.

Before they departed, David hugged Sakuri and promised he would stay in touch. She responded with a gentle kiss on his cheek and hugged him back. She knew full well this moment could be the last she would ever see David. Even though the hurt was hard to bear, she did want him to chase his dream and sincerely wished him well. They released their embrace and each went their separate way without any more words. As he walked away, David couldn't help but think if he had made the right decision or if he would ever see the exotic Asian beauty again.

CHAPTER THIRTY-SEVEN

David arrived at his home in Oceanside at five-forty and found nobody home. Tina was at work on her new job, so he unpacked his bags and went into his office to recap the day and begin to plan for his business launch. The skeleton plan was put together but now that Jefferson had offered his help with the materials he would provide, David was in position to accelerate the launch and get started quicker than he originally anticipated. He was excited to share the news with Tina and could hardly wait for her to come home. Tonight he would take her to dinner for her own celebration as he promised, and they would include his good news as well.

He was twenty minutes into the work he laid out when he heard the front door open. Tina walked in and headed straight for David's office. She knew he was home when she saw his car parked out front.

"Hi David, how did everything go this weekend?"

David felt a warm glow come over him as he looked up to see Tina, who had broad smile on her face and a look that depicted a child-like curiosity with the question she asked. It was obvious she had a genuine interest in David's pursuit and wanted to see him succeed as much as she wanted her own success to come. After all, David was there to save her from her desperate situation and she felt a genuine love and respect for him. He was much more than a friend, but she had to contain what she truly felt so as to not derail either of them from the career path they each sought. David stood and walked around the desk to greet Tina with a hug. She was a bit surprised at his action, especially since they experienced the awkward moment they had prior to his trip, but she enjoyed the embrace nonetheless.

"Tina, I promised you we would go out and celebrate your new job when I returned. Get ready, because we are going to the harbor for a night out. There's some news I want to share with you too."

"Okay, that sounds good to me. Give me a few minutes to freshen up."

Tina always looked fresh and lovely as far as David was concerned. She had a youthful appearance and usually carried herself in a positive manner, exuding confidence and a generally positive energy with everyone she interacted with. It took only five minutes for her to slip on a nicely printed summer dress and grab a light shawl in case the harbor was a bit cool. She touched up her face, but there wasn't much to do there. Tina had a natural look that didn't require much time in front of the make-up mirror. When she walked back into David's office he looked up and took a deep breath. He tried to hide it, but he was obviously taken by her natural beauty. In that very moment David realized he loved the young woman who stood there in front of him with a glow of light all about her. She was all he could want in a partner and it would be fruitless to carry-on in the manner in which he had been. She was attracted to him as well and he knew that to be certain. David stood again and walked around the desk to where she stood and took her by the waist with his hands.

"Tina, you're beautiful and I just can't fight this anymore... I love you too."

Tina thought back to what she had said to him before he left for Las Vegas and smiled. Her head dropped momentarily and then she looked back up at him with her eyes filled with tears. The emotion of the moment had caught her off guard and she began to lose control of her usual calm, collected demeanor.

"Tina, why are you crying?"

"Oh David, I love you too. I have loved you for quite some time now, but I know you had other things you had to give your attention to. I'm so sorry, I really didn't mean for it to slip before you left for Las Vegas. I don't ever want to be a distraction in your life, I want nothing but the best for you; for all that you have done for me."

David pulled her by the waist into his body and then wrapped his arms around her. He hugged her tight and spoke softly.

"There is nothing to be sorry for Tina. This is the way I feel and it isn't because of any obligation I feel for what you said or anything like that. It's real, and it's not going to go away. I want you to stay here with me for as long as you want to be here."

Tina composed herself and gently pushed back from his embrace. She looked deeply into his eyes as she began to speak.

"David, I will stay under one condition."

He looked at her quizzically.

"What would that be?"

"Nothing changes as far as our personal pursuits are concerned. If nothing else, we help each other continue down the path we have started on. If we give up on our dreams in lieu of this relationship, it will be something we may regret later, and for the rest of our lives. I don't want to live with that David."

David was actually relieved that she had stated as much. He planned to have the discussion of that very topic over dinner, but now they would just enjoy each other's company, their time together, and the benchmarks they each had to celebrate.

Upon their return home from the harbor, David went to the patio and turned on the fountain, took a seat in his favorite Adirondack chair and relaxed in the moonlight of the evening. Tina took the chair next to his and they sat in quiet solitude for several minutes before David broke the silence. He stood up and entered the townhome, turned on soft jazz and returned to the solitude of the tropically decorated patio.

"It's beautiful out tonight."

Tina sat with her head leaned back into the padded chair, eyes closed, and relaxed as if she had not a care in the world, and in that moment, she didn't.

"It is so beautiful David, and you made it even more beautiful."

David grinned shyly and reached for her hand. He engulfed her petite hand in his and leaned back into the headrest of his own chair. A little over twenty minutes had passed when David's eyes popped open and he looked toward Tina.

"Shall we go to bed?"

Tina wasn't sure what he meant by the question, but she followed his lead and rose from the chair to trace his path to the master bedroom. Once there, David turned around to face her and gently pulled her toward him by her shoulders. He leaned forward and kissed her on the mouth with a passion that had swelled inside of him for what seemed to be years. Tina responded with passion that equally matched his and the two began to embrace, kiss, and gently tear at each other's clothes until they lay with their fully naked bodies facing each other on the bed. David moved slowly and gently with intent to love her totally and not just have a sexual experience. He craved her body in a manner he had not experienced in almost a year since he and Laura had split, but he also felt a longing to love Tina in a way he had never experienced before. The two made love passionately for what felt like hours into the early morning, when finally they were each thoroughly exhausted and the love-making culminated in a tight embrace. They dosed into a deep slumber and slept in each other's arms until the mid-morning hour when the bright morning sun shone through the blinds and woke them almost simultaneously.

David stroked his hand through Tina's dark, thick hair and smiled at her when her eyes popped open to see him propped on his elbow, looking down on her. He leaned downward and kissed her gently on the lips.

"I love you Tina."

"I love you too David."

Their new life together had begun.

CHAPTER THIRTY-EIGHT
A YEAR HAD PASSED – JUNE
OCEANSIDE, CA

It had been a full year since David launched his business and it developed in a manner which he and Jefferson had never anticipated. The accelerated growth put David in the forefront of the self-help industry and he appeared on several radio broadcasts as well as a couple morning television shows to promote his method for achievement in life, a change of course, or simply to eliminate an otherwise bad habit. David Christian was on a high, and had rapidly ascended the ranks in the world of self-realization and self-help. The wave he now rode established his star among followers, as well as with inquisitive people who sought help with their daily challenges. The sales from the books, pamphlets, and self-hypnosis recordings on the website soared.

David's popularity had grown rapidly and he was in demand to speak at conferences, business meetings, graduations, and several other varied attractions in which he could deliver his message and sell the tools to an audience which sought relief from their problems or a change of course in their lives with any means they could obtain to help them. He had the answers they looked for and the fact he continued to practice the methods he learned from his lessons with the master, Jefferson Paul, and stuck to his ritual of daily self-hypnosis sessions in which he authored his own success, had become the validation he needed to convince others he had what they needed. Everything in David's life seemed to go as he planned and he had Jefferson to thank; for it was through the exercise and continued practice of self-hypnosis he had become a believer and not only owned the direction he had set for his life, he was the creator of it all.

He helped Tina with the lessons he had learned from his mentor Jefferson, and she too, experienced achievements with the execution of the same method of self-hypnosis David had learned and practiced daily. She had become a real believer as she developed her career in what took shape as a promising move into the theater group of the La Jolla Playhouse. She had long since left her job to wait tables and took a position with the theatre group which gave her plenty of opportunity to audition for roles and participate in various ways to learn all she could about theater production.

In fact, she took some of her experience in theater and worked with David to develop his business further. With Tina's help, David would include more theatrics and turn his regular speaking engagements into presentations filled with entertainment which were targeted to move more and more product. The show as it were, would continue to evolve and eventually turned David into a star almost as significant as his mentor and stage stalwart, Jefferson Paul.

It was late Thursday afternoon and David sat at his desk. It was the day before he would leave for a seminar in Las Vegas in which he would speak with a medium sized group of real estate professionals. The phone rang and he noticed it was Jefferson.

"Jefferson, how are you my friend."

David loved to hear from Jefferson and his gratitude came through each time they spoke.

"I am well David. I understand you will be the keynote speaker at the real estate seminar this weekend. Will you have time to meet for lunch or maybe a late night snack?"

Without hesitation David committed to see Jefferson at his convenience.

"You know I will always make time for you Jefferson. Just let me know when and where. You can count on me to be there."

Jefferson knew if they met at the café after his show there would be no chance of a schedule conflict so he went with it.

"How about if we meet Friday after my late show at the café, sound good?"

"Of course, that's our spot. I'll see you there around eleven fifteen."

As David hung up the phone, he reflected for a moment on all the times he and Jefferson had spent in that café. The wisdom Jefferson had passed on to him over their late night meetings and afternoon conversations had impacted David's life in ways he could never have imagined when he first met the master. All he looked for the night they met was a little advice from someone he didn't even know. What he ultimately got was a genuinely great friend and more knowledge of the manner in which life really worked than he could have ever bargained for in any self-help seminar. David placed his face in his hands and cried. He cried from the joy he felt inside at the way Jefferson had taken him and helped him from the depths of where he had come. His life was magical now and he owed it all to the man he called the master, his best friend, Jefferson Paul.

He and Jefferson would meet at the café that Friday night. They would enjoy each other's company, but Jefferson would never really know how thankful David was for all he had done for his friend. He felt as if he owed Jefferson his life and in many ways he did.

David attempted to express his gratitude, but Jefferson would only remind him to pay it forward as he had asked long ago when they embarked on their mission together. David would do just that every time he spoke to an audience or sold a recorded affirmation, a book of wisdom, or a self-help manual to somebody in search of guidance in their life. He would do it again the next day.

CHAPTER THIRTY-NINE

Saturday afternoon at the Las Vegas Convention Center and the crowd was a buzz. The prospect of hearing David Christian speak had the group of Real Estate professionals in a clamor for the good seats in front of the stage. The auditorium had filled quickly and the noise settled down as the convention got underway. As usual, there would be some housekeeping, legal reviews, and conversation about the current state of the housing market in Las Vegas. The usual business took the morning and a portion of the early afternoon, but it was now time to bring on the guest speaker. Everyone in the place anxiously looked forward to the message they would hear from David and it made his job easier to know they wanted to learn what he had to teach them. The convention's moderator approached the stand which was set to the right side of the stage and grabbed the microphone from its stand.

"Ladies and gentlemen, it gives me great pleasure to introduce to you our keynote speaker for the seminar. This is man who has vaulted to the top of his industry in a relatively short span of time with the effective use of the tools he will speak to us about. He is a man on a mission to help others and will stop at nothing to provide you with the tools and techniques for achievement in this field or with whatever else it is you would like to pursue in life."

He pauses for effect and then announces

"Ladies and Gentlemen, I give you the man himself... Mister David Christian!"

David came on stage to a loud ovation and he settled into the presentation he had worked out with the help of Tina. The scene was very familiar. He had played this scenario over in his mind so often that the actual presentation came with relative ease. He was like a cat as he prowled along the edge of the stage and spoke with fluctuations in his voice that gave emphasis to the points he had identified as important lessons to learn and keep for future use. The crowd hung on to his every word and many jotted notes on the tablets. There was not a sound other than David's voice, which seemed to boom through the speakers hung from the ceiling of the stage. David was certainly in his element on stage and anyone could see he had developed into a very effective public speaker. His sales training and professional experience provided him with the skill he needed to persuade others to believe in what he sold, but it was the subject and specific material he spoke about that gave him the passion which drove him to believe in what he pitched. He delivered the message he had come to provide with such energy and enthusiasm, it was virtually impossible for any in the audience to doubt him. He delivered the material in such a manner it was as though he had somehow channeled the master himself into the presentation. Little did he know, Jefferson stood behind the stage curtain and watched as David delivered the presentation with such conviction, it even moved him.

This was actually Jefferson's first time to view live the new presentation David had created, with Tina's help, and he felt proud to see him perform with such positive energy and assuredness. It was now apparent David had made a very wise choice long ago when he decided to change his life. Not only had he overcome his demons with drug abuse, he changed his whole outlook and vision of how life could be lived. He had managed to create significant change in his life over a short period of time and it was obvious to Jefferson as he watched the presentation, David would change the lives of many others in his path as he continued his quest.

David continued with an extraordinary passion for approximately an hour until the end was finally near. As he stepped forward to the edge of the center stage and made eye contact with those in the first few rows he closed with his usual question.

"... and so I ask you now, will you be a master of your mind, and thus your destiny, or will you be a servant to the uncontrolled thoughts that take harbor in your head and control your mind?"

With those words David ended and turned to walk off stage to the eruption of applause from the crowded auditorium. He caught a glimpse of Jefferson standing back behind the curtain as he strolled to his right and walked over to him, took his hand and pulled him in for a hug. He whispered softly in Jefferson's ear.

"Hey Jefferson, I'm delighted to see you here. You didn't tell me you would be in attendance."

Jefferson laughed as the two separated from their brotherly embrace. He looked at David with an expression of love for his close friend. His student had become a master in his own right and Jefferson let him know how proud he was.

"You were good David, very good."

David placed his hand on Jefferson's shoulder.

"Well, I learned from the best Jefferson."

"What you did out there David, that was certainly not anything I could have taught you. You delivered with a passion I never possessed in the days I considered that path for myself. I guess that could be why I stuck to the entertainment side of hypnosis."

David brimmed with confidence as Jefferson

continued to praise his work.

"You will surely impact many lives. Keep doing the work David, and you will grow to be an icon in the industry. I can't tell you how proud I am of what you have become, and to be able to call you my friend makes it even more special."

The two men embraced once again then turned shoulder to shoulder and walked together into the darkness of the back stage. Jefferson was filled with pride as he realized the success David had achieved in a short period of time. He looked favorably on the advancements his protégé had made in his life's quest for change and knew he played a significant part in that transformation. David, on the other hand, would continue to grow in his recognition as a prominent leader in the field of self-realization, only to one day come face to face with the toughest battle of his life... literally.

To be continued...

ABOUT THE AUTHOR

Joe Frazzette is a fiction writer, with professional experience in sales, and marketing. He also holds a certification, in clinical hypnosis. He effectively utilizes his past experiences in these fields, to contribute to the characters he develops, for the stories he writes.

Joe is an enthusiastic individual who approaches life with a zest for adventure and risk taking. He enjoys the great outdoors and spends much of his time exploring the wonders of nature, as well as, the individuals that occupy the space he travels in.

Through his own personal adventures, as well as, other various examinations of life, Joe has developed an ability to vividly depict everyday life in its rawest forms. He writes about characters that have an edge, but are also authentic, and with whom his many readers can typically identify.

Novels By: JOE FRAZZETTE

MASTER or SERVANT
Recapture the Power Within

DEADLY SLUMBER

Coming Soon By: JOE FRAZZETTE

DEADLY SLUMBER
   SHATTERED

More Books From Perfect Publishing

Your Book Here

www.PerfectPublishing.com

Printed in Great Britain
by Amazon